Future of Business and Finance

The Future of Business and Finance book series features professional works aimed at defining, describing and charting the future trends in these fields. The focus is mainly on strategic directions, technological advances, challenges and solutions which may affect the way we do business tomorrow, including the future of sustainability and governance practices. Mainly written by practitioners, consultants and academic thinkers, the books are intended to spark and inform further discussions and developments.

More information about this series at http://www.springer.com/series/16360

Hermann Troger

Human Resource Management in a Post COVID-19 World

New Distribution of Power,
Individualization, Digitalization
and Demographic Developments

 Springer

Hermann Troger
Brixen, Bolzano, Italy

ISSN 2662-2467   ISSN 2662-2475   (electronic)
Future of Business and Finance
ISBN 978-3-030-67469-4   ISBN 978-3-030-67470-0   (eBook)
https://doi.org/10.1007/978-3-030-67470-0

This Springer imprint is published by the registered company Springer Nature Switzerland AG.
The registered company address is: Gewerbestrasse 11, 6330 Cham, Switzerland

Preface

Not so long ago, the world of work was turning at an alarming pace under the influence of the megatrends of globalisation, digitalisation and demographic shifts.

I had spoken to entrepreneurs in Berlin, London, Milan and New York: they all complained with remarkable unanimity about the current crux of the world of work: there are not enough suitably qualified specialists, the existing workforce is too old, too expensive and increasingly demanding. The head of HR for a German automotive supplier complained to a French colleague about the lack of motivation of young employees and, in the same breath, about the reduced performance of many older ones.

Against this backdrop, I had decided to write a book about these phenomena of the new world of work: about the shift in the balance of power between employers and employees, about generational conflicts, digitalisation and a VUCA working world 4.0.

Then—halfway through this project—a tiny little virus unceremoniously exposed the marginal importance of all this to me and the entire world. Since March 2020, the corona virus has been the dominant subject—in politics, in families, in schools and, of course, in companies. There, instead of employer branding programmes and further training courses, the focus was now on short-time work and redundancies.

And although, in one sense, we can call it a watershed, the coronavirus also fits very well into this context: COVID-19 is fundamentally nothing other than the exponential expression of our VUCA (working) world. Nothing describes the fragility and complexity of the world of work better than the consequences of this virus. For years, we have been experiencing the dawn of a new era in the world of work in an economic, social, socio-political and an individual-psychological sense. The coronavirus, as it were, represents the culmination of this process.

The question now is: What does effective HR management look like in times like these?

There is little doubt that HR professionals are currently experiencing nerve-wracking times: On the one hand, they face a seemingly insurmountable number of challenges in relation to *New Work*, and on the other, they run the risk of slipping into insignificance if they fail to meet these challenges. Over the past 30 years, they have gladly embraced the ideal of being a strategic partner for the top decision-makers in the company; but never before has the opportunity to actually fulfil this role in daily practice been as great as today. To achieve this, the HR experts in turn need a partner, in this case the managers from the various operational areas. Only together can they make use of the numerous opportunities for shaping the working world 4.0—with or without the coronavirus—to ensure effective and sustainable HR processes.

The practical way to achieve this will be described in this book.

How This Book Is Structured

Part I (Chaps. 1–3) describes the framework conditions for today's HR work. The current situation is presented from three points of view. From a **macro-economic perspective**, the focus is, among other things, on the proportion of employed persons in the total population, their qualifications, their income and the relevant occupational profiles. In addition, socio-political developments, such as the dominance of certain family models or the employment rate of women also play a role. And over all of this hovers an unfavourable demographic development like the sword of Damocles, threatening to pose considerable difficulties for HR management for decades to come. The speed at which the corona virus has entered our world stands in stark contrast to these long-term developments, and yet its impact is as far-reaching as it is immediate.

Consequently, the **micro-political perspective** can be summed up quite easily: Companies are facing enormous challenges. There are fewer highly skilled workers; and those that are available are becoming more diverse and demanding. Age, gender, ethnic and cultural background, religious values or simply a variety of different interests make every employee a unique individual who needs to be integrated and managed effectively—a task that has been made all the more difficult by the pandemic since it is now often done remotely.

For this reason, an additional third perspective is taken into account in the description of our challenging starting situation: that of the individual, the **ego perspective**. The complexity of an economic world 4.0 presents itself to employees through a working world of near limitless possibilities. Especially for the younger generation, *New Work* offers virtually unfettered freedom of choice. The world is open to them in the truest sense of the word—even if at the moment it is a world full of question marks on account of the coronavirus.

Having described our complex starting point, Part II of the book first focuses on **what today's employees expect from their employers** (Chap. 4). To this end, among other things, an empirical survey of 4500 employees will be discussed, showing employees' expectations of what constitutes a good job. This is followed in Chap. 5 by the (common) solutions to the HRM debate as proposed by HR experts; and here, too, different views on the subject are presented: The most influential approaches from the field of HRM over the past 80 years will be contrasted with the many different roles that HR managers have assumed in practice. Rounding off these 'solutions' are various experts' suggestions for organisational adjustments right up to the provocative end of the spectrum where calls for the dissolution of HR departments have gained attention.

By comparing the complex starting situation with the expectations of the employees and the insufficient answers and solutions, the first five chapters aim to lay the foundation for the book's central argument: **A new, clearly defined form of cooperation is needed between HR specialists and the leaders from the various operational departments.**

Effective HR work can only succeed in close cooperation between the HR department and line managers. Although this approach is easy to describe and to understand, it is not always easy to implement in practice. It neither requires major organisational changes nor an increase in resources. Nor is it a question of decentralisation or hierarchical assignment. What is necessary, however, is that this idea finds support in the minds of the individual actors. Then, at the operational level, it is a matter of constructive cooperation in all phases of the HRM process.

How this approach can contribute to achieving the goal of good HR management—i.e. increasing the success of the company through the effective management of staff in terms of economic and social efficiency—is described in Part III (Chaps. 6–9).

For this purpose, HR work is divided into three key processes:

1. **The recruitment process**, which comprises four operational steps: staff planning, HR marketing, selection and hiring;
2. **The staff management process**, including elements such as staff deployment, feedback and remuneration, as well as a number of specific leadership challenges related to the overall diversity of the workforce. And, of course, HR management takes on a whole new dimension in 'times of pandemic'.
3. **The staff development process**, which includes sections on education and further training, and career planning.

Alongside the description of the essential elements and the particular challenges of current HR management tasks, the division of responsibilities between the line managers and the HR professionals is discussed throughout, with particular reference to the role of line managers. They are called upon to no longer leave the field of HR work solely in the hands of HR departments, but to take on a much more active role in this process. HR management finds its most direct expression in the relationship between supervisor and employee. And since this relationship has become many times more complex, it is high time that the supervisor took the reins again.

The Shoulder-to-Shoulder Approach

The old cliché 'anyone can do HR' has now been replaced by 'anyone must do HR'—at least every manager should do it. But let there be no doubt: Of course the HR department is still needed. In fact, the technical and methodological competence of HR professionals is becoming more important than ever—but it must be combined much more strongly with the leadership competence of direct superiors. Good HR work will be less a question of the organisational integration of the HR department or the role of the HR manager, but rather a question of dealing with the individual employee, of responding to his or her interests and needs. And for this very reason, efficient HR work requires a close relationship between HR staff and line managers.

Brixen, Bolzano, Italy   Hermann Troger
1 December 2020

Acknowledgments

My heartfelt thanks go to my friends who are entrepreneurs, my colleagues and my students for the stimulating discussions, to my family for their loving patience, and to Dr. Prashanth Mahagaonkar and his team for their trust and professional support. I would also like to take this opportunity to express my special thanks to my expert translator Ute Elford, whose outstanding feeling for language has been invaluable to make this book a reality. It was a pleasure to work with her on this project!

Contents

Part I A New World of Work

1 The Global Perspective: Macro-political Considerations 3
  1.1 Demographic Changes 3
      1.1.1 The Old Are Getting Older 5
      1.1.2 Shrinking Numbers of Young People 6
      1.1.3 A More Diverse Society 8
  1.2 Socio-political Trends 9
      1.2.1 'Family' Can Mean Many Things 10
      1.2.2 The Rise of Living Alone 11
      1.2.3 Gender 12
  1.3 Generational Diversity and the Battle for Distribution 14
      1.3.1 Traditionalists and Baby Boomers 15
      1.3.2 Generation X 15
      1.3.3 Generation Y 16
      1.3.4 Generation Z 16
      1.3.5 The Failure of the Intergenerational Contract 17
      1.3.6 Generational Equity and the Distribution of Scarce
             Resources 18
  1.4 Economic Factors 19
      1.4.1 Employment 19
      1.4.2 Qualifications 21
      1.4.3 Jobs in a World Shaped by Industry 4.0 22
  1.5 The Coronavirus-Effect 24
      1.5.1 Demography and Social Policy 24
      1.5.2 Generational Conflicts 24
      1.5.3 Social and Economic Policies 25
      1.5.4 World of Work 25
      1.5.5 Digitalisation and Remote Work from Home 26
  References 26

2 The Company Perspective: Micro-Political Considerations 29
  2.1 The Interminable Shortage of Skilled Workers 29
      2.1.1 The Gripes of Entrepreneurs vs. Labour Market Research . . 29

	2.1.2	The Choice Between Study or Work	30
	2.1.3	STEMs	31
	2.1.4	Digital Transformation: Solution or Problem?	32
2.2		Diversity in the Workforce	33
	2.2.1	Generational Diversity	34
	2.2.2	Multiculturalism	36
	2.2.3	Diversity of Interests	39
2.3		Performance (Dis)Orientation	41
	2.3.1	Do Young People Lack Motivation?	41
	2.3.2	Does Productivity Decrease with Age?	43
2.4		Industry 4.0	46
	2.4.1	Increased Productivity	46
	2.4.2	Impact on the World of Work	47
2.5		The Coronavirus-Effect	48
	2.5.1	Work-Life-Blending Versus Work-Life-Separation	48
	2.5.2	Homeworking Works!	49
	2.5.3	The Generation Gaps Just Got Smaller	50
	2.5.4	Adopting a 'Feel-Good' Management Style	50
	2.5.5	VUCA *Plus* Covid-19	51
		References	51

3   The Ego Perspective: Workforce Considerations 53
3.1		A Working World of Unlimited Opportunities	53
	3.1.1	'We Have Time'	53
	3.1.2	'The World Is Open to Us'	55
	3.1.3	Knowledge Is Relative	55
3.2		A New Distribution of Power	56
	3.2.1	From Baby Boomers to Gen Z	56
	3.2.2	From Employer to Employee Market	57
	3.2.3	Increased Expectations	58
3.3		We Are All Individuals	60
	3.3.1	Variety of Interests	60
	3.3.2	Work-Life Balance	61
	3.3.3	Individual Career Paths	62
3.4		The Coronavirus-Effect	63
	3.4.1	Decline in Loneliness	64
		References	65

Part II   Expectations of Good Work Opportunities—and the Sobering Reality

4   Expectations of a Good Job 69
4.1		What Is a 'Good Work Opportunity' Today?	69
	4.1.1	Increased Expectations	69
	4.1.2	Diversity of Interests and Values	71
	4.1.3	The Attractive Employer	73

	4.2	Survey: Employee Expectations of a Good Job	75
		4.2.1 The Research Question	76
		4.2.2 Survey and Method	76
		4.2.3 The Results	77
		4.2.4 Conclusions	85
	4.3	The Coronavirus Effect	86
		4.3.1 Stress and the Anxieties of Employees	87
		4.3.2 Working from Home	87
		4.3.3 The Deal: Loyalty in Return for Accommodations	88
		4.3.4 Conclusions	89
	References		89

5 Taking Stock: Multiple and Complex Challenges, But No Effective Solutions 91

	5.1	Stakeholder Dissatisfaction	91
		5.1.1 Role Conflicts	91
		5.1.2 Cost Pressure	92
		5.1.3 Self-Image/External Image	93
	5.2	Economic Science Approaches	93
		5.2.1 Transaction Cost Theory	94
		5.2.2 The Principal Agent Theory	94
	5.3	Behavioural Science Approaches	96
		5.3.1 Social Exchange Theories	96
		5.3.2 Motivational Theory Approaches	97
	5.4	Historical Development	99
		5.4.1 Scientific Management vs. Human Relations Movement	99
		5.4.2 The Current HRM Controversy	101
		5.4.3 Reorganisation or Dissolution of the HR Department?	102
	References		105

Part III Effective HRM in an Individualized and Fragile Working Environment

6 Rethinking Human Resources Management 109

	6.1	Personnel Management vs. Human Resources Management	109
		6.1.1 Leadership Is Relationship	109
		6.1.2 Human Resources Management	111
	6.2	A Single Process with a Single Aim	112
	6.3	The HR Actors	115
		6.3.1 The Top Management	116
		6.3.2 The Line Managers	117
		6.3.3 The HR Professionals	117
	6.4	The Shoulder-to-Shoulder Approach	118
	References		119

7 The Recruitment Process 121
  7.1 Staff Planning 121
    7.1.1 Quantitative and Qualitative Staffing Needs 121
    7.1.2 Challenges Within the New World of Work 122
    7.1.3 Long-Term Planning Under Uncertainty 123
    7.1.4 Practical Tips and the Division of Responsibilities
          in Staff Planning 124
  7.2 HR Marketing 125
    7.2.1 Informing, Encouraging Action—and Brand Building! 125
    7.2.2 Target Groups 126
    7.2.3 Employer Branding: Methods and Channels 129
    7.2.4 Practical Tips and the Division of Responsibilities
          in HR Marketing 132
  7.3 Staff Selection 133
    7.3.1 Phase 1: The Starting Situation 134
    7.3.2 Phase 2: Candidate Screening 135
    7.3.3 Phase 3: Selection Interviews 135
    7.3.4 Phase 4: Recruitment Tests 136
    7.3.5 Phase 5: The Decision 137
    7.3.6 Practical Tips and the Division of Responsibilities
          in Staff Selection 137
  7.4 Staff Hiring 139
    7.4.1 The Formal Employment Contract 139
    7.4.2 The Psychological Employment Contract 140
    7.4.3 Employee Onboarding 141
    7.4.4 Practical Tips and the Division of Responsibilities
          in Staff Hiring 142
  References 143

8 The Staff Management Process 145
  8.1 Staff Deployment 145
    8.1.1 Delivery on a Promise 145
    8.1.2 *What* Work Should Be Done? 146
    8.1.3 *Where* Should Work Be Done? 147
    8.1.4 *When* Should Work Be Done? 148
    8.1.5 Smart Working (from Home) 150
    8.1.6 Practical Tips and the Division of Responsibilities
          in Staff Deployment 151
  8.2 Feedback Process 153
    8.2.1 *Day-to-Day* Feedback 153
    8.2.2 360-Grad-Feedback 154
    8.2.3 Annual Staff Appraisals 155
    8.2.4 Management by Objectives 155

	8.2.5	Performance Evaluation	156
	8.2.6	Practical Tips and the Division of Responsibilities in the Feedback Process	156
8.3		Remuneration	158
	8.3.1	Principles of Remuneration	158
	8.3.2	The Goal: Work Delivered by Satisfied Employees	160
	8.3.3	Remuneration Strategy	161
	8.3.4	Personalisation Through Flexible Cafeteria-Style Plans	162
	8.3.5	Practical Tips and the Division of Responsibilities in Remuneration	164
8.4		Leadership Challenges of the Coronavirus Crisis	165
	8.4.1	Diversity Management	165
	8.4.2	Individual Work-Life Balance	167
	8.4.3	Employee Well-Being as Part of Company Culture	170
	8.4.4	Practical Tips and the Division of Responsibilities in Dealing with Leadership Challenges	172
		References	174

9 The Staff Development Process ... 175
9.1		The Revival of Staff Development	175
	9.1.1	How Did We Get Here?	176
	9.1.2	Employability	178
9.2		The Staff Development Process	180
	9.2.1	The Seven Stages of the Staff Development	180
	9.2.2	Education and Training	182
9.3		Life-Phase Oriented Staff Development	185
	9.3.1	A Question of Age (or Not)	185
	9.3.2	Personal Development Plans	188
	9.3.3	The Perfect Career Wave: Not Ladder!	190
9.4		Staff Development from an Organisational Perspective	191
	9.4.1	Knowledge Transfer	191
	9.4.2	Succession Planning	191
	9.4.3	Employee Retention	192
	9.4.4	Career Planning Options	192
	9.4.5	The Question of Return on Investment	193
	9.4.6	The Actors	194
9.5		Conclusions and Practical Tips	196
		References	198

Part I

A New World of Work

The Global Perspective: Macro-political Considerations

The Economic and Social Framework

Starting from the premise that HR management—as an expression of a new world of work—can only be understood and implemented within a contemporary context, we should make a brief analysis of this context. The following chapters focus on some economic and socio-political factors that can influence the micro-political decisions of a HR manager. From a macroeconomic perspective, we are concerned with the proportion of the working population in the total population, their qualifications and income, and the relevant job profiles. From a socio-political perspective, we also consider developments such as the dominance of certain family structures or the employment rate of women. This book begins with a few parameters from an area that has long received little attention. In recent years, however, it has become a somewhat fashionable field of research for various social sciences: demography.

1.1 Demographic Changes

The twentieth century has seen the largest population increase in the history of mankind to date. Around 1900, world population stood at about 1.5 billion people. By 1950, this figure had risen to 2.5 billion, and by the end of 2019 it had reached 7.9 billion. In just a few decades, the population of the world had multiplied many times over.

Every second, about four children are born worldwide. This amounts to about 80 million births per year. By contrast, just under two people die every second, or around 55 million a year. The result is an additional 25 million people every year. The United Nations forecasts that the global population will increase to 9.7 billion people by 2050 (see Fig. 1.1).

Despite this significant increase in world population, many of the highly developed regions of the world are discussing a contrary phenomenon: a dramatic decline in population and the associated negative social and economic effects. This is due to the fact that the above-mentioned growth is taking place almost exclusively in developing nations. The population there is expected to grow from the current six

© The Author(s), under exclusive license to Springer Nature Switzerland AG 2021
H. Troger, *Human Resource Management in a Post COVID-19 World*, Future of
Business and Finance, https://doi.org/10.1007/978-3-030-67470-0_1

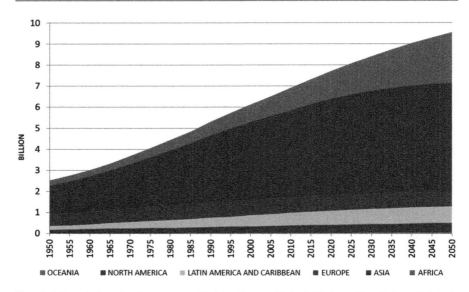

Fig. 1.1 Population development worldwide. Source: United Nations (Population Division): World Urbanization Prospects, the 2019 revision

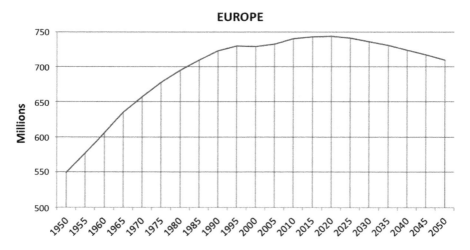

Fig. 1.2 Population trends in Europe. Source: United Nations (Population Division): World Urbanization Prospects, the 2019 revision

billion to over seven billion within three and a half decades. In industrialised nations, by contrast, it will remain stable. Many European countries are projected to see an even bigger decline in population (Fig. 1.2). Italy, for example, is expected to see a decline from today's 60.5 to 52.5 million people by 2050. In Greece, the population is facing a drop from 10.4 to 8.7 million, in Japan from 126 to 102 million. It is

Fig. 1.3 Basic shapes of age
structure graphs

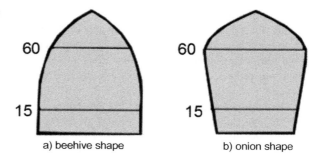

a) beehive shape   b) onion shape

interesting to note that the demographic forecasts for European countries have
changed considerably over the last 5 years. For example, in 2015 it was still expected
that Germany would have 70 million inhabitants in 2050. Today, this figure is
estimated at 80 million. The situation is similar for most central European countries.
The reason for this is immigration. In recent years, immigration has become a
significant factor in Europe—a factor that is both fixed and difficult to quantify.

The now ubiquitous debate on demography not only focuses on the numerical
composition and geographical distribution, but also on the age structure of a
population. The so-called beehive shape (see Fig. 1.3a) is considered ideal because
it represents a population that is neither increasing nor decreasing. The slow conver-
gence of this age structure is the result of high life expectancy with a constant birth
rate of just over two children per woman on average. Over the last 30 years, most
central European countries have moved further and further away from this ideal.
Their age structure graphs have increasingly taken on the 'onion shape' so feared by
demographers (cf. Fig. 1.3b). The reason for this development is a lower birth rate
combined with increasing life expectancy. The inevitable consequence of this is an
ageing population.

The following chapters outline the three main aspects of this unfavourable
demographic trend.

1.1.1 The Old Are Getting Older

In the middle of the nineteenth century, men in Europe reached an average age of
35 years and women an average age of just under 40 years. Only 40 years later, life
expectancy had risen to 47 for men and 51 for women. Between 1913 and 1993, life
expectancy rose steadily by a further 30 years in just 80 years, with men reaching an
average age of 73 and women an average age of 79. Over the last 25 years this
upward trend has continued, albeit at a much slower pace, so that today we have an
average life expectancy of 79 years for men and almost 84 years for women. The
leaders are Japan with a female life expectancy of 88 and Iceland with a male life
expectancy of 82 (see UN World Population Prospects 2020).

Since the 1990s, much greater progress has been made in poorer regions of the
world. According to the World Health Organisation (2020), life expectancy in

developing countries has increased by more than 9 years over this period. This is mainly due to successes in the fight against child mortality and a number of diseases. Of course, the economic improvements experienced by many developing countries have also contributed to the global trend towards living longer. In Ethiopia, for example, projected life expectancy has risen from just 45–64 years over the past 20 years.

The impact that an increase in life expectancy has on global ageing can be seen in the old age dependency ratio, defined as the ratio between the number of older people who are generally inactive (65 years and over) and the number of people of working age (15–64 years). The EU's old age dependency ratio is expected to reach 57% in 2100 (Eurostat 2020a, f), almost twice as high as in 2019 (31%). This means that there will be less than two people of working age for every elderly person aged 65 and over. Across Europe, the old age dependency ratio is expected to be highest in Poland (63%), followed by Italy, Malta and Finland (all 62%) and Croatia (61%). Iceland (49%) is expected to have the lowest ratio.

The proportion of elderly people is also increasing throughout Europe. Compared to 1950, the number of people aged 80 or over has quintupled and now stands at 5%, a figure that is expected to rise to 13% by the middle of the twenty-first century. However, individual countries within Europe show considerable differences (cf. Statista 2020a, b). In 2019, Germany and Italy had the highest proportion of citizens over 65 in Europe, at around 22%. At the other end of the scale was Turkey with only 7%. Somewhere in the middle were Spain with 18% or the Netherlands with 17%. When viewed globally, however, the differences are even more pronounced. Countries like Angola (2.5%) or Sierra Leone (1.9%), for example, have an extremely low proportion of older citizens. For a discussion of the impact of Covid-19 on these figures, see Sect. 1.5. However, we can anticipate here that the current pandemic—although it highlights the vulnerability of an ageing population—has not yet changed the upward trend in overall life expectancy.

The next figures make it clear that the ageing of a population is neither a given nor an immutable fact: while the average age in Germany and Italy is expected to be around 51 years in 2050, the population of the UK is expected to be almost 10 years younger by comparison (UN World Population Prospects 2020). Given otherwise similar parameters, it can be deduced that this is due to a significant difference in birth rates, a topic we will look at in more detail in the next section.

1.1.2 Shrinking Numbers of Young People

According to the Federal Statistical Office (Destatis 2020), almost 780,000 children were born in Germany in 2019. Although this is a considerable increase since the low birth rate of 2011 (663,000), it is still only just over half of what it was in 1964, when more than 1,357,000 births were registered in both West and East Germany combined. Today, these 57-year-olds can claim to have been born in the year with the most births of all time, a record that may never be broken. Despite this increase in the last 10 years, the fertility rate[1] in Germany and most other central European countries still lags far behind that of America, Asia and above all Africa. The situation in Germany is comparable to Austria or Switzerland, in Italy it is even worse. However, considerably more children are born in the Scandinavian countries. Great Britain also has a higher birth rate than most central or southern European countries. France has been a notable exception for many years, with a birth rate of 2.1 children per woman of childbearing age. This means that France's population structure is almost perfectly in line with the hive form that is considered ideal by population scientists.

The crude birth rate[2] illustrates the problem of low birth figures in some central and southern European countries even more clearly (cf. Eurostat 2020b): in 2019, it was at a level of 7.3 births in Italy, 7.9 in Spain and 8.1 in Greece, while in France and the United Kingdom the rate was 11.5, and in Ireland it even reached just under 12.5.

The reasons for these low birth rates are as varied as they are controversial: changes in lifestyle, a general increase in the number of people choosing to live alone, greater economic prosperity, the family policies of the countries concerned, higher levels of education, the desire for professional fulfilment, which in turn places even greater demands on the individual, and last but not least, a general anxiety about the future. Demographers and sociologists observe a negative correlation between the educational level and social status of the family, on the one hand, and the number of children on the other. Relationships between university graduates, for example, statistically produce fewer children, they are older when they have their first child, and the number of childless couples in this group is also higher than in the group with a lower educational level.

There is no scientific evidence on how economic conditions affect birth rates. For example, while the birth rate in Greece is stagnating, it is rising steadily in Lithuania, despite the fact that both countries have experienced economic difficulties in recent years. However, there seems to be a clear link between the birth rate and either family policy or the unemployment rate of a country. For example, the high unemployment rate in some southern European countries (Greece, Spain, Italy) has a particularly strong influence on the decline in births.

Finally, a look at family policy shows that from a statistical point of view, it is striking that countries which actively support the reconciliation of work and family life through official policies (e.g., France or the Scandinavian countries) currently have the highest birth rates in Europe.

Even without a more in-depth analysis of the issue, it can be safely assumed that the flattening of the age structure of the European population is linked to the sharp decline in births over the last 40 years. However, readers over 50 should not reproach

---

[1]Put simply, the fertility rate expresses the average number of children of all women in a country between the ages of 15 and 49.

[2]The number of live births in 1 year in relation to the average population in the same year. The value is shown per 1000 inhabitants.

themselves for having contributed to the pension crisis because they may not have brought enough children into the world. The general ageing of the European (and even more so the Japanese) population is due less to falling birth rates than to the rapid increase in life expectancy—an overall highly desirable development.

1.1.3   A More Diverse Society

According to the European statistics portal Eurostat (2020c), 21.8 million people from outside the EU (i.e., non-EU nationals) were living in the European Union on 1 January 2019. This represents 5% of the total population. EU citizens with a migration background are not included in this statistic, of course. In 2018 alone, 3.9 million people immigrated to one of the 27 EU countries, while 2.6 million people emigrated from the EU. In addition, an estimated 1.4 million people move from one EU country to another every year. On 1st January 2019, the largest numbers of non-nationals across the 27 member states of the EU were found in Germany (10.1 million), Italy (5.3 million), France (4.9 million) and Spain (4.8 million).

Since WWII, Europe has provided a safe haven for citizens of former European colonies and for war refugees from countries such as the former Yugoslavia, and more recently, Romania and Syria. Germany, the country with the highest immigration rate, had a surplus of about 1.2 million people in 2015. This means that 1.2 million more people moved to Germany that year than left Germany. In the same year, the United Kingdom and Austria had a surplus of approximately 400,000 and 123,000, respectively. At the other end of the spectrum, Greece saw about 35,600 more people leaving than arriving. Romania fared only slightly better with a negative net migration of 35,000 (Eurostat 2020c).

With the media focusing heavily on armed conflicts and economic migration, it could easily be forgotten that these are not the only reasons for migration to Europe. Other important motivating factors relate to education, religion or health.

A 2009 Gallup poll showed that 38% of adult Africans wanted to emigrate, and about half of them said they would choose Europe if they did. This illustrates an important point. The population of 650 million at the time of the survey has now risen to 1.2 billion and is expected to double again by 2050. As the economic, climatic and political situation is not expected to improve significantly by then, this would mean that around 950 million people could become migrants—with half of them heading for Europe (Gallup 2009).

In view of these forecasts, some experts believe that any efforts to improve living conditions through international development aid will at best be a stopgap solution with little impact on migration flows. The predicted population decline in European countries, at least in the traditional immigration countries, must be seen in this context. In any case, demographic changes will continue to be strongly influenced by migration to other countries. While this is likely to have little impact on the size and age structure of the European or American population as a whole, the impact at national, regional and local level will be significant.

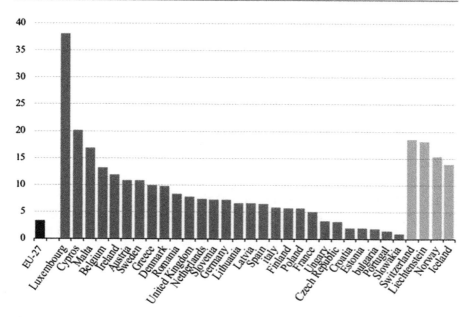

Fig. 1.4 Immigration in Europe. Data: Eurostat (2020c)

At this stage, we should not be too concerned with detailed calculations of population estimates for 2035 or 2050. However, in the ongoing debate on demography, the immigration aspect will most likely need to be reassessed. Immigration will mitigate the declining population growth of the central European nations and it will also slow down the ageing of the population, due to the low average age of migrants and their higher fertility rate.

Overall, the inherently predictable, slow and unexciting nature of demographic developments acquires a new dynamism and an element of suspense when combined with the volatility of migratory flows. And whether we like it or not, a discussion of the pros and cons of immigration is beyond the scope of this book—our world will undoubtedly become more diverse. Politicians will be called upon to address this new situation and hopefully find solutions that work for everyone. Immigrants will have to be successfully integrated. The impact of immigration on the labour market and the implications for businesses are discussed in more detail in Chap. 2 (Fig. 1.4).

1.2   Socio-political Trends

The demographic developments discussed above, which are slow and gradual, have long-term consequences that should serve as a warning to future generations. Today's social interactions are also determined by various trends. The most important of these will be briefly outlined below.

1.2.1 'Family' Can Mean Many Things

The 'normal' nuclear family, consisting of father, mother and child, is no longer the norm. Our ideas about what a family looks like are changing and they now encompass a range of different family structures. The number of single households, same-sex marriages and mixed families is increasing. Because of the diversity and complexity of these arrangements, there are no precise statistics.

Regardless of family structure and composition, all these new variants help to ensure social cohesion as they prepare the next generation to lead independent lives of their own.

1.2.1.1 The Erosion and the Revival of the Family

The many different family living arrangements clearly indicate an erosion of the traditional family model. However, today's sociologists and psychologists never tire of emphasising the importance of family culture, awards are given for family-friendliness, modern companies have recognised the motivational effect of family-friendly staffing policies, and children spend more time with their grandparents than ever before.

After several decades of being radically challenged, the family is now enjoying renewed societal and political appreciation as one of the core building blocks of society, and as a place of safety and regeneration for individuals. We can see this in the wealth of measures designed to support the family. While this trend was initially driven by political decision-makers, it is now increasingly supported and complemented by businesses. The reasons for this targeted support for families are falling fertility rates and the associated demographic and labour market implications.

For the younger generation, too, family is 'on-trend' and is no longer seen as narrow-minded and stuffy. Young people now perceive it as a place of safety—a benefit that, given the many modern-day threats and uncertainties, is even appreciated by teenagers. It may further play a role here that the generation born between 1985 and 2000 has generally had positive experiences with their families—while growing up in a time characterised by staff cutbacks, unstable working conditions and high property prices, which often made it impossible for them to climb the property ladder. Family support networks provide a stark contrast to the harsh realities of the business world. The Europe-wide phenomenon of 'boomerang kids' is a side effect of this.

1.2.1.2 Friendships

The renaissance of the family is facilitated also by a much broader definition of what family means. Compared to earlier generations, we think of it in a wider context. For example, many people today see their closest friends as their extended family. Co-parenting has become an accepted way of raising a child, regardless of whether the parents have ever had a romantic relationship or not. Friends are no longer limited to being part of separate spheres of our social life, they can play a much more important role. Friends are the new family.

The traditional family model has proven to be fragile. Therefore, many people see friendships as a suitable substitute.[3] Katja Thimm (2014) even speaks of a 'third way' in the German news magazine *Der Spiegel*, pointing to the results of a Jacobs Study from 2014, according to which 85% of those surveyed by the Allensbach Institute (2014) considered having good friends to be of particular importance. The categories 'family' and 'relationships' followed behind.

Sociologist Janosch Schobin (2016) speaks of a much more 'friendship-driven' society (in German: *Verfreundschaftlichung*) and an accompanying increase in consideration and caring for one another.

1.2.1.3 Family Is Everything

New partnership models, multi-generational households and friendships are modern forms of living together that demonstrate that a new family culture, based on a strong sense of togetherness, is flourishing—contrary to the widely perceived collapse of family values. The conservative view of traditional family models has been replaced by the concept of the family as a generic term for a variety of trusting, warm and caring relationships between people. In this context, family really *is everything*. This is also the view of German futurologist Horst Opaschowski (2014), who sees the family as the only reliable and safe haven: It offers us connection through enriching relationships and at the same time protects us from the risk of poverty. He calls it 'the best life insurance' because it is cheap and compassionate.

1.2.2 The Rise of Living Alone

Alongside the new models of family life, another—opposite—trend can be observed: the trend towards individualisation or, in other words, towards a 'single society'. More and more people want to live alone.

There has been an enormous increase in single-person households across central Europe over the last 15 years, and they have now become the most common type of household. A growing number of people seem to disregard the societal pressure of having to be in a relationship and choose to live alone. According to statistics from the British Office for National Statistics (2016), married women are now in the minority in England. At the beginning of the 1970s, around 85% of all women were married by the age of 30. Today, this figure is only around 30% in the UK, and around 41% in Germany—another country with an above-average proportion of single-person households compared with the rest of Europe (Statista 2020c). There are big differences between rural areas, where traditional models of co-habitation still dominate, and urban areas, where single-person households seem to be the model of the future. Munich is Europe's 'singles capital', according to a report by münchen.tv from 23 January 2015, which claimed that more than half of all households in the city were occupied by singles.

---

[3]This explicitly omits social media friendships between young people.

Given the high divorce rates, the main reason for this rise in single-person households could be seen in the failure of the 'together for life' model. However, surveys also show that values such as independence, personal freedom or flexibility are consistently rated very highly by people and are perceived as something one should aspire to.

Another indication of why single life is attractive to people comes from the tourism industry: holidays for singles are the fastest growing tourism segment in recent years. According to a study by tourism researcher Constanza Bianchi from Queensland University of Technology in Australia, the main motivation for single travellers is a desire for relaxation, freedom, and self-discovery.

Gender differences can also be observed in this rise of living alone. On average, women live alone more often than men—but only from their mid-50s onwards. Younger men are more likely to live in a one-person household than women of the same age. This is only reversed at an older age.

Women over 70 are predominantly living alone (many of them widowed). Among men of this age group, the proportion of singles is only around 25% (Bianchi 2015).

For many young adults today, living with their parents and delaying the start of their own family is another attractive option that is linked to the rise in single-person households. According to the German Federal Statistical Office (Destatis 2016), in 2014, 42% of all young Germans between the age of 18 and 29 were still (or again) living with their parents. In the past, this phenomenon was only common in the southern European nations. Many people who choose not to live with a partner evidently regard living at home as a more attractive alternative to living in a single-person household.

1.2.3 Gender

When the discussion about a women's quota first emerged in Germany, there was an astonishing amount of whining and protests throughout the large corporations—and not only at board level. 'A blanket quota of 30% would not benefit employee participation if it meant that women could be given a seat at the board without the backing of their co-workers', wrote Michael Brecht, chairman of Daimler, in 2014. At the time, women accounted for around 20% of Daimler's workforce.

A survey of DAX 30 listed companies by the auditing firm KPMG, before the quota came into force (January 1, 2016), showed that women in management positions were more likely to be in charge of communicative and creative areas, such as human resources, PR and communications. In this 'pink ghetto', women were supposedly able to make the most of their strengths (KPMG 2016). The women's quota came and with it—albeit slowly—women started to move into the executive and supervisory boards of corporations. The concerns that were raised in the KPMG survey turned out to be unfounded. According to the results of a further study by consulting firm Korn Ferry (2020), the largest group of female board members was not confined to human resources, but instead, the women were heading up core business activities.

1.2.3.1 Male vs. Female Leaders

The classic stereotype sees the male boss as a tough and uncompromising 'doer' and the female counterpart as a team player willing to compromise. Evidence to the contrary was provided by Russell Reynolds Associates (2016): The management consulting firm surveyed over 4300 female and male decision-makers in 25 countries on classic gender stereotypes at an executive level. They concluded that the more women were represented in the management structure of a company, the less their behaviour differed from that of their male colleagues. The study suggested that, at a fundamental level, men were significantly more competitive and assertive, whereas women were more concerned with their social environment. As the proportion of women at executive level increased, however, the attitudes and behaviours of male and female managers gradually converged. When the female proportion had reached a minimum of 22%, it was observed that female leaders were starting to mirror male assertiveness levels. A proportion of 26% and higher meant that there were no longer any significant differences in competitiveness.

At the same time, the social aspect took a back seat with female leaders. Both genders were observed to be more focused, more competitive, and thus more successful—but 'tougher'. The author of the study, Joachim Bohner, summed up the results: 'Regardless of gender, when the proportion of women increases, managers adapt to embody the ideal characteristics and competencies of a top decision-maker or CEO. These are highly performance-oriented individuals, with the strength and emotional ability to motivate people and win them over, yet they do not shy away from tough decisions if the transformation processes require it. Gender-specific differences lose their relevance'. (cf. ibid.)

1.2.3.2 The Female Employment Rate

Raising women's employment rate and increasing the national birth rate are considered key economic objectives in most EU countries. These seemingly contradictory goals are both important pre-requisites for the future financing of pensions and for overcoming the current shortage of qualified workers.

The northern European nations are leading the way (cf. Eurostat 2020d). While in Italy in 2019, for example, only 54% of women were participating in the labour force, in Sweden it was 80%, almost the same as for men (84%). In some EU member states there is still a considerable gap between the employment rates of men and women, even if the rise in general unemployment rates, caused by the economic crisis, is taken into account. In 2019, this gap was highest in Italy and Greece (20% points), followed by Poland (15.5). The smallest gender employment gaps, by contrast, were recorded in Latvia (3.5) and in Sweden (4).

Although the level of women's qualifications is generally rising—half of all students in Europe are now female—the number of mothers in highly qualified positions is still relatively low. This is due to the persistence of traditional gender roles for men and women. Despite theoretical equality, when children or vulnerable relatives need to be looked after and cared for, it is mostly women who take on this responsibility. For many of them, full-time employment is then no longer an option. It is therefore not surprising, that a recent study by the German Institute for Employment Research showed that two thirds of all part-time positions in Germany were held by women.

1.2.3.3 Part-Time as a Career Killer

For most women, starting a family marks the end of their full-time employment and with that also their chances of promotion to management positions. Many experts, both male and female, believe that the decision to go part-time is the biggest career killer for women. Although it can now almost be taken for granted that most organisations offer a range of part-time employment options, this does not apply to executive positions. According to a study by AT Kearney (2018), almost a third of the women asked deemed career and children incompatible, and 77% of the female managers featured in the survey had remained childless.

In light of increasing staff shortages at executive levels, attitudes towards part-time work may need to change. Yet society, and more specifically companies, are still reluctant to explore different approaches that involve part-time work because long working hours and overtime are still widely regarded as a prerequisite for professional success and as a sign of commitment and loyalty. Regardless of this, there are now numerous studies around the world that suggest that job sharing can be a viable alternative for some executive positions. Any organisational or cost disadvantages would likely be offset by a number of benefits, such as flexibility, representation and productivity. It seems, therefore, that our attitudes towards attendance and full-time work may have to change to allow for new ways of working in the future.

1.3   Generational Diversity and the Battle for Distribution

For most people today, the term 'generation' has several meanings. We use it to categorise people of different ages into older and younger groups, and it also evokes a variety of stereotypes. In relation to our own family—our parents and perhaps our own children or even grandchildren—the meaning of 'generation' seems very clear as we base it on our own experience of the multi-generational family structure. In this context, age only plays a minor role. If we look at the term in a more differentiated way, and not just as a distinction between 'old' and 'young', or tied to the degree of kinship, then a 'generation' can also be understood as a group of people in a comparable temporal and social context. Such cohorts create a common social identity through similar values, characteristics, and actions (cf. Lüscher et al. 2014).

This shared identity, based on a connection to historical events or simply the year of birth (e.g., the post-war generation, or millennials) is linked to their social perspective and manifests itself in the way they think, feel and act.

This last definition of 'generation' is the most relevant for our purposes because it best explains the interests and behaviours of people in organisations. The following overview lists the five generations of employees based on their year of birth (cr. Troger 2019).

1.3.1 Traditionalists and Baby Boomers

The oldest cohort is often referred to as the traditionalist or post-war generation. They were born in the post-war era, between 1922 and 1945, and the majority of them have already retired. However, some people in their mid-70s still hold the reins of political and economic power. They often share positions of power with members of the subsequent generation—the baby boomers. The 'boomers', born between 1943 and 1964, are by far the largest cohort and also the wealthiest of the five generations. Many of them are in top executive positions of companies, organisations or political parties, and consequently, they are the main decision-makers of our time. This, perhaps inevitably, turns them into the automatic enemy for younger generations. The secret of the baby boomers' success is their adaptability. Their engagement with the company or organisation is remarkably high, they are very idealistic and also very sensitive in discussions about themselves or their values.

1.3.2 Generation X

Gen X, named after the novel by Douglas Coupland, published in 1991, describes those born between 1965 and 1980. They dislike the clichés and moral values of their parents as much as they dislike the idea of a lifelong commitment to a single employer. A certain feeling of having arrived 'too late' in this world is compounded by justified concerns about a real shortage of resources and high national debt. The prosperity of the previous generation can no longer be reproduced; instead, this generation has experienced periods of great economic and political uncertainty (oil crisis, the Cold War, etc.).

Today, most Xers have reached the end of their (short) career ladder. The next level is often still occupied by a baby boomer, who will probably soon vacate their position for a millennial to take over. This lack of prospects is commonly reflected in fairly moderate levels of work motivation. It is no coincidence that this cohort has frequently been characterised as 'slackers', alienated and disaffected. Due to the uniformity and predictability of their behaviour, the Gen X employee generally does not pose any major challenges in terms of HR management.

1.3.3   Generation Y

The term Gen Y is used for those born after 1980. They take networking and global thinking for granted but resent being pigeon-holed. Their strong sense of individualism is reflected in many different worlds they inhabit—from socially committed environmentalists to materialistic hedonists—this population cohort encompasses everything. The Internet, or rather their relationship to media in general, is their common denominator. It is no coincidence that they are the first generation that is often referred to as 'digital natives'. Last but not least, we know them also as 'millennials', because they began to immerse themselves in the world at large around the turn of the century, when they were teenagers.

Gen Y is very well-educated. There has never been a higher proportion of graduates. Sentiments like: 'Why can't I travel the world and still have a successful career?' may well sum up the typical Gen Y attitude. The old systems and methods for doing things are challenged, if they threaten to impact the millennial's life plan, and important life decisions are made according to the immediate advantages and disadvantages for the individual's well-being. Millennials are optimistic and self-confident, but they have little confidence in politics. They generally prefer to keep all their options open, both professionally as well as in their private lives, and have a strong drive for personal autonomy and self-actualization.

The tech-savvy millennials prefer to work in virtual teams rather than in rigid company hierarchies. As employees, they demand more freedom as well as fulfilling tasks and opportunities, while also demanding more time for family and leisure activities. They are no longer willing to prioritise work above all else and instead expect to achieve the much vaunted 'work-life balance'. Gen Y fiercely insists on the compatibility of career and private life and in the process it does not shy away from breaking some old taboos—equal opportunities, same-sex marriage, paternal leave and alternative family structures have all become part of normal life.

1.3.4   Generation Z

In contrast to Gen Y, the cohort that follows them no longer sees the digital world as a parallel universe that one dips in and out of. The post-millennial generation—also a generation of 'digital natives'—live entirely in the digital world. Visions of microchip implants have lost their fear factor among this age group. 'From the very first images of our birth, we live on the web and control our world with tablet and smartphone', says Philipp Riederle (2013) in his 'autobiography' of his generation (transl. from German: *Who we are and what we want*). The renowned academic Christian Scholz (2014) describes Gen Z as a 'work-shy mollycoddled cohort', whose radical self-centredness is now starting to spread across to other generations.

Gen Z is even more strongly influenced and disillusioned by the economic and financial crisis than Gen Y. These young people have been growing up with mass redundancies, youth unemployment and insecure working conditions on the one hand, and multi-million salaries for board members on the other. For Scholz, this is the main reason why Gen Z rejects any notion of an emotional attachment between employee and company and insists on a clear separation between professional and private life. The millennials have already rejected the emotional commitment to the company, but they are still much more likely to form emotional attachments to individuals within that company. Gen Z no longer seeks these connections. They are interested foremost in themselves and, at best, in projects they find appealing.

1.3.5   The Failure of the Intergenerational Contract

Since the nineteenth century, most European societies have based their welfare system on an unwritten intergenerational contract: There is a contributing active generation and a receiving generation of pensioners. By bringing up a third, subsequent generation, the contributing generation can expect to be provided for when it is time to retire. This intergenerational contract has its origins in the traditional family structure: parents care for their young and also support their own parents. When the children have grown up, the circle is repeated. Until the 1970s, this system worked without any problems: Employees made financial contributions to pension funds, which directly benefited pensioners. At the same time, the contributors themselves also acquired the rights to a pension, which was then financed by the next generation of workers.

Due to the shortage of young people (birth rates have halved since the 1960s in many central European countries), this system has long ceased to function as it was intended: a shrinking number of young people now bear the burden of financing an increasing number of older people. In Germany, for example, there were 40 pensioners for every 100 contributors in 1995. By 2015, this had increased to 60, and in 2035 it will be an estimated 80 pensioners. The situation is even more serious in Italy and other southern European countries, where the effect is exacerbated by high youth unemployment and negative migration balances. In 2019, there were on average 2.9 people of working age for every person over 65 in Europe. In 2070, this ratio is expected to drop to 1.7 (cf. EU-Commission 2020). The continuous rise in life expectancy aggravates this problem because it leads to increased pension payments. In 1960, the average time spent drawing a pension in Europe was 10 years—today it is already 17 years, and the upward trend is continuing.

In hindsight, the failure of the intergenerational contract was only a matter of time since it was based on two false premises: a birth rate and a life expectancy that were both assumed to be consistent. Instead, the former declined, and the latter increased. As a result, policy-makers in most European nations face major challenges. The beneficiaries of the existing redistribution system have a steadily growing political majority in the population, which creates the potential for social conflict. While the 'injustice' of this situation is growing, the power of those who have to endure it is diminishing.

1.3.6   Generational Equity and the Distribution of Scarce Resources

Given this widely perceived injustice, what are the criteria are for a fair distribution of resources between the generations? The Intergenerational Justice Index-Iji by Pieter Vanhuysse (2013) provides an answer. Vanhuisse's study was published by the Bertelsmann Foundation for the European Centre for Welfare Policy and Research. He used the following four criteria, or 'dimensions' as he calls them, to determine the Intergenerational Justice Index for the 29 OECD countries:

- The 'ecological footprint' as a unit of measurement for the amount of resources consumed.
- Public debt rates per child.
- Child poverty in relation to old age poverty.
- The ratio of elderly to non-elderly public spending as a bias indicator.

The country with the most positive assessment was Estonia. South Korea, Israel, New Zealand, Hungary and the northern European countries of Norway, Denmark, Sweden and Finland also took the top positions. Germany was ranked 13th, in the middle, while the USA, Japan, Italy and Greece were firmly at the bottom of the table.

Within organisations and companies, competition between the generations manifests itself to varying degrees. Alongside the financial contributions towards retirement provision, there are a number of other resources and their scarcity, as can be expected, determines the intensity of the discussion about their distribution. Leadership positions, decision-making power, income, leisure time, work-life balance, or the job itself—all these are limited—or at least there is the perception that they are—and therefore they are increasingly contested in terms of intergenerational distribution.

The prevailing differences in salaries between older and younger employees are one of the main causes of envy and frustration among the younger generations—especially since a skill comparison often speaks in favour of the younger colleague. The appointment of executive positions is also frequently based on years of service rather than performance. Despite the much-cited battle for young talent, older employees continue to win the battle for distribution—quite simply because demographically they are and remain in the majority and therefore, they have control.

Economic and socio-political considerations aside, no matter how harmonious and value-based a company's culture may be, it will not be possible to satisfy all employees equally when it comes to the distribution of scarce resources. A management position, a salary increase, participation in a development program, a company car, the security of a permanent contract or a vertical part-time contract, an assistant, a desk by the window—all these are incentives or improvements that can normally only be granted to a limited number of people. Accordingly, these privileges will be contested to a greater or lesser extent.

1.4   Economic Factors

From the point of view of HR management, it is useful to start with a description of the macroeconomic situation by looking at the employment situation within the population. However, it should also include a discussion of the 'right' qualifications, meaning the jobs that offer the best future prospects.

1.4.1   Employment

For most people, in addition to securing their livelihood, gainful employment contributes greatly to their sense of social belonging and is therefore an essential prerequisite for quality of life. In the coming years and decades, the demographic changes mentioned earlier will have a direct impact on the working age population. This will affect the labour market in four different areas: the general availability of workers, their age, their qualifications and their origin. A high employment rate, and in particular a highly skilled workforce, is a major contributor to a country's prosperity.

1.4.1.1 Employed Population

In 2019, more than 240 million people aged 20–64 were in employment in Europe (see Eurostat 2020d). This represents an employment rate of around 73% of the population of that age. By comparison, this figure was 69% in 2005. In many EU countries the consequences of the financial and economic crisis continued to be felt on the labour market for many years after 2008. At the same time, however, all EU Member States saw GDP rise again. But while Sweden and most other EU countries in northern Europe had employment rates between 75% and 80%, the countries in southern Europe (i.e., Spain, Italy, Greece) had employment rates of 60% and below. Of course, the pandemic has had a significant impact on this important statistic, which will be discussed below. But regardless of Covid-19, the wide gap between northern and southern (and eastern) Europe remains.

1.4.1.2 Unemployment

First things first: The lack of young talent due to low birth rates, unfortunately, does not have a positive effect on (youth) unemployment, which is usually based more on short-term parameters. While unemployment rates in the economic strongholds of Europe and America have fallen continuously since the financial crisis of 2008, this is not the case in most southern and eastern European countries. They face the critical challenge of having to cope with perhaps the most negative aspect of all demographic changes: low birth rates combined with extremely high youth unemployment.

At least this was the situation before the pandemic. In March 2020, Covid-19 was added to the mix and with it came an immediate slump in sales and a general uncertainty about the future, leading to an employment crisis in economic sectors previously considered safe and invulnerable. Everything was suddenly called into question. By and large, staffing costs are among the items of expenditure that can be adjusted downwards faster than others, and it is relatively easy to terminate employment contracts. Despite the fact that the governments of many countries have introduced measures, bans and incentives to prevent redundancies, countless people are currently (August 2020) losing their jobs, and the hiring of new staff has been postponed, cancelled or replaced by short-time work. An end to this trend is not yet in sight. More on this in Sect. 1.4.

1.4.1.3 Employment of Older Workers

When Otto Bismarck introduced legislation on old age and disability provision in 1889, a worker in Germany could retire at the age of 70. In 2019—130 years later—the retirement age in most industrialised countries will only begin about 3–5 years earlier, although working conditions have improved considerably. The average life expectancy of an employee in Germany in the late nineteenth century was around 40 years, whereas today it is almost twice as high.

According to calculations by the European Commission (2012), the number of Europeans over 65 will have more than doubled by 2060. The proportion of people over 80 will almost quadruple in that period. By contrast, the proportion of 20–64-year-olds will fall significantly: only one in two Europeans will belong to this age group, which is particularly productive in economic terms. Against this background, it is clear that the main challenge for European pension systems is to achieve or maintain adequate pension levels, while at the same time not overburdening future workers. Although life expectancy in Europe is growing steadily at around 3 years per decade, adjustments to the retirement age are being made only very hesitantly. The adjustment to 67 years has been hailed as a great success in the countries for which it applies, but it will be far from sufficient. Sooner or later the situation will call for greater flexibility in linking retirement age to life expectancy. For about 100 years, people could retire at around 65, but life expectancy increased by about 30 years during this period. In essence, life expectancy relative to retirement age is as unrealistic today as it was around 1900 when pensions were first introduced.

1.4.1.4 Employment of Foreign Workers

Free movement within the European Union enables EU citizens to take up work in any of the member states—and a growing number of people are taking advantage of this opportunity. In 2019, a total of 9.5 million EU citizens were working in another EU country without holding citizenship of that country. In 2009, it was only around 6.0 million, which means that their number rose by 60% in 10 years (cf. Eurostat 2020a, f). The EU-wide number of workers from countries outside the European Union increased by 14% from 7.6 to 8.7 million in the same period.

The total number of foreign workers in the EU rose from 13.1 to 17.5 million between 2009 and 2019. Of the 17.5 million workers with foreign passports in the EU, 4.5 million worked in Germany. The UK (3.5 million), Italy (2.4 million) and Spain (2.0 million) were also large labour markets for foreign workers. The proportion was particularly high in Luxembourg, where in 2019, more than half (51%) of all workers had a foreign passport (cf. Eurostat 2020c).

With regard to the labour market, it is interesting to note that foreign workers are on average younger than domestic workers. In 2019 across the EU, around 69% of all foreign workers were younger than 45 years, compared to 54% for domestic workers (cf. Eurostat 2020c). On 1 January 2019, the median age of the national population in the EU-27 was 45 years, while the median age of non-nationals living in the EU-27 was 36.

Last but not least: In the EU-27, more than one fifth (21.8%) of workers born outside the EU were employed on a temporary fixed-term contract in 2019, compared with 13.0% for domestic workers and 15.2% for workers born in another EU member state (cf. Eurostat 2020c).

1.4.2 Qualifications

The right qualifications are a crucial prerequisite for participation in the labour market. Qualifications are classified according to the International Standard Classification of Education (ISCED). They distinguish between low, medium and high qualifications, taking into account the highest officially recognised educational attainment. In recent years, the skill levels of the EU labour force have increased significantly. While around 26% of the labour force had a high level of education in 2007, by 2017 the figure had risen to 34%. Ireland had the highest rate in the EU at 48%. In seven other countries, the proportion was also already above 40% (cf. Destatis 2018).

In recent years, women have significantly increased their educational advantage over men. In 2017, on average in the EU, women (38%) were significantly more likely than men (30%) to have a university degree or equivalent qualification. Germany was the only EU country where the labour force included more men (31%) than women (27%) with a high level of education.

The proportion of low-skilled workers has decreased significantly over the last 10 years. For women, it fell from 22% to 16% and for men from 25% to 20%.

1.4.2.1 Continuing Education and Training

Despite the increased complexity of the world of work, the behaviour of the working population with regard to continuing education and training has hardly changed in the last 10 years. This is reflected in surveys that looked at the recent participation of people aged 25–64 in all types of training.

Many people, especially in the northern European countries, take it for granted that they will engage in continuing education during their working lives. In 2017, around 30% of employed 25- to 64-year-olds surveyed in Denmark, Finland and Sweden reported that they had participated in education or training events in the 4 weeks preceding the survey. The EU average for recent participation in a training event was 12%. The unemployed (10%) were on average slightly less likely to attend training than the employed (12%). Among the employed, training rates varied according to gender, type of contract or size of the company. Across the EU as a whole, women (13%) were more likely to participate than men (10%), and those on fixed-term contracts (16%) were more likely to participate than those in permanent employment (12%). High rates of participation in continuing training across the EU were found particularly in the social professions: In the area of 'education and training', 20% of employees had participated in CET in 2017, in 'health and social work' it was 19% (cf. Destatis 2018).

1.4.2.2 Qualifications of Immigrants

On average, newly arrived immigrants are 10 years younger than the native population. Moreover, they are no longer less educated—far from it. While the proportion of university graduates among immigrants was only 16% in 2004 (i.e., roughly the same as the proportion within the native population), by 2014 43% of new immigrants had a university degree or comparable qualification. As many as 35% of them still had intermediate vocational training (cf. Eurostat 2020e).

This trend towards higher educational levels among immigrants is also reflected in the cohort without school-leaving qualifications or vocational training: The share of immigrants without qualifications fell from 36% in 2004 to 22% in 2014. Nevertheless, the above-average share of university graduates is still offset by an almost equally above-average share of low-skilled workers.

Despite this, over a third of immigrants with tertiary education had worked in a position that did not require that level of education (ranging from 34.3% for those born in the EU to 36.2% for those born elsewhere), compared to around 20% of the native population (ibid.).

1.4.3 Jobs in a World Shaped by Industry 4.0

What will the world of work look like in the coming years and decades? Which jobs will be in high demand and which will disappear? On behalf of the German Federal Ministry of Labour and Social Affairs, an international team of experts drew up a projection for Germany up to the year 2030. It assumed average annual growth of the German economy of 1.5%, an annual increase in productivity of 1.7% and a rise in real per capita income of 1.9% (cf. Bundesinstitut für Berufsbildung 2014).

According to the results of this prognostic study, Germany (like most central European countries) is predicted to continue to grow, especially in the service sector. However, declines are expected in the administrative and especially the manufacturing sector. Demand for the education professions will also decline due to low birth and infant rates. The demand for nursing and care services, by contrast, is expected to increase significantly. In general, all health care professions will experience a marked increase.

In the area of graduate jobs, the largest share is expected to go to people with degrees in law, economics and the social sciences. However, a strong increase in employment opportunities is also predicted for the much-needed technical professions. The experts conclude that although the German labour market will be subject to considerable changes over the next 15 years, these changes will be easy to manage with well-chosen employment policies and also thanks to the flexibility of

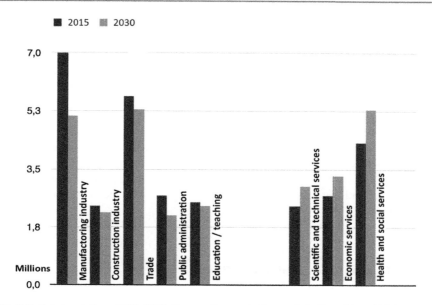

Fig. 1.5 Job descriptions 2015–2030. Source: Economix Research & Consulting (2016)

the labour market. Figure 1.5 gives an overview of the biggest changes to be expected in job profiles between 2010 and 2030.

Industry 4.0 has been a much-discussed topic lately, and one of its characteristic features is the increasingly widespread digitalisation of the working world. This transformation is impacting entire sectors, job profiles and qualification requirements, and it is changing established structures and business processes. When it comes to assessing the possible effects of this digital transformation of work and value creation processes, the opinions of experts differ. According to Carl Benedikt Frey's polarisation thesis (2013), the advancing automation in capitalist societies leads to a split into a smaller proportion of highly qualified technical and scientific workers on the one hand and a larger proportion of still unqualified workers on the other. This stands in contrast to the so-called upgrading thesis, which predicts a general upgrading of qualifications.

There is no doubt that these new technologies will have tangible and lasting consequences for industrial processes. The dissemination of these new digital technologies is still in its infancy and their impact on the world of work has not yet been fully explored. It is therefore not yet possible to make any general statements about a possible devaluation or upgrading of jobs and qualifications. Any changes must be considered in their specific context and in relation to the larger structure to which they refer.

1.5   The Coronavirus-Effect

There is little doubt that the year 2020 will go down in the annals of history. Sars-CoV-2 represents the biggest health, social and economic challenge since the end of the Second World War. The pandemic has changed society almost overnight—at a local and a global level. Government-imposed quarantines, school and factory closures, curfews, border closures—the drastic measures and the associated restrictions of personal freedoms knew hardly any limits and were previously unthinkable in most democracies. Even if the virus were to disappear completely, its legacy will continue to shape the way we live and work for a long time to come.

Continuing our macroeconomic considerations, some aspects of the Covid-19 pandemic are outlined below—with the caveat that this is neither an exhaustive nor a detailed list.

1.5.1   Demography and Social Policy

The pandemic has highlighted the demographic changes described earlier in this chapter. It has caused the greatest suffering to the oldest generations because they are the most vulnerable in this crisis. Not only because they are at greater risk of developing more severe complications from the virus itself, but also because they are the most affected by social distancing and other restrictive measures that were introduced in many places—making them the most isolated and the most affected by this social isolation. In other words, the ageing of the population and other trends—such as isolation and the rise of single-person households, high population density and urbanisation—are linked to the impact of the pandemic, making it much more difficult to counter its effects.

1.5.2   Generational Conflicts

While it is true that the older generations are more directly affected by Covid-19 (despite greater adherence to measures that restrict leisure and social activities and the wearing of masks), the indirect costs of the pandemic will affect the younger generations much more, and they will feel this impact for much longer. These indirect effects relate mainly to higher costs of living and long-term prospects in the face of increased public debt. Together with the current demographic trends (fewer young people in an ageing population), we may end up with a situation that feeds a certain 'generational malaise'. The post-pandemic recovery of Europe and the rest of the world must therefore have active solidarity between generations (as well as between nations) at its core.

1.5.3 Social and Economic Policies

The restrictions imposed by the authorities on social activities and the loss of household incomes, inevitably lead to a general reluctance to spend money, which in turn results in less investment by businesses. Consequently, aggregate demand will decline and, without government intervention, the economies affected will head straight for recession. Expert estimates in individual countries predict a decline in economic output of between 5% and 30% this year (as of August 2020).

What was striking in this time of crisis was the speed and cross-party unity with which politicians everywhere exceeded each other in their commitment to providing financial support to the population and to businesses. The ensuing increase in public debt, on the other hand, is rarely discussed, nor is the inevitable tax increase that will eventually follow, or the threat of inflation.

The fact remains that government influence has increased and will continue to increase across countries. This applies to social redistribution—for example, through higher taxation of wealth—but it also means direct state intervention in operational processes in certain economic sectors (basic services, transport, health). In view of the rise in unemployment expected in the short and medium term and the resulting social and health implications, many countries are now talking about unconditional basic incomes again.

1.5.4 World of Work

Covid-19 is changing the world we live in and it has also had a profound impact on the world of work. It has seen millions of people lose their jobs as industries were obliterated and businesses closed down. The crisis has put enormous pressure on the labour market and has exacerbated the existing problem areas described above. What will be the long-term impact of the pandemic on the labour market? The hope is that the downturn will be followed by an upturn in the market. This would be a 'normal' development in terms of economic cycles.

At the moment, however, no one knows where we currently stand and how long we will stay there, or whether there will be further drops. It is also possible that there will be prolonged ups and downs as a result of the relaxation and reintroduction of restrictive measures. Apart from the considerable economic costs, a growing VUCA[4] world like this would mean one thing above all for the labour market: that the speed of reaction is more crucial than ever.

A key question for the future will also be how the coronavirus crisis will have affected the balance between job vacancies and job seekers on the labour market. In other words: Which jobs will still be available after the pandemic, and which professions will have fallen victim to the crisis?

---

[4]**V**olatility, **U**ncertainty, **C**omplexity, **A**mbiguity.

1.5.5   Digitalisation and Remote Work from Home

The pandemic has given the migration to digital technologies a huge boost (home/coursework, webinars, online meetings, etc.) and this drive for digitisation could well provide the impetus for significant long-term growth. Without digital technologies, the current level of work from home would be unthinkable. The proportion of employees working from home across Europe has more than doubled in recent months from 12% to 25% in recent months. This does not take into account the fact that without digital technology, the education of pupils and students would also have largely come to a standstill.

Both the proponents and the opponents of the two megatrends digitalisation and homeworking recognise one fact: they represent sustainable solutions for the (professional) everyday life of the future.

References

Bianchi, C. (2015). *Reise zum Selbst. Psychologie heute*, p. 28.

Bundesinstitut für Berufsbildung. (2014). BiBB–Report 23(8).

Destatis. (2016). *Press release No. 246, 14 Jul 2016*. Retrieved August 15, 2020, from https://www.destatis.de/DE/PresseService/Presse/Pressemitteilungen/2016/07/PD16_246_12421.html.

Destatis. (2018). *Arbeitsmarkt auf einen Blick. Deutschland und Europa*. Retrieved August 17, 2020, from https://www.destatis.de/DE/Themen/Arbeit/Arbeitsmarkt/Erwerbstaetigkeit/Publikationen/Downloads-Erwerbstaetigkeit/broeschuere-arbeitsmark-blick-0010022189004.pdf?__blob=publicationFile.

Destatis. (2020). *Geburtenentwicklung Deutschland und EU*. Retrieved August 10, 2020, from https://www.destatis.de/DE/Themen/Gesellschaft-Umwelt/Bevoelkerung/Geburten/_inhalt.html.

Economix Research & Consulting. (2016). *Arbeitsmarkt 2030—Wirtschaft und Arbeitsmarkt im digitalen Zeitalter, München*

European Commission. (2012). *Employment, Social Affairs & Inclusion. Annual Report 2011*. Retrieved August 13, 2020, from file:///Users/hermanntroger/Downloads/EF1232EN.pdf.

European Commission. (2020). *European Commission Report on the Impact of Demographic change*. Retrieved August 16, 2020, from https://ec.europa.eu/info/sites/info/files/demography_report_2020_n.pdf.

Eurostat. (2020a) *Old dependency ratio*. Retrieved August 13, 2020, from https://ec.europa.eu/eurostat/en/web/products-eurostat-news/-/DDN-20200713-1?inheritRedirect=true&redirect=/eurostat/en/news/whats-new.

Eurostat. (2020b). *Fertility statistics*. Retrieved August 13, 2020, from https://ec.europa.eu/eurostat/statistics-explained/index.php?title=Fertility_statistics.

Eurostat. (2020c). *Migrant integration statistics*. Retrieved August 13, 2020, from https://ec.europa.eu/eurostat/statistics-explained/index.php/Migrant_integration_statistics_-_employment_conditions.

Eurostat. (2020d). *Employment rate*. Retrieved August 14, 2020, from https://ec.europa.eu/eurostat/statistics-explained/index.php?title=Employment_annual_statistics#Female_employment_rate_increases_over_time.

Eurostat. (2020e). *Statistics on education and skills*. Retrieved August 17, 2020, from https://ec.europa.eu/eurostat/statistics-explained/index.php?title=First_and_second-generation_immigrants_-_statistics_on_education_and_skills#Educational_attainment_level.

Eurostat. (2020f). Retrieved August 15, 2020, from https://ec.europa.eu/eurostat/statistics-explained/index.php/Migration_and_migrant_population_statistics.

Frey, C., & Osborne, M. (2013). *The future of employment: How susceptible are jobs to computerisation?* Retrieved August 17, 2020, from https://www.oxfordmartin.ox.ac.uk/downloads/academic/The_Future_of_Employment.pdf.

Gallup. (2009). *World desire to migrate.* Retrieved August 14, 2020, from http://www.gallup.com/poll/124028/700-million-worldwide-desire-migrate-permanently.aspx.

Institut für Demoskopie Allensbach. (2014). *Jakobs Studie 2014: Freunde fürs Leben.* Retrieved August 13, 2020, from https://docplayer.org/17600956-I-n-s-t-i-t-u-t-f-ue-r-d-e-m-o-s-k-o-p-i-e-a-l-l-e-n-s-b-a-c-h-jacobs-studie-2014-freunde-fuers-leben.html.

Janosch, S. (2016). *Freundschaft heute: Eine Einführung in die Freundschaftssoziologie, transcript 2016.*

Kearney, A. T. (2018). *Beyond gender diversity. Inclusion 2.0.* Retrieved August 16, 2020, from https://www.kearney.com/diversity-and-inclusion/article?/a/beyond-gender-diversity-inclusion-2-0-article.

Korn Ferry. (2020). *Advancing women worldwide.* Retrieved August 15, 2020, from https://www.kornferry.com/content/dam/kornferry/docs/fact-sheets/advancingwomenworldwide-factsheet.pdf.

KPMG, Women's Leadership Study. (2016). Retrieved August 12, 2020, from https://home.kpmg/content/dam/kpmg/ph/pdf/ThoughtLeadershipPublications/KPMGWomensLeadershipStudy.pdf.

Lüscher, K., et al. (2014). *Generationen, Generationenbeziehungen.* Konstanz: Generationenpolitik.

Office for National Statistics. (2016). *Percentage of single parents.* Retrieved August 15, 2020, from https://www.ons.gov.uk/aboutus/transparencyandgovernance/freedomofinformationfoi/percentageofsingleparentsinsouthwark.

Opaschowski, H. (2014). *So wollen wir leben. Die Welt 25 Sep 2014*, p. 5.

Riederle, P. (2013). *Wer wir sind und was wir wollen.* München: Knaur.

Russel Reynolds Associates. (2016). *Jeder zweite DAX 30-Vorstand ist eine Frau. Press release 25 Jan 2016.* Retrieved August 15, 2020, from http://www.presseportal.de/pm/67171/3351229.

Scholz, C. (2014). *Generation Z. Wie sie tickt, was sie verändert und wie sie uns alle ansteckt.* Weinheim: Wiley.

Statista. (2020a). *Bevölkerungsentwicklung.* Retrieved August 10, 2020, from https://de.statista.com/statistik/daten/studie/548267/umfrage/anteil-der-bevoelkerung-ab-65-jahren-und-aelter-in-deutschland/.

Statista. (2020b). *Migration in Europe.* Retrieved August 15, 2020, from https://www.statista.com/topics/4046/migration-in-europe/.

Statista. (2020c). *Ein-Personen-Haushalte in Deutschland.* Retrieved August 15, 2020, from https://de.statista.com/statistik/daten/studie/156951/umfrage/anzahl-der-einpersonenhaushalte-in-deutschland-seit-1991/.

Thimm, K. (2014). Der dritte Weg. *Der Spiegel, 1*, 114–117.

Troger, H. (2019). Ein neuer Generationenvertrag. In H. Troger (Ed.), *7 Erfolgsfaktoren für wirksames Personalmanagement* (2nd ed., pp. 117–134). Heidelberg: Springer Gabler.

UN World Population Prospects. (2020). *The 2019 revision.* Retrieved August 15, 2020, from https://population.un.org/wpp/Download/Probabilistic/Mortality/.

Vanhuysse, P. (2013). *Intergenerational Justice in Aging Societies: A Cross-national Comparison of 29 OECD Countries.* Gütersloh: Bertelsmann.

World Health Statistics. (2020). *Health statistics.* Retrieved August 15, 2020, from https://www.who.int/gho/publications/world_health_statistics/2020/en/.

The Company Perspective: Micro-Political Considerations

2

Business Economics and Company Policy Aspects

2.1 The Interminable Shortage of Skilled Workers

2.1.1 The Gripes of Entrepreneurs vs. Labour Market Research

For decades, the issue of skilled labour shortages has been a hot topic for large and small entrepreneurs alike, and it has also been the subject of algorithms and much statistical analysis devised by labour market experts. A successful entrepreneur, nowadays, is almost expected to voice concerns about the difficulty of finding suitable staff. The research reports of the various labour market institutes are far from unanimous in their assessment of skills shortages. On top of this, their predictions are regularly contradicted by reality.

For example, there had been predictions that from 2015 onwards there would be major shortages of qualified workers in the most industrialised regions of the EU, especially in the technical areas. The reality, though, was different: In 2020 (pre-pandemic), the number of people employed in these regions had reached an all-time high—despite the expected demographic decline. One reason for this is the increased participation of women and older workers in the labour market in recent years. The main reason, however, is that migration to these regions has been much higher than anticipated.

Incidentally, it is now almost taken for granted that entrepreneurs should 'gripe' about a lack of 'good employees' (a practice that can also serve to distract from any weaknesses in their HR management). Sometimes, this can help to create a certain atmosphere within a particular industry. For example, the strongly made calls for skilled workers in a certain economic sector can also be used as skilful self-advertising and can achieve a more rigorous selection of staff and more favourable wage levels from the employers' point of view.

Nevertheless, the shortage of skilled workers in certain sectors is real and cannot be dismissed as mere conjecture. A look at the different job markets across Europe shows that the demand for qualified staff, including executives, is increasing annually in all sectors.

2.1.2 The Choice Between Study or Work

Developments in the labour market are not only influenced by demographic and economic factors, but also by the educational choices of the population. The latter determine which skills and qualifications people bring with them when they enter the market and thus have a bearing on whether the supply can meet the demand. Against this background, there has been a worldwide debate in recent years about the increasing proportion of university graduates or, more generally, about the 'overeducation' of society. While this trend towards higher education is seen as a positive development by OECD education experts, many entrepreneurs (especially in skilled crafts and trades) remain somewhat critical of it.

It is undeniable that many more young people are choosing to go to university, while apprenticeships and vocational training are losing their appeal for them.

In most OECD countries, the proportion of 25–30-year-olds with a degree has risen significantly in the last 15 years (cf. Sect. 1.4.2). The OECD average today is 44.5%. In France, 47% and in Great Britain, 50% of the population between 25 and 34 years of age have a tertiary degree. The record is held by the Republic of South Korea, where in 2019 almost 70% of this cohort had graduated from university (cf. OECD 2019). In Germany, Austria and Switzerland, this proportion is lower at around 25–30%, due to the dual education system there. Tellingly, the latter are also the countries with the lowest youth unemployment.

However, it should be noted that it is inherently difficult to compare higher education rates internationally. In Finland and the USA, for example, nurses have a 'bachelor of nursing' and kindergarten teachers are classified as 'graduates,' while in England hairdressers can hold a 'diploma in hair dressing' from a higher education institution. Moreover, a high rate of graduates does not necessarily pose a problem for companies. Such a problem only arises if the rise in qualification levels leads to widespread over-qualification of candidates in the labour market. For example, the German Institute for Employment Research (IAB 2016) has found that in Spain, Portugal, Italy and Greece around 29–52% of all employees are over-qualified in positions that only require medium-level qualifications. This may be explained through a lack of practice-oriented in-house training and development opportunities. And it is perhaps no coincidence that these countries also suffer from the highest youth unemployment in Europe.

As far as medium and long-term recruitment strategies are concerned, companies can generally assume that positions that require high-level qualifications are going to be easier to recruit for while many non-graduate level jobs that require a relatively high level of skill will continue to be affected by a lack of young talent. Companies can only counter this development with internal training and development opportunities—otherwise the only option is higher wages or more attractive working conditions.

2.1.3 STEMs

STEM stands for science, technology, engineering and mathematics—in other words, subjects with high economic viability. It has also come to be associated with the large skills gap in human resources that many companies in Europe are facing. For example, the electrical engineering sector, or the mechanical and vehicle engineering sector, which are high-turnover and export-oriented, need an above-average proportion of STEM graduates in order to remain competitive.

Many employment experts now also include the health professions, health technology and social sciences under the STEM umbrella. It matters less whether the term is used in its pure form or in a broader context, what is certain is that our lives have become increasingly characterised by a profound structural shift towards a technology-oriented and knowledge-based society. New forms of energy production, the widespread use of state-of-the-art information and communication technologies, and the rapidly increasing digital transformation of many areas of society (not only in the IT sector) are driving a boom in STEM vacancies. Germany is a good example: According to the German Federal Employment Agency (2016), around 7.5 million specialist workers were employed in 2015 in 'MINT' fields—the German equivalent of STEM (it stands for mathematics, information technology, natural sciences and technology). This figure corresponds to almost a quarter of the total workforce. Most of them—86%—fall under 'T' for technology, they might work as mechatronics or electronics engineers or as engineering technicians. 9% of them work in the field of Information Technology and only 5% are employed as mathematicians or natural scientists. In terms of qualification level, the proportion of skilled workers with dual or school-based vocational training is a striking 61%. A good 20% have qualifications as master craftsmen or technicians, and only 16% chose a traditional university education.

The general trend of higher graduation rates thus seems to be particularly pronounced in the STEM occupations and if the high uptake of STEM related university courses is anything to go by, there will be no shortage of young talent coming through. By contrast, the number of skilled workers without degree-level qualifications (who account for two thirds of the workforce) has been declining markedly for several years. According to research conducted by the German Economic Institute (IW) in November 2019, there was a shortage of around 263,000 skilled workers from the 'MINT' fields, despite the Europe-wide economic slowdown. In the IT sector alone, the gap has more than doubled since 2015 due to digitalisation. German companies are particularly short of workers with 'MINT' vocational training (cf. IW 2019). Skilled workers, master craftsmen or technicians account for two thirds of all vacancies. In the experts' opinion, this shortage of skilled workers in non-graduate 'MINT' occupations will worsen considerably in the future across all European countries.

2.1.4   Digital Transformation: Solution or Problem?

The debate about the future of the labour market—in terms of supply and demand—is currently dominated by two opposing factors: On the one hand, there is the hypothesis that the demand for labour will fall significantly in the coming years due to the digital transformation of the economy—cue Industry 4.0. On the other hand, the ongoing unfavourable demographic trend is feared to result in declining numbers of young talent coming through—cue skilled labour shortages. From a purely mathematical point of view, the problem of securing skilled workers could therefore resolve itself. However, it will not be as simple as that. The digital transformation will change the entire working world and with that the socio-political realities of the twenty-first century in ways that are both radical and varied.

We may already be more prepared than we realise for the digital transformation, and we have certainly become accustomed to some of its benefits. While I am having dinner at a restaurant with my family, for example, I quickly skim-read an important email from a customer on my smartphone. My wife, who realises she forgot to leave some lights on to deter burglars, uses her phone to turn several lights on in our home, which is about 15 km from where we are. At the same time, my oldest daughter shares pictures of her food with friends on Snapchat, while her sister quickly makes detailed plans for the weekend with a group of friends. Not even 5 min later we all turn our attention to each other again as we choose our desserts—via an app that 'reads' the 'menu card'.

2.1.4.1 Will Automation Cause Large-Scale Job Losses?
What impact will the ongoing digital transformation of our world have on the working world? Who will win, and who will lose (possibly their job)?

In the past, progress worked in such a way that technological development made old ways of working redundant, but it also created new jobs that made society—as a whole—more prosperous. Now, however, futurologists and a great many economists believe that the digital revolution will destroy jobs en masse. In January 2016, the World Economic Forum in Davos predicted the disappearance of five million jobs in the industrialised nations by 2021, based on a survey of top executives of the 350 largest corporations in the world (cf. WEF 2016). Today, at the end of 2020, there is little evidence of this—despite the coronavirus crisis. And as early as September 2013, the two Oxford professors Carl Osborne and Benedikt Frey famously joined the ranks of cyber-pessimists and caused a stir when they published a working paper that concluded that around 47% of all jobs in the USA could fall victim to growing automation (cf. Frey and Osborne 2013). In their research, they had examined 702 job profiles for their susceptibility to computerisation. While social workers or craftsmen, for instance, were less at risk, they deduced that employees in finance, administration, logistics, shipping, and especially manufacturing could be replaced relatively easily by automation.

There have been comparable studies in Europe with similar predictions. According to a study by the ING DIBA (2015), 59% of all jobs in Germany are at risk because they can sooner or later be replaced by robots and software. Examples include secretarial work, delivery services, warehouse management, sales, as well as cleaning or catering services.

2.1.4.2 Opportunities Through Digitalisation

The consulting firm PwC, together with the WIFOR Institute in Darmstadt, also conducted research in this area and analysed the effects of digitalisation on the German labour market. Their overall conclusions were far less gloomy (cf. PwC 2016). Although they forecast that demand for labour will fall in some sectors, for example, by 19% in the transport and logistics sector or by 17% in the retail trade, they also predicted a significant increase for other sectors. In technology, media and communications, for example, they predicted an 11% increase in labour demand, and a 6% increase in the health and pharmaceutical industries. In particular, the study stresses that the expected labour shortage of 4.2 million by 2030 could be reduced to an estimated two million through digitisation. Various futurologists also question the hypothesis that digitisation will inevitably destroy jobs or recognise its potential for creating new jobs and upgrading existing ones, and the results of their research support this. They argue that, historically, technological innovation has never led to a reduction in jobs.

2.1.4.3 Conclusion: Winners and Losers

While the debate about the digital transformation of our world is often emotionally charged and controversial, there is little doubt that this transformation will bring about drastic changes for individuals, for most companies and for society as a whole. Digitisation is already in full swing, but the predicted large-scale negative effects have not materialised. Both employers and employees will continue to adapt. Both employers and employees will continue to adapt. There will be winners and losers, and considerable efforts are needed to ensure that the losers will not fall behind completely. New areas of activity will emerge, and new opportunities will be created. There will undoubtedly be a general upgrading of job profiles. New 'digital' skills will be needed and valued, but 'real-life' attributes, such as creativity, the ability to work in a team and other interpersonal skills, will not lose their importance.

2.2   Diversity in the Workforce

Most leaders consider the professional handling of diversity in the workplace a challenge. The reason for this is that good diversity management, more than ever, is now recognised as a key success factor for the effective leadership of staff and organisations. The differences between employees can have many dimensions and relate to age, gender, education, nationality, language, ethnic origin, race, religious beliefs, social class, or simply different interests—they all contribute to making each and every employee a unique individual to be integrated and managed within the company. This section looks at workforce diversity in relation to age, cultural background, and the individual interests of employees.

2.2.1   Generational Diversity

Chapter 1 presented several meanings associated with the term 'generation', in particular their typological classification in relation to a comparable temporal and social context as the basis of a common identity expressed through similar values, characteristics and actions. Such a classification helps to understand the employees of an organisation and to take their expectations and interests into account effectively. However, given the great differences in attitudes and behaviour, this is also one of the great challenges for the leaders within an organisaiton, from board level to the line manager.

2.2.1.1 From the Post-War Generation to Gen Z

The five generations that are present in today's workforce will be outlined briefly once again, this time with a focus on their behaviour in everyday working life (cf. Troger 2019a, b).

The 'Traditional Generation' (1922–1943)

Also called the 'Silent Generation' or 'Greatest Generation', these people are born between 1922 and 1943, and they can still be in positions of power, especially in family businesses. Sometimes they are a CEO, but more often a chair of an administrative or supervisory board. Famous examples include Ingvar Kamprad (IKEA), Leonardo del Vecchio (Luxottica) or Bernardo Caprotti (Esselunga, an Italian supermarket chain).

The Baby Boomers (1943–1964)

The baby-boom generation refers to those born between 1943 and 1964. In many companies this is still the most strongly represented cohort. Baby boomers are often at the top of companies and organisations and successfully defend their position—mainly thanks to their adaptability. They are very involved in 'their' company, but can also be particularly sensitive to criticism.

What are the typical behavioural characteristics of baby boomers in the workplace? Put simply, you could say that they just want to do their job and be left alone. Their biggest concern is the security of their pension.

The baby boomers' recipe for success was and is their ability to adapt and to fit in. That is how they have lasted and had time to learn that nobody can beat them. This applies equally to CEOs (with their well-known staying power), as to the average employee.

The boom generation employee is consensus-driven, respects authority and has a high moral compass. They are not easily at risk of dismissal and their retirement—in about 10 years' time—may represent a considerable loss of knowledge and skills for the company and is therefore often viewed with concern.

Generation X (1965–1976)

Gen X employees have a problem with the lifelong commitment to a single employer, especially since they often feel that they have already reached the end of their career ladder—either because they are blocked by a baby boomer or because they have been overtaken by a Gen Y colleague. Due to their general disillusionment, this cohort is commonly more difficult to motivate than older or younger colleagues. They tend to be sceptical of organisational changes because they do not expect them to improve anything either for themselves or in general. Their perceived lack of prospects is often reflected in rather moderate work motivation and correspondingly average productivity levels. Gen X employees unequivocally and openly put personal concerns before company interest, and life outside of work is much more important to them than it is to baby boomers. Overall, though, the Gen X employees do not generally pose any great challenges in terms of HR management, due to their conformity and their easily predictable behaviour.

Generation Y (1977–1996)

Millennials are currently the most discussed generation. For them, networking and global thinking are a matter of course. Other generations want to compare themselves to them and rub shoulders with them. Companies see them as the future. Millennials do not like to be pigeon-holed—not that this would be an easy task, given their strong drive for individualism, which has led to every conceivable lifestyle being represented in this generation. But one could argue that this in itself has become their trademark characteristic. Thanks to their high levels of education and their self-confident and optimistic outlook, the world is their oyster. They strive for the highest degree of individual freedom and give it priority over seamless professional advancement.

In organisations, the technology-minded Gen Y employees prefer to work in virtual teams rather than rigid hierarchies. They demand a maximum of creative freedom and opportunities for self-actualization from their leaders, but they also expect more time for their life outside work. This generation will no longer accept having to put work first, like previous generations have done. Instead, they expect to achieve the perfect work-life balance. The German social researcher Klaus Hurrelmann refers to them as 'Egotaktiker' (translated: *Ego-tacticians*)—a term he coined to describe their pragmatic approach of always keeping their options open.

This generation understand that their high levels of motivation and their flexibility can pay well. Their commitment to the company is less than that of previous generations, but they develop loyalty to individuals within the company. This is reflected in the fact that they can be excellent team players.

Generation Z (1997–2012)

The fully digitalised Gen Z is only just entering the labour market and they are already no longer surprised about anything. In the last 10 years, these 20–24-year olds have witnessed multiple financial crises, the collapse of large corporations and small companies, as well as unemployment and precarious employment. They have watched CEOs retire in disgrace, but with huge severance packages. These 'digital natives' have yet to find their feet in the workplace, but in the meantime they will post and comment and 'like' their way through social media. Author and consultant Phillip Riederle (2013) compares the workplace to a party on Facebook: 'Whoever turns up, will be there and will bring some food'. For Riederle, punctuality, order and structure date back to the time of the Industrial Revolution. A rigid lifestyle is no longer an option, and the thought of strict deadlines amuses him.

Saarland University professor Christian Scholz (2014) describes Gen Z as a work-shy, mollycoddled cohort whose radical egocentricity is now starting to spread to other generations. Effort and hard work are not a matter of course for them. They treat the workplace like they treated school: praise and recognition are expected. Leaders must be prepared that the post-millennial generation will neither show much respect for nor be very engaged with the job or the company. The best way to inspire them is with an exciting project. But whether we (baby boomers, Gen X, or Gen Y) like it or not: the future belongs to Gen Z.

2.2.1.2 Generational Diversity Management

Whereas the intergenerational distribution struggle described in Chap. 1 still has clear economic features, the diversity of the age groups working in an organisation also poses concrete challenges for the company and the individual. The aim is always the effective cooperation between all parties—despite generational affiliations—while keeping the company's aims and objectives at the core. And this is precisely where the difficulty lies: Gen Y and baby boomers rarely speak the same language, and a digital native just starting out in their career may find a traditionalist's remarks on 'work ethics' hard to fathom, even if they share a similar geographical and social background. An effective feedback culture would recognise that a millennial may need praise just for showing up on time on a Monday morning, while their Gen X colleague does not expect to be lauded for choosing to work overtime at the weekend.

The big challenge, therefore, is how to manage this generational diversity in an organisation. Effective diversity management does not aim to eliminate these differences, but recognises—from a strengths-oriented perspective—that genera- tional diversity has great potential to contribute to the overall success of the company.

2.2.2   Multiculturalism

As described in Sect. 1.1.3, our society is becoming increasingly diverse. According to official statistics, around 25% of the population in Europe are either first- or second-generation immigrants. If we look at the age distribution, it is safe to assume that this percentage will continue to rise (cf. Eurostat 2020): In 2019 in Europe, already more than a third of all children under five were first- or second-generation immigrants, while the proportion in the 35–45-year-old cohort was still at 27%. So, what is the situation in companies?

The importance of foreign-national workers in the European labour market is growing, especially in the economically strong countries of central and northern Europe. The free movement of workers—one of the pillars of the EU economic area—is increasingly being taken advantage of. The EU-wide number of foreign workers rose from 13.1 to 17.5 million between 2007 and 2017. In 2007, around 5.4 million EU citizens worked in another EU country, and this figure was expected to rise to 8.8 million in 2017. That is an increase of 61%. The total number of employees from outside the EU rose by 14% from 7.6 to 8.7 million over the same period. If we factor in a second generation of immigrants, together they will make up an estimated one third of the EU's workforce.

Of the above-mentioned 17.5 million workers with foreign passports, Germany hosted 4.5 million in 2017 (this corresponds to about 12% of the labour market). The labour markets of the UK (3.5 million), Italy (2.4 million) and Spain (2.0 million) were also popular with foreign-national workers. However, the highest proportion was recorded in Luxembourg, where in 2017 more than half (54%) of all workers had a foreign passport.

A study conducted by the German Economic Institute in 2016 produced interesting results: almost 1000 companies were asked about their experiences with hiring foreign-national employees. The results showed that 57% of all 987 companies surveyed had employed migrant workers within the previous 5 years. In large companies this was 92%, in medium-sized companies 81%, and in small companies it was 55% (cf. IW 2017).

Three quarters of these companies (75%) had recruited employees from EU member states, and around two thirds (65%) of the employees came from non-EU member states. A noteworthy detail here is that only 40% of the 987 companies surveyed had employed female migrants.

We can therefore say that most companies now have a degree of cultural diversity. Nevertheless, there are still certain obstacles to overcome in recruitment—at least according to the aforementioned study: 83% of all HR managers surveyed considered language skills to be a difficulty when recruiting migrant workers. 64% said that they lacked information about the candidates' level of qualification when presented with foreign qualifications, and 55% stated that the process of employing migrants took more time and effort. Many HR managers (33%) also mentioned problems in connection with the right to remain.

From the HR manager's point of view, therefore, the difficulty in employing foreign nationals does not so much lie in cultural differences as in the prevalence of genuine obstacles.

2.2.2.1 Cultural Differences

If we assume that in just a few years' time between 20% and 30% of the European labour force will be made up of first or second-generation immigrants, the effective integration and management of these workers represents a key challenge that must be met. Cooperation and the management of employees take on a new dimension when language barriers, cultural idiosyncrasies, and (in the case of transnational collaborations) physical distance have to be overcome. In this context, a German study points to a surprising finding: 352 professionals from various industries and company sizes within Germany were asked about their language skills, their experience in an international environment, and the degree of internationalism in their company, among other things. The aim of the survey was to find out how far the internationalisation of the German economy had progressed, how internationally oriented leaders were, and how the cooperation between leaders and employees at different locations was organised. The results were surprising: despite the frequently lamented shortage of skilled workers, foreign experts still played a very minor role: almost 40% of the professionals and leaders surveyed stated that they did not have a single foreign-national colleague or employee in their company.

And although almost one in three leaders said that they were managing one or more employees with whom they could not communicate in their own language, 50% of them said that their companies did not pay attention to the composition of the teams. They stated that nationality, age, or gender were given no consideration (cf. Akademie für Führungskräfte der Wirtschaft 2015).

Nationality, ethnicity, race, language, religion and social class are important elements of a person's cultural background. It is through the lens of our cultural background that we see the (working) world and interpret what happens to us and around us. Our cultural identity influences our motivation and our approach to problems. But first and foremost, employees from a different country may speak a different language. What does this mean for internal communications? Usually, there is an official company language, but messages that are not written in one's own native language can easily be misinterpreted and lead to misunderstandings. In case of doubt or critical situations, I recommend using the language that the employee understands best.

I have frequently witnessed classic examples of linguistic and cultural differences in the assessment centres of big international corporations during the selection of executives. Although all participants had an excellent command of English, the cultural and linguistic diversity of their backgrounds meant that they had different interpretations of the exercises, different approaches to solutions, different behaviours in the group, and different ways of communicating the results. These differences were unmistakably influenced by the individual's cultural background.

2.2.2.2 Integration

Cultural diversity in companies is not only a reality in today's world, but it is largely viewed as enriching. Various studies have highlighted the strength of multinational teams and the problem-solving skills generated in transnational teams. However, in order to reap the benefits of such collaborations, a number of measures are necessary, starting with the selection process. When assessing candidates for a position, we must always question how our own cultural lens influences the way we perceive others. During the induction phase, we should not only help the foreign-national employee come to grips with the technical requirements of their job, but we should also pay special attention to aspects of well-being. This can include a range of things, from a personal mentor or assistance with childcare, to helping the employee's spouse or partner with planning their career. However, none of these measures alone will suffice unless there is also an accompanying atmosphere of intercultural openness at all levels of the organisation. Creating and maintaining a company culture that promotes intercultural competence and cultural sensitivity is therefore of paramount importance for any international and culturally diverse organisation.

The term 'Willkommenskultur', which is used in German-speaking countries (translated: *Welcoming Culture*), describes the concept of a positive and welcoming attitude towards foreigners, especially towards migrants. Although the term is politically controversial today, this kind of positive attitude will be a critical success factor for companies all over Europe when it comes to the effective integration of foreign-national and culturally diverse employees.

2.2.3   Diversity of Interests

As a general rule, the employer–employee relationship begins with a written contract. This contract includes the mutual expectations and interests, such as the salary or the tasks required by the position, and it usually lists the rights and responsibilities of both parties. Other aspects, such as teamwork, loyalty, or the quality of work are usually discussed verbally and mutual expectations are raised, but they are not formalised. On top of this, hopes or fears might arise but not be expressed verbally and certainly not written down. And so, the contracting parties begin their working relationship with a mutually signed legal contract and a unilaterally conceived, so-called psychological contract.

2.2.3.1 The Psychological Contract

Psychological contracts are generally defined as the non-formalised mutual expectations and obligations between employer and employee that exist beyond the legal employment contract. Fundamental issues of the psychological contract are, for example: How secure is the position? How much effort—for example in the form of overtime—is expected? Will my market value increase if I work for this company, and by how much? Or, on the employer's side: How will this person get along with their colleagues and how long will they last?

Contrary to the expectations that originate from the formal employment contract, the parties are usually unaware of the expectations that are placed on them based on this psychological agreement. Broadly speaking, the psychological contract covers all areas of the employer–employee relationship and—unlike the legal agreement— is subject to continuous change.

The main actor on the employer's side is the employee's superior, and over the course of the working relationship, the cooperation with this superior will decide whether the parties consider the contract to be fulfilled or not. The consequences of a failure to fulfil the psychological contract are well illustrated by the results of the Gallup Engagement Index, which is published annually. It shows the degree of employee engagement: Currently, only 15–16% of employees in Germany fall into the category of highly engaged employees, while the same proportion of people have already internally decided to terminate their contract. The rest, about 70% of employees, do no more than what is expected of them. Interestingly, the percentages on employee engagement are broadly similar across European countries, while the proportion of highly engaged employees in US companies is regularly much higher—between 25 and 30% (cf. Gallup 2019).

2.2.3.2 Negotiating Interests

The emotional commitment in the employer–employee relationship is based on the interests of both parties. Our interests are, in effect, the motivations for our actions. This raises the question: What are the fundamental—intrinsic and extrinsic— motivations that drive our wants and actions?

The central task of the HR manager and, consequently, of the employee's respective superior, is to recognise the employee's interest structure and take it into account when shaping the working relationship with them. It is as important to understand the openly stated interests, such as money, free time, leadership responsibilities, company car, as it is to understand the underlying fundamental motivations, such as power, harmony, perfection, recognition—and the connection between the two.

Generally, the job interview is the beginning of this 'negotiation process'. Mutual expectations are discussed, as are interests—although the latter tend to relate mostly to leisure activities. Although recruiters are psychologically training in this area, they sometimes still find it difficult to identify the actual interests of candidates in relation to their basic needs, which would give clues about their personality profile.

The identification of interests is a growing challenge for companies due to the continuous shift in the balance of power between employer and employee (as a result of demographic developments and the shortage of skilled workers). However, the consideration of individual interests is made even more difficult by the large number of diverging interests in today's workforce. We experience this diversity on two levels: On the one hand, we see it through the simultaneous work of four, sometimes even five, generations in the same company. (Their diverging interests and expectations regarding the employment contract were described above.) On the other hand, even within the same generational cohort we can sometimes see major differences in lifestyle and interests. Particularly within the two youngest generations, Gen Y and Gen Z, ideas about work, career and leisure time differ widely. Generalisations and a uniform incentive system will therefore be less and less successful at achieving the desired results, even if the latter has been designed with generational expectations in mind. Nowadays, not even a baby boomer's request for parental leave to start a second family, for example, should come as a surprise to HR staff.

Whether the interests relate to generational or individual matters, whether they are written down in the formal employment contract or are the implied expectations of both parties involved in the psychological contract—identifying them, understanding them, and goal-oriented negotiation are perhaps the most crucial and far-reaching components of effective leadership. Due to their complexity and diversity, they are also the most challenging.

2.3 Performance (Dis)Orientation

Rationally speaking, the significance of an employee to an organisation can be defined according to their (measurable) benefit for the organisation. This economic benefit—social or societal benefits are not considered here—is most easily measured in relation to the employee's productivity. For this purpose, the costs incurred through the employee are set in relation to their productivity. In practice, however, defining productivity is not always easy. Apart from the production-line worker, whose output is put in relation to their salary in line with their learning curve, it is often difficult to measure the productivity of individuals. The classic productivity indicators 'value added per employee' or 'contribution margin per employee' refer to the average values that apply to the company or a workgroup. The measuring of productivity, both in terms of individuals and in relation to age cohorts, is also recognised as a challenge in the field of labour economics.

The feeling among business owners is somewhat different. In debating the issue of productivity, there is a rare show of consensus among them when they lament that older people are less able to perform or that young people lack motivation. An interesting scientific approach to describing and evaluating the productivity of employees, in the broadest sense, was devised in Finland in the 1980s. The 'Work Ability Index' describes the extent to which employees are able to do their jobs successfully. A high WAI value indicates a high degree of alignment between business requirements and individual motivation, while a low value indicates an imbalance (cf. Ilmarinen and Tuomi 2004). Chapter 9 deals with the WAI in more detail.

2.3.1 Do Young People Lack Motivation?

We generally associate young employees with energy, flexibility and creativity. They are also known for their quick comprehension and excellent memory. Of course, younger people are also physically more resilient and do not tire as quickly. All these talents and strengths are of little use, however, if they are not accompanied by the necessary motivation to put them into use in everyday working life. 'Young' employees today belong to two generations: Gen Y and Gen Z, which were discussed above. A considerable amount of research on the work ethic of millennials has already been done, and there are now also some early observations of regularities in the work behaviour of Gen Z employees, who are just entering the workplace. Although typologies of this kind are always clouded by over-simplifying generalisations, we will investigate how these young people differ from their role models of earlier generations. To this end, some central aspects of working life will be briefly outlined (cf. Troger 2019a, b).

2.3.1.1 Competencies
Baby boomers, and even more so Gen X, place greater emphasis on the development of social competencies, while professional competency is expected as a matter of

course. Millennials and Gen Z, by contrast, try to distinguish themselves above all through their affinity for technology and other 'hard factors'. In terms of personal strengths, boomers and Gen X are mainly concerned with adaptability and team integration, while Gen Y and Z are primarily concerned with personal dynamics and the adoption of new technologies.

2.3.1.2 Priorities

Work to live or *Live to work*? This question is seen very differently by different generations. While the baby boomers were brought up on the premise 'we live to work', this applies to a much lesser extend to Gen X, which instead adopted the new mantra 'Work to live'. Gen Y follows a mixed approach (depending on need), while Gen Z—whose members are still very young—again shows a clear desire to keep work and life separate with a clear preference for 'life'.

2.3.1.3 Working Hours

In line with their priorities, a working day for the baby boomer generation typically lasted (or lasts) from 8 a.m. to 8 p.m., while the typical Gen X worker is more likely to be on duty from 9 a.m. to 5 p.m. Millennials are more flexible in terms of working hours—they are used to sitting behind their computer when they come home from work. For Gen Z, it is (still) mainly about working as little as possible to maximise the time they have for their life outside work.

2.3.1.4 Attitude Towards Authority and Leadership

Baby boomers have grown up with a certain belief in hierarchical structures and therefore have no problem fitting into a subordinate role. Gen X is much more sceptical about hierarchies and expects a common agreement on objectives. The same applies to the typical millennial, although respect for hierarchies is even less pronounced in this cohort. What counts, however, is the professional competency of the expert. Gen Z does not yet differ significantly from their colleagues in this respect, however, the personal relationship to experts plays an even greater role.

2.3.1.5 Employee Engagement

In this area, the generational comparison is simple: employee engagement decreases from generation to generation, i.e., it declines proportionally with the age of the employees. Observations have shown that Gen Y employees form bonds with certain people within the company, while the youngest cohort of employees mainly engage with exciting projects.

2.3.1.6 Motivation

The basic motivation for baby boomers is to use their job as a means to a rewarding life for themselves and their family. Their career came about almost 'by chance'. This, however, has generally been interpreted as a problem by Xers, who have seen it as an obstacle to their own advancement. The last two generations are not so much focused on a seamless career, as they are on monetary incentives and, above all, on fun and variety at work.

2.3.1.7 Work Ethic

The differences in motivation, therefore, give an interesting overall picture in terms of work ethic. Since baby boomers were mainly driven to make a good life for their family, their work ethic was relatively average. People worked a lot, but not so much out of idealism as to live well. The members of Gen X are often frustrated because their career expectations have not been met. They frequently do as little as they can without neglecting their contractual obligations. Work morale is generally higher among millennials. They have clear (short term) incentives, and they are often offered the prospect of a promotion to a management position. Work morale is equally high among young Gen Z colleagues when they are given the chance to work on exciting, innovative projects. In addition to the motivational factors of fun and money, recognition also plays an important role for them, as does—what may seem surprising at first—job security. Status and prestige, on the other hand, play a secondary role.

In summary, it is clear that there is no general lack of motivation among the younger generations. However, they are placing much higher expectations on their employers in terms of job content, opportunities for participation, and flexibility. Young employees do indeed want to work, but they demand a new world of work and working conditions that reflect this. Their self-confident optimism often means that they see no limits and—especially the younger members of Gen Z—are not prepared to compromise. More than any generation before them, they expect that companies and their leaders rethink the old ways and adapt to their demands. In other words, they expect companies to treat them as their parents treated them. While growing up, they were supported in exploring a multitude of different directions, were allowed to take part in decision-making processes from an early age, and were encouraged to develop freely. They were always given a choice. If their expectations are met, they are willing to commit fully. The CVs of millennials and Gen Z candidates are proof of this: unpaid internships, time spent abroad and social involvement bear witness to their work ethic and commitment. Young workers obviously have high expectations not only of their employers but also of themselves.

2.3.2 Does Productivity Decrease with Age?

Employers seem to have a different problem with older workers. The concern that an ageing workforce will create a productivity disadvantage is still widespread. Lower resilience and increased sickness absence among older workers are often quoted as the reasons for this. The issue of staff age averages, which reflects this concern, seems to be present in most board meetings.

However, the long-prevailing youth craze appears to be subsiding. Demographic developments, but also the high turnover of young workers, as their expectations are increasingly difficult to meet, have brought a certain disillusionment with young workers. There is an underlying sense, nevertheless, that the leadership teams of most companies are still keen to keep staff age averages as low as possible. For this reason, it is still the declared aim for most HR managers to be particularly attractive to young applicants and to recruit as many of them as possible (cf. Troger 2019a).

But are younger employees really much more flexible, more innovative, more willing to take risks, more agile, more resilient, more adaptable, and better at learning new things than older employees?

Such sweeping generalisations are never accurate. Although studies in the field of labour economics show an inverted u-shaped progression between age groups and company productivity, it is not possible to determine exactly where the cusp lies. The actual usability of this research for companies is rather limited, due to the high level of aggregation within it. Studies from the fields of gerontology and sociology show that physical performance and certain cognitive skills decline with age, but experience and general education increases. Generally, it is more difficult for a 60 year old to learn a new language than for a younger person. After a short adaptation period, however, the older person can usually compensate for a potentially lower cognitive speed with experience, perseverance, patience and—last but not least—diligence.

2.3.2.1 Age Is Relative

The concept of age has been relativised. We should consider two aspects: Firstly, the average fitness level of a 60 year old today is the same as that of a 50 year old in the 1970s. Statistically speaking, we gain more than 2 years of life expectancy per decade. And as longevity increases, so does the lifespan of physical fitness. An employee today, is therefore 'too old' much later than they would have been in the past. However, a 60 year old is deemed 'old'—or at least that is what the United Nations decided at the 2nd World Assembly on Ageing 2002 in Madrid (2002).

Secondly, the question should be 'too old for what'. Given the diversity of tasks and responsibilities in companies, is it really plausible that someone will become 'too old' for everything within the span of just a few years? Age may at best be suitable for statistical purposes within the company, but not for a qualitative assessment. Suitability for a task is determined by rather different factors: Training, knowledge, motivation, willingness to take on responsibility, social skills—all these are qualitative characteristics that are essential for professional success, and they are only conditionally related to the employee's age.

The following may serve as further evidence of the relative insignificance of age within the company context. I presented 15 HR managers with a list of generally recognised competencies and characteristics with the request that they assign them either to younger (25–45 year old) or older (46–65 year old) employees:

Professional expertise—methodological competence—social competence—personal skills—commitment and engagement—goal-orientation and initiative—creativity and solution-orientation—ability to learn—resilience—flexibility—intercultural competence—leadership skills.

The results were surprising even for me. Only in two aspects—methodological competence and flexibility—did the younger employees come out on top. In all other areas, more trust was placed in the older employees.

2.3.2.2 Resilience

The ability to work under pressure is a desirable quality and a sensitive subject, especially since it is often put into question in connection with older employees. We should therefore look at it more closely. In psychology, the term resilience generally refers to the physical and psychological resources that a person can mobilise in order to react to objective stressors.

Science does not provide a clear answer to the question of whether older workers are in principle more or less resilient than their younger colleagues, but points to the individual history or the personality structure of the person. One thing is clear, though: in view of the constantly increasing professional (and private) demands, resilience is seen as an important quality.

Being resilient also means being able to deal with defeats. It means being persistent and not always taking the path of least resistance. A somewhat carefree outlook can also be helpful. Self-discipline, balance, and a certain amount of stress resistance are also part of resilience.

Although some of the above characteristics are considered innate and therefore age-independent, in most cases we recognise that life experience is essential. The light-heartedness of youth may be lost with increasing age, but instead we gain qualities such as self-discipline, stamina or calm. Above all, we gain experience in dealing with difficult situations or the occasional defeat, and therefore, we are more likely to stay calm and focused in a crisis.

2.3.2.3 Strength-Oriented Task Allocation and Diversity Management

In summary, there is no empirically proven general decline in productivity as people grow older. Depending on individual motivation and external conditions, older employees do not necessarily have less positive qualities, but they have different qualities. From the HR manager's point of view, therefore, the ageing of the workforce should be met with a strength-oriented allocation of tasks and the support of the employee throughout their entire time in the organisation. The strengths of employees are not a question of age, but rather of their individual characteristics, skills and interests. These must be brought into line with the requirements of their respective positions.

Above all, overall performance is not only about performance capacity, but also about motivation. And motivation usually has nothing to do with age.

2.4 Industry 4.0

While for many 'Industry 4.0' only means the continuation of 'lean production' using new technologies and large amounts of data, others see it as the 4th industrial revolution in the true sense of the term. In any case, Industry 4.0 is first and foremost a technical concept involving sensors, auto-ID technologies, automation, IT systems engineering, virtualization and simulation techniques, big data and internet technologies. The economic goal is to create more efficiency through minimal idle costs, scalable batch sizes and the establishment of data-driven new products and business models.

2.4.1 Increased Productivity

For the entrepreneur, Industry 4.0 is mainly about three operational processes: automation, virtualization and networking. Systems and products must be controlled by computer technology using algorithms; digital networking with customers and suppliers guarantees continuous interaction throughout the entire value creation process. According to expert opinion, digitalisation enables improvements in the value creation potential of about 15–20%. For example, machine downtimes can be reduced by 30–50% through remote monitoring and preventive maintenance, which can extend the service life of equipment and reduce staffing costs. Digitisation also creates greater performance transparency. Instead of the classic quality control at the end of the production cycle or at the end of a shift, deviations from the standard can be detected in real time in the digital world and processed directly.

Nonetheless, Industry 4.0 is not purely about IT, but leads to further fundamental business considerations. For example, increasing automation of value creation processes can make production in high priced European countries interesting again. Delivery times can be shortened, freight costs avoided and increased customer proximity ensured.

Industry 4.0, therefore, is about technology and people. The real increase in value creation results from a combination of new technologies, data analysis and human expertise. Technical solutions that use robots and algorithms for data analysis are relatively easy to obtain already. But for the optimal design of value chains and the accompanying process modelling, experts with interdisciplinary knowledge are needed.

The consultancy firm McKinsey (2015) also points out the great potential of Industry 4.0 in its *'Digital Compass'*. According to their research, 300 experts in 100 companies in Germany, Japan and the USA suggest that companies can benefit from the digital revolution in the following areas in particular:

- **Resources and processes:** Productivity in this area can be increased by 3–5%. This is achieved through intelligent energy consumption, storage of information ('intelligent lots') and real-time profit optimisation.

- **Machinery and equipment:** The remote controlling and monitoring of equipment and preventive maintenance can reduce machine downtime by 30–50%.
- **Work:** According to the results of the McKinsey survey, automation steps can increase productivity in technical jobs by 45–55%. Here too, it is a question of controlling and monitoring remotely, as well as the management of knowledge work. In this area, the cooperation of man and machine is particularly important.
- **Time to market:** According to the '*Digital Compass*', time to market can be reduced by up to 50%: Industry 4.0 allows fast experimentation and simulation, as well as simultaneous technical processing. The direct involvement of the customer during product development accelerates the process further.
- **Customer service:** Costs in the area of after-sales can also be reduced by 10–45%. The previously mentioned remote maintenance avoids costly warranty services, and the introduction of products requiring explanation can also often be done remotely.

2.4.2 Impact on the World of Work

The use of new technologies and the systematic use of large data sets open up many possibilities for the automation and flexibilisation of value creation processes. The concrete effects on the working world are currently the subject of much controversy: Which jobs will be lost, and what new job profiles will emerge?

The German Economic Institute in Cologne (IW 2016) has conducted a survey of nearly 1400 companies and asked them about the possible effects of digitalisation on the number of staff. Two responses stood out: Firstly, only one in ten of the significantly digitalised companies planned to cut jobs in the short term. Secondly, over 35% of them intended to hire additional employees within a year, while only 16% within the group of less digitalised companies intended to do so.

From my experience of working with HR managers and entrepreneurs, and the many conversations we have had on this topic, the shaping of the industrial and working world by Industry 4.0 will have three specific implications for job profiles:

Firstly, the increased technologisation of the working world and the accompanying new knowledge and skills will lead to a general 'upgrading' of jobs in terms of technology. Increased communication between humans and technology will make additional training necessary for many professions, while some—usually very simple—tasks will disappear.

Secondly, it can be assumed that new job profiles will emerge, especially in the field of data management and human-machine communication.

Finally, as a result of the above-mentioned 'upgrading', there will be an even greater polarisation between skilled jobs requiring qualifications and low-skilled jobs for simple tasks that cannot be automated yet.

Automation, digitisation and networking: the interaction of these three key elements is behind Industry 4.0 and the resulting consequences in the world of work. Machines work and communicate with, instead of, and for us humans—and also with each other. And according to most experts, this development is still in its early stages of implementation.

2.5   The Coronavirus-Effect

Around the turn of the year, the economy in the prospering countries of central and northern Europe began to cool down, and in southern Europe, the threat of recession had been looming for some time. And then came Covid-19. In most industry sectors and companies, operations came to a sudden and crashing halt. Almost overnight, entrepreneurs and decision makers were confronted with a new and unexpected reality. The most important goal since, has become to save as much as possible on variable costs. First and foremost, this has meant one thing: reducing staff.

In recent months, the main task of HR managers has been to find the right balance between short-term survival, and making staffing decisions that might be damaging in the medium to long term. Redundancies, the implementation of short-time work or the rejection of top candidates have led to many difficult discussions with employees. It would go far beyond the scope of this book to address a specific coronavirus response in terms of HR management. However, some important developments that would not have occurred without Covid-19 should be pointed out, as they will have a lasting impact on the world of work.

2.5.1   Work-Life-Blending Versus Work-Life-Separation

The 'magic formula' of work-life blending, which has enjoyed popularity in recent years, is beginning to show cracks. It was hailed by most as the pinnacle of the 'new work', but since entering the era of Covid-19, people have begun to experience its less positive aspects.

An effortless transition between work and private life, no constraints of time and space, maximum work autonomy: many workers had dreamed of this. Autonomous time management, answering e-mails from the hammock or team meetings by the pool seemed to finally guarantee an optimal work-life balance. Even before the pandemic, however, several experts had already warned of the negative side effects of work-life blending: not being able to switch off, exploitation or self-exploitation, internal conflicts, burnout (cf. inter alia Scholz 2018), but they were largely dismissed as pessimists or leftists.

Most parents today are familiar with this situation: when the children get sick, their painstakingly constructed fragile system begins to crack and with a moment's notice everything has to be rescheduled. The normal daily routine often involves constant juggling and stringing together all kinds of tasks. Early in the morning—when everyone is still asleep—or late in the evening—when they are asleep again—we can work efficiently. After all, noise, restlessness and the feeling of having to satisfy two worlds at once are strong stress factors. During the pandemic, this fragile system has been put to the test more than ever. This is partly because some of the usual options have not been available (e.g., help from grandparents), but also because the demands of work and family now have to be managed over much longer periods than under normal circumstances.

Against this background, employees are expressing the wish for a clearer distinction between work and family or leisure time. Efficient planning in times of coronavirus, is therefore a central challenge for employees and employers alike.

Although flexibility is still highly valued on both sides (more so than ever during the pandemic), a somewhat sharper separation between work and private life would protect workers from the possible negative consequences of a hypothetical '24-h working day' and would therefore be more sustainable.

2.5.2   Homeworking Works!

Homeworking was the most immediate and will perhaps be the most lasting impact of Covid-19 on everyday working life. According to a survey conducted by Xing in Germany, Austria and Switzerland at the beginning of May 2020, around 70% of the Xing members surveyed worked either partially or exclusively from home.

40% of those surveyed were in favour of the more flexible working hours. Many employees, however, seemed to miss their 'real' office. 51% of them said that they were looking forward to working in an office again. They stated that they missed their colleagues and the social interaction on site the most, and 91% of them had a desire to return to work for their employers. 66% said that work and family life could be better separated there than when working from home. A further 41% cited better equipment as a reason. And finally, 37% of respondents believed that they were more productive in the office than while working remotely from home (cf. Xing 2020).

So much for the perspective of employees, which is somewhat different from that of most employers. Pre-pandemic, the latter used to view their employees' desire to work remotely mainly as the striving for more independence and more free time, with perhaps the added bonus of a saving on office space. Entrepreneurs and leaders regarded the impact of remote work on themselves above all as a loss of control. How should tasks be coordinated and how could their correct and efficient execution be inspected if superiors only saw their staff occasionally?

Covid-19 forced companies to convert to working from home on an unprecedented scale and changed the minds of those who still had doubts. They have seen that it is indeed possible to digitise processes and tasks and to do them from home. In doing so, the employees are very productive, some even more productive than in the office, and all without close supervision. There has been a general awakening: working from home works and could be capitalised on. Siemens, for example, is planning to allow 140,000 employees to continue working from home 3 days per week after the pandemic (cf. *Handelsblatt* from 16.07.2020). Remote work is now also seen as an effective strategy to mitigate the shortage of skilled labour.

2.5.3 The Generation Gaps Just Got Smaller

The different generations' views and approaches to work have already been described earlier. Especially young employees of generations Y and Z generally have very different ideas compared to their (older) managers and employers: 'new work', as they see it, has no fixed working hours, high flexibility and a lot of free time—following the examples of Google and others. Pre-pandemic, this is how they expected to achieve the perfect work-life balance. Unfortunately, most companies could not fulfil the majority of these wishes, and neither did they want to. There was a lack of understanding for these wants and a perception that such a work model was destined to failure. Both sides were frustrated, and divisions widened.

It took the coronavirus pandemic to bring the parties back together and to focus their joint attention on other priorities. Young workers were suddenly prepared to make greater sacrifices for their job, while the older generations saw that new work models could work well. Either way, they seem to have been united in their hope of avoiding redundancy.

2.5.4 Adopting a 'Feel-Good' Management Style

It might be tempting to think that so-called feel-good managers are not particularly needed to keep employees happy in the difficult times we are currently living in. After all, those who are still able to work can count themselves lucky. However, their role and purpose can also be viewed from a different angle: Feel-good managers support the workforce in overcoming this crisis. They provide moral support and encouragement. In many cases, they also provide practical help. For example, help in creating the right conditions to work from home or help with digitising work processes. However, dedicated feel-good managers are still thin on the ground and are usually only found in some larger companies. In addition, the problems that they deal with are mostly very individual and can rarely be solved across the board. For these reasons, I believe that it is particularly important for leaders and direct superiors to take responsibility. They should address the well-being of their staff and, where necessary, provide moral support. If the work is done remotely from home, they must adapt their organisation to these special circumstances. Delegation, feedback and control need to be rethought and individually designed.

In general, many leaders like to keep the personal out of their leadership relationship with employees. They keep communication limited to professional topics. In times like these, however, many employees feel the need to talk about their personal issues and worries. The topic of 'job security' has suddenly gained significance even for 'high performers', and clear information and transparency are expected from superiors. This requires a high degree of sensitivity on the part of the superior and can present them with previously unknown challenges.

2.5.5   VUCA *Plus* Covid-19

For several years now, the VUCA working world has been on everyone's lips—long before any of us had ever heard of a novel coronavirus. We had become somewhat accustomed to the volatility of a world of work filled with uncertainty and unpredictability. *New Work*, in the context of the digital transformation, offered promising ways of dealing with the complexity and the sometimes contradictory nature of situations and facts. Some even believed that VUCA could make our working world more interesting and varied. All that was needed, they argued, were the right methods and approaches to cope with the many VUCA challenges.

But Covid-19 shone a new light on things. In the broadest sense, the current pandemic meets the characteristics of VUCA more than all other developments, trends and events. The (fundamental) difference lies solely in the scale of the individual parameters: their magnitude makes the Covid-19 crisis almost unmanageable for the world of work.

The virus, essentially, is the *perfect* expression of our VUCA world, or something like a scaled-up and amplified element of it, and it forces businesses to confront their very own, previously unknown VUCA situations. Traditional approaches to dealing with VUCA are only partially effective in this instance—yet they are needed more than ever:

- Adaptable and agile organisational structures that can react quickly and flexibly to specific situations.
- Vision and mission statements and a value-based culture can provide orientation.
- A clear focus on the essentials reduces complexity and increases the ability to act effectively and quickly.
- Technology as a driving force for change.

The speed with which the pandemic has spread around the world took everyone by surprise and its ongoing effects are posing enormous challenges to business leaders and politicians everywhere. In addition to its impact on health and the economy, we are still not able to make a clear and conclusive assessment of what the future holds. The only thing we know for certain is that a post-Covid world will still be a VUCA world.

References

Akademie für Führungskräfte der Wirtschaft. (2015). Internationale Arbeitswelten. *Akademie-Studie, 2015*, 21.

Avaris-Konzept. (2014). *Ego-Taktiker? Interview zur Generation Y*. Retrieved August 22, 2020, from https://www.avaris-konzept.de/ego-taktiker%2D%2D-interview-zur-generation-y.html.

Eurostat. (2020). Retrieved August 20, 2020, from https://ec.europa.eu/eurostat/statistics-explained/index.php/Migration_and_migrant_population_statistics.

Frey, C. B., & Osborne, M. A. (2013). *The future of employment: How susceptible are jobs to computerisation? Working paper, Martin Oxford School.* Retrieved August 20, 2020, from https://www.oxfordmartin.ox.ac.uk/publications/the-future-of-employment/.

Gallup Engagement Index. (2019). Retrieved August 20, 2020, from https://www.ing-diba.de/pdf/ueber-uns/presse/publikationen/ing-diba-economic-research-die-roboter-kommen.pdf.

German Federal Employment Agency. (March 2016). *Der Arbeitsmarkt in Deutschland—MINT-Berufe, Nürnberg 2016.*

IAB. (2016). *Bildungsbericht 2016.* Retrieved August 17, 2020, from https://www.bildungsbericht. de/de/bildungsberichte-seit-2006/bildungsbericht-2016/pdf-bildungsbericht-2016/wichtigste-ergebnisse-bildungsbericht-2016.

Ilmarinen, J., & Tuomi, K. (2004). *Past, present and future of work ability. Research Reports 65, Finnish Institute of Occupational Health.*

ING DIBA. (2015). *Economic Research: Die Roboter kommen. Folgen der Automatisierung für den deutschen Arbeitsmarkt.*

Institut der deutschen Wirtschaft Köln. (IW 2016). *Digitalisierung, Industrie 4.0, Big Data. In: IW-Report 24-2016.* Retrieved August 20, 2020, from https://www.iwkoeln.de/studien/iw-reports/beitrag/roman-bertenrath-hans-peter-kloes-oliver-stettes-digitalisierung-industrie-4-0-big-data-293203.html.

Institut der deutschen Wirtschaft Köln. (IW 2017). *Personalpanel 2016.* Retrieved August 20, 2020, from https://www.iwkoeln.de/fileadmin/publikationen/2017/329215/IW-Personalpanel_Beschaeftigung-Migranten.pdf.

Institut der deutschen Wirtschaft Köln. (IW 2019). *MINT-Herbstreport 2019.* Retrieved August 20, 2020, from https://www.iwkoeln.de/fileadmin/user_upload/Studien/Gutachten/PDF/2019/IW-Gutachten-MINT-Herbstreport-2019.pdf.

McKinsey Digital. (2015). *Industry 4.0: How to navigate digitization of the manufacturing sector.* Retrieved August 20, 2020, from https://www.mckinsey.com/business-functions/operations/our-insights/industry-four-point-o-how-to-navigae-the-digitization-of-the-manufacturing-sector#.

OECD Education Data. (2019). *Adult Education Level.* Retrieved August 17, 2020, from https://data.oecd.org/eduatt/population-with-tertiary-education.htm.

PwC. (2016). *Der Einfluss der Digitalisierung auf die Arbeitskräftesituation in Deutschland, Frankfurt am Main.*

Riederle, P. (2013). *Wer wir sind und was wir wollen.* München: Knaur.

Scholz, C. (2014). *Generation Z. Wie sie tickt, was sie verändert und wie sie uns alle ansteckt.* Weinheim: Wiley.

Scholz, C. (2018). *Mogelpackung Work-Life-Blending.* Weinheim: Wiley.

Troger, H. (2019a). Demografieorientierte Personalbeschaffung. In H. Troger (Ed.), *7 Erfolgsfaktoren für wirksames Personalmanagement* (2nd ed., pp. 35–56). Wiesbaden: Springer Gabler.

Troger, H. (2019b). Ein neuer Generationenvertrag. In H. Troger (Ed.), *7 Erfolgsfaktoren für wirksames Personalmanagement* (2nd ed., pp. 85–134). Wiesbaden: Springer Gabler.

UN, Department of Economic and Social Affairs. (2002). *Second world assembly an aging, April 8–12, Report.* Retrieved August 22, 2020, from https://www.un.org/development/desa/ageing/madrid-plan-of-action-and-its-implementation/second-world-assembly-on-ageing-2002.html.

World Economic Forum Davos. (2016). *Mastering the fourth industrial revolution.* Retrieved August 20, 2020, from http://www3.weforum.org/docs/WEF_AM16_Report.pdf.

Xing-Survey. (2020). Retrieved August 20, 2020, from https://recruiting.xing.com/de/wissen-veranstaltungen/wissen/digitalisierung-im-hr-bereich/umfrage-unter-mehr-als-1200-personalern.

The Ego Perspective: Workforce Considerations

3

3.1 A Working World of Unlimited Opportunities

Last year, at a career's day for graduates, I surprised a hall full of 25-year-olds with the statement that I could not make any recommendations for their further professional development, nor would this even be necessary. After disappointment and confusion had spread, as expected, across the faces of an already insecure audience, my explanation followed. I told them that, firstly, the world of work was characterised by a multitude of trends and just as many counter-trends, and secondly, that each of them was going to have almost unlimited freedom of choice—due to the fact that in the coming years they would have to compete with fewer graduates like themselves than their predecessors.

Today, we are witnessing a working world of near unlimited possibilities, thanks to the complexities of an economic world shaped by Industry 4.0. This 'working world 4.0' is rife with trends and phenomena, but one of its most fascinating features is its seemingly contradictory nature: *New Work* means digital yet it also means human, it stands for global yet individual, automated yet decelerated, virtual yet local. The following chapters will examine some aspects of this world of work from the workforce's perspective.

3.1.1 'We Have Time'

In 1889, when Germany, under Otto von Bismarck, introduced legislation on old age provision, those entitled to a pension had to be at least 70 years old. At that time, the average life expectancy of a working class person was just above 40 years. Today, life expectancy has almost doubled, while the retirement age has remained virtually unchanged. Combined with an extremely low birth rate, this development will inevitably lead to the collapse of pension systems unless more and more people work longer and longer in the future. Any reform that attempts to redress this imbalance is likely going to affect only generations X, Y and Z (the latter two in

© The Author(s), under exclusive license to Springer Nature Switzerland AG 2021 53
H. Troger, *Human Resource Management in a Post COVID-19 World*, Future of
Business and Finance, https://doi.org/10.1007/978-3-030-67470-0_3

particular), but not the baby boom generation, as they form the largest cohort of voters and therefore represent a major political electorate. But even among those who could retire in 5–10 years under the current rules, there is growing distrust of state pension funds. Members of the three generations most likely to be affected must therefore assume that, firstly, they will have to work much longer and, secondly, that they will have to take responsibility for their own economic stability in old age (as opposed to the post-war generation who could safely assume that the money they paid into their pension fund would provide for their parents and grandparents).

A job today does not only mean financial survival and provision for the future. Many employees (especially the younger generations) associate their profession with a sense of identity and meaning. They enjoy their work, or rather, they expect it to be motivating and rewarding. It is not only seen as a duty but also as a right, and in many countries this right is even enshrined in the constitution. Work is also seen as an opportunity for self-fulfilment, and there are fewer and fewer age restrictions on professional self-actualisation. As life expectancy has increased due to improved health conditions (see Chap. 1), the length of one's working life has also increased significantly in recent decades. In theory, a large number of 70-year-olds could now pursue their chosen profession without major restrictions. This applies all the more to today's 20-year-olds.

The factor 'time' in connection with a person's working life is increasingly being redefined. Why should a 19-year-old high-school graduate not take time out and go on a trip around the world before beginning their university studies? Why should a 30 year old not end their career as a banker at 30 to study music and spend the next 25 years working as a teacher? What keeps you from listening to that inner voice telling you to pursue your dream of running a small restaurant in a beautiful location? A previous career as a manager of a software company or a degree course in electrical engineering may have been chosen under parental pressure rather than out of personal conviction.

One might expect and understand such thoughts and actions from a 20 or 30-year-old member of Gen Y. After all, they still have most of their working life ahead of them. They may have witnessed the frustration of many of their older co-workers who have been in their jobs for 30 or more years and heard them say that they would do many things differently 'if given a second chance'.

But even among the 50-year-old members of Gen X, there is an increasing number of people who leave their jobs and rethink their careers. What motivates them to embark on a new start? They may have experienced changes in their private life, feel frustrated about a lack of professional development opportunities or shudder at the prospect of spending another 20 years in the same rut. The courage needed to make such a consequential decision is fueled also by the recognition of the general shortage of skilled workers and by the existence of numerous retraining opportunities. So why not start a second career at 50?

In summary, despite the much-cited fast pace of life in today's working world, it is evident that a different kind of outlook is gaining momentum: 'We have time'.

3.1.2   'The World Is Open to Us'

The business world, or rather the employers, have been operating for some time now in a world characterised by internationalism and globalisation. Whether international conglomerates, production facilities in low-wage countries, sales offices around the globe or simply business relations with international customers: The majority of commercial enterprises today work internationally.

But it is not only the business world that operates internationally; the world has also moved closer together for the individual. Cheap flights and budget airlines allow students and low-income earners to travel all over the world. Many Europeans today are growing up bilingual, many primary schools already have a choice of several foreign languages, and learning is routinely supported by internships and study trips abroad. It is therefore no great surprise that the vast majority of job-seeking university graduates can offer some, now almost expected, 'experience abroad'.

When young people enter the working world today, the whole world is open to them, quite literally—especially as any international experience gained in the first few years of working life will almost certainly be seen in a very positive light by potential employers in the future. Due to the globalisation of most companies mentioned above, it makes sense to ensure that the composition of your workforce is as international as possible. The 'open world' has yet another characteristic: one does not have to be on site physically in order to operate abroad. At a pinch, a 'virtual' office will suffice. A seller of household goods, for example, can provide efficient support online through website administration, call forwarding, mail service, etc., in order to assist their clients all over the globe. And if a young software developer prefers not to be transferred to an office abroad, they can, without much effort, set up their office from home and work remotely, thus relieving their employer of the task to create the necessary space and working environment for them. In today's electronic age, many professions can easily be practiced remotely, whether from home or from anywhere in the world, as long as there is access to the Internet.

Global digitalisation and people's growing desire to live multilocal lives have led to a new category of workers—the 'digital nomads'. These bon vivants combine their love of travel with their job as copywriters, programmers, graphic designers or writers. They work online and conduct their activities independent of time and place. They communicate with their clients via Skype, store documents in the cloud, and rent their short-term accommodation via Airbnb.

3.1.3   Knowledge Is Relative

'Knowledge is power'—this statement may still be valid, but in the last 10 years we have had to redefine it. After all, knowledge, whether general or industry-specific, has become easily accessible for all. For our grandparents' generation, attending higher education was all too often still the privilege of a select few. Today, social class no longer plays the same role in the acquisition of knowledge.

This firmly ties into the next point: the diversity of knowledge sources. From free copies of daily newspapers to open access to public libraries, from Internet cafés to higher education distance learning courses—the acquisition of knowledge has almost no limits in terms of sources, time and place.

The re-evaluation of the way we think about knowledge includes a third, less positive aspect: its transience. The so-called half-life of knowledge is shrinking faster than ever in many areas, especially in the digital sciences, where it is now measured in months. In the past, it was assumed that about half of everything learned at school would be obsolete after about 20 years. The more specialised the field is, the faster this knowledge deteriorates as a result of new developments and findings.

3.1.3.1 What Does This Development Mean for the Employee?

Firstly, the above-mentioned decreasing half-life of knowledge makes a commitment to lifelong learning and continuous professional development imperative in order to keep pace. Secondly, age plays only a marginal role (experience helps, at best, to process new knowledge better). Thirdly, the relatively easy accessibility of knowledge gives everybody a second, and perhaps even a third chance at self-actualization through work. We are by no means tied to our previous education choices. And finally, in this time of inflationary knowledge diversity, actions speak louder than words. More than ever, it is less about what I know, but rather how I translate this knowledge into concrete action.

In this working world of unlimited possibilities, it is never too late for a new beginning, as long as you are motivated and willing to take a chance.

3.2   A New Distribution of Power

Although much has changed over the last decades in terms of economic environment and operational processes, the distribution of power and the roles of the main actors have always been clear. The age structure of an organisation used to be threefold: the generation of the 'old', who sat at the levers of power and gradually handed it down to the generation below them. Then, at the lowest level, there was the 'youth', who had just entered the organisation and were gaining their first experiences. They had to wait patiently until it was their turn, and it was most likely not appreciated if they raised any complaints.

There was a second dynamic between employers and employees. Here too, the roles were usually clearly defined and the rules were set accordingly. In recent years, a gradual shift in these traditional power relations has begun in both areas.

3.2.1   From Baby Boomers to Gen Z

When highly trained, young and motivated Gen Y and Gen Z workers enter the labour market, they are likely to come across people of retirement age who are still fit for working life. But the older colleagues—they might be baby boomers or perhaps even of the post-war generation—are not thinking of handing over the reins just yet. A generational change, the way it happened just a few decades ago, is no longer the norm. Instead, we live in an era of parallel societies where three, four or even five generations work together. The demographic developments described in previous chapters—increased life expectancy with a low birth rate and empty pension coffers, which has led to longer working lives and also the need to work longer—mean that different age cohorts with very different interests, methods and goals now work together, probably in the same department. Conflicts cannot be avoided. On the one hand, the younger generations Y and Z are numerically outnumbered, and they are usually hierarchically subordinate to members of older generations. (In top management, too, one will mostly find either baby boomers or generation X.) On the other hand, the Y and Z generations provide the most sought-after talent on the labour market. Decades of declining birth rates have created a shortage of young professionals across almost all of Europe. Despite this, the power constellation between the generations will not change, at least not in the short term. The 'older generation' will continue to determine the rules.

Nonetheless, the new generations of employees are challenging the established rules. They have different ideas about work and life than their predecessors. They may wonder why they have to stay in the office until 6 p.m. when there is nothing left to do, or question why they are not allowed to write private emails during working hours yet are expected to answer work emails on a Saturday. Older colleagues of equal standing usually do not understand this attitude or may even react defensively, while their superiors (who are probably older too) are torn and may decide to try and keep them happy. Yet no one admits that these young people, unlike their older colleagues who have influence in the company, have nothing to lose and therefore have no motivation to adapt. Career, in the conventional sense, is usually not very important to them. Money and status symbols mean far less to millennials and Gen Z than they did to their 'role models'.

In summary, the situation is a paradoxical one in which there is formal power on the part of the older generations and partially visible or invisible power on the part of the younger generations.

3.2.2 From Employer to Employee Market

In HR management, we speak of either an employer or an employee market. Depending on the economic situation, i.e., the situation between labour supply and labour demand, it is a question of who has more influence on the parameters of a new position. An employee market exists when companies need to recruit qualified specialists and the number of vacancies is greater than the number of available workers. This is precisely the situation we find ourselves in at the moment, not only with regard to highly qualified specialists, but increasingly also when it comes to ordinary positions. This phenomenon will intensify in the coming years due to the demographic trends already mentioned. Very soon, the power in the labour market will no longer lie with the employers.

Against this backdrop, companies will have to reinvent themselves to raise their status with potential employees. Good *employer branding* alone will no longer suffice if there are no available skilled workers on the market. The only solution will be to poach them from other companies. Consequently, the much-cited *war for talent* is now reaching a whole new level and living up to its name. That said, workers—whether young or experienced—will gain great negotiating power.

3.2.2.1 The Power of the Candidates

The job interview of the future will be different—and in many industries it already is. The recruiters' standard question 'Why should we choose you over other candidates?' will likely only be posed confidently when looking to fill a high-ranking position. The well-educated Gen Y candidates can counter this with much more self-assurance than their parents and grandparents and reply with another question: 'Why should I accept this position? What do you offer that the competition doesn't?'

The power of employers is crumbling and the employer market is gradually turning into an employee market. Within the next 15 years, the number of Germans of working age—according to research—will drop by up to six million. This means that the labour market will increasingly be driven by employees who will be calling the shots. Companies will have to ensure that they are perceived as attractive, young and innovative, and they will be applying for candidates, rather than the other way round. The potential candidates, on the other hand, will sift through their offers and select their favourites. The best employers will then be allowed to introduce themselves personally. Elaborate recruitment fairs of the future may result in a dry 'I'll get back to you' and the HR manager may, at best, hope for a phone call or two.

We can already see this shift in the balance of power in the wording of job advertisements today. Employers introduce themselves in detail and describe at length what they can offer their employees. Only then follows the list of skills and attributes required of applicants, and even these are often presented more as a wish list than as a set of requirements.

Therefore, more than ever, effective HR management will start with good employer marketing. Recruitment, for that matter, is becoming a key element of HR work.

What does this mean for me as a qualified specialist? I select the company according to the criteria that are important to me and I trust that a good HR manager or a company executive will define a role within the company that is suitable for me and adapt the structure of the organisation accordingly.

3.2.3   Increased Expectations

'Seeking permanent position in a leading role. The job must include varied and rewarding tasks, allow me to manage my own time, and offer opportunities for advancement. I'm willing to give my best for 20 h of work per week, for an attractive salary'. This could be the suggestion of a 25-year-old freshly graduated candidate to a recruiter of an international engineering company. Said recruiter, on the other hand, might have different ideas: 'We are looking for an ambitious trilingual mechatronics engineer with a university degree in business informatics and a master's degree in international business law, with 3 years of professional experience and excellent social skills to start immediately. We offer—after a 2-year training period—an appropriate salary and the classic incentives'.

Unsurprisingly, these two actors in the job market are unlikely to seek and find each other. As a matter of fact, expectations have been rising on both sides in recent years (Troger 2019). The demands that employers place on employees are becoming ever higher—in view of the growing challenges of globalisation—yet, at the same time, hiring success is declining. This is because, in addition to falling numbers of available candidates, the expectations that the latter place on an available position, have also been rising. It is therefore becoming more and more difficult for entrepreneurs, HR departments and line managers to respond to the wishes of existing and potential employees. Creating attractive working conditions used to be much easier for previous generations and was primarily a question of having the right budget. Today, the compilation of cafeteria-style benefit plans shows how much more complex it is to manage the great diversity among its beneficiaries. A 55-year-old engineer, for example, may not be very interested in the availability of a childcare facility, while a 25-year-old computer scientist has no use for a company's partial retirement policy.

The increased expectations on the part of employees have three components: Firstly, people generally demand more of life (and their career). Secondly, there is now a much greater variety of expectations amongst employees. And thirdly, there has been a clear shift in the balance of power between employee and employer.

A survey of 1500 HR managers in Australia, Germany, France, the United Kingdom, the Netherlands and the USA, commissioned by SAP (2012), revealed significant differences between baby boomers, Gen X and Gen Y in terms of expectations and requests from job candidates and employees. Overall, generation X was the least satisfied with the current situation and made the most demands. This was the cohort that was most likely to request a higher job title and more pay, among other benefits. The millennials, or Gen Y, were more interested in personal development than any other cohort: 41% said that training and additional leisure time were important to them. The baby boomers were clearly the most satisfied. Their most frequent request, if they made one at all, was for a small increase in leisure time.

Another study by PwC (2013) confirms that millennials and Gen Z are not the only generations that have high expectations and are keen to take advantage of their market power. While there were some 'stereotypical' differences in behaviour between the generations in terms of the demands and expectations placed on employers, there was a surprisingly high degree of similarity between all three employee cohorts. For example, all respondents insisted on more flexibility and autonomy in choosing where and when to work. There was also intergenerational agreement on leadership style: an authoritarian leadership style with one-way communication is no longer adequate. The old motto 'silence is praise enough' must be rejected by today's leaders if they want to be successful.

The PwC survey revealed one thing above all: a high level of self-confidence among employees when it comes to asserting their expectations. This applies not only to the demands of the job itself, but also to the much-debated balance between work and private life. All age groups consistently requested more leisure time, among other things, and stressed the importance they placed on achieving work-life balance.

3.3   We Are All Individuals

Today's workforce, as mentioned above, has become increasingly heterogeneous in terms of age, origin, education, religion and other factors. As a result, the interests and wishes of the workforce are just as diverse. Due to the increase in bargaining power, workers are now in a much stronger position to communicate and assert these wishes. Naturally, each individual wants to find solutions to shape his or her work-life balance in a way that makes sense to them.

3.3.1   Variety of Interests

The current shortages of qualified applicants explain the constant stream of new studies and employee surveys—especially among young people. They aim to find out which criteria are most important to people when making job decisions. The following factors are often mentioned as the most influential:

– Does the job represent a fresh challenge?
– A well-blended team,
– Opportunities for personal development.

Salary and company benefits range somewhere behind this in importance. But despite the congruence in expectations at a certain level, the ideas and interests of employees differ depending on their age, personal goals and current life situation. The main purpose of the above-mentioned international study by PwC (2013) was to investigate the job expectations of millennials and to compare them with those of non-millennials (baby boomers and Gen X). Among PwC's approximate 44,000 employees, significant generational differences came to light. For example, a good 60% of millennials expected to work for the same employer for 9 years or more, whereas for non-millennials it was 70%.

Another such difference is the desire for direct and timely feedback on performance, which is much more pronounced among younger workers (41% vs. 30%). Not surprisingly, mobility is also a factor: 37% of millennials would regard a job transfer abroad as a pivotal moment of their career, while only 28% of older employees showed an interest.

While our parents and grandparents aspired to earn as much as possible in secure employment, drive a company car or be guaranteed a company pension, the millennial is far more attracted by exciting projects, the opportunity to be part of a young, hip team, and plenty of free time. Status and power are losing their significance for the younger generations, while self-actualization is increasingly taking centre stage.

However, we must not fall into the trap of thinking that the different ideas and interests of employees can easily fit into four simple 'generational pigeon holes'. By living and working together, the generations learn from each other and recognise the value and strengths of their differently aged colleagues. This mutual enrichment across generations makes generalisations difficult or even counterproductive. We feel like individuals and we want to be treated as such.

3.3.2 Work-Life Balance

Work-life balance is often defined as a balanced and healthy relationship between work and private life. Organisations, companies and managers are keen to claim awareness of its importance, yet cases of burnout and sickness absence related to mental health are on the rise. More overtime, the expectation to be contactable at all times, and rarely having time for oneself are signs that work-life balance is getting increasingly out of kilter almost everywhere in Europe. It appears, that this buzzword represents an idea that is closer to wishful thinking, at this point, than to lived reality.

Gen Y employees have clear advantages over their older colleagues when it comes to balancing work and private life. As digital natives, they have learned to optimise their working hours with a variety of technological tools, and companies are trying to win them over with flexitime offers and opportunities for remote work. All this makes working life more comfortable, but it does not mean that they do less work. A millennial simply aims to reconcile all three: self-actualization, professional life and private life.

The fact that this reconciliation is becoming increasingly difficult in most European countries, is also shown by the Better Life Index (2019), which was compiled by the Organisation for Economic Cooperation and Development (OECD). This study examines how well people in OECD countries are able to reconcile their work and family life. According to the survey, many people are still worried about work-related issues outside working hours. Fewer and fewer people are able to switch off completely or use their free time for leisure activities. Many also reported that their own heavy workload had started to affect their family and friends as well.

How should we deal with this? We could follow the example of Thomas Vollmoeller, who decided to take a 3-month sabbatical in 2016 while he was CEO of the listed German company Xing. At that time, the company he was heading was flourishing and his unprecedented decision was intended to set an example of flexibility and work-life balance. Although the German business newspaper *Handelsblatt* (2016) praised his move and announced that they expected him back 'with a suitcase full of fresh ideas', time off at this level of senior management is still seen by many as an admission of weakness (even if it is not spoken out loud).

Alternatively, we could follow into the footsteps of former organisation consultant Ron Ashkenas (2012), who, as early as 2012, questioned whether the hype surrounding the 'work-life balance' was not perhaps prompting us to chase after something unattainable, and instead proposed that we consider it to be a 'work-life blend'.

Ashkenas suggested that a healthy balance between work and private life was an illusion, especially for the generations of digital natives. His argument: stop trying to fight the influence of smart phones and constant accessibility, but embrace them as part of our current reality. In return, workers should be given the autonomy to determine their own working hours instead of having to adhere to rigid office hours. A 2-h lunch break should not be a problem if the work gets done in time.

Another idea for the reconciliation of work and private life comes from Scandinavia: the 'Hoffice Concept'. Swedish psychologist Christofer Gradin Franzén's does not simply suggest to work remotely from home, but he encourages people to share their private work space with others by letting them into their homes. The aim is to create structure, exchange ideas and receive feedback, and to share existing resources. However, this alternative co-working model has not yet gained widespread support.

All in all, it can be expected that the classic 9–5 office job will die out, mainly as a result of employee needs. The children have to be picked up on time from the day care centre, the elderly parent suffering from dementia might need to be looked after at home, and the fitness-loving software developer may prefer to do his training after breakfast. Companies will have to respond to these challenges and preferences in the lives of their employees and find ways to meet their demands.

3.3.3   Individual Career Paths

To get the best out of employees and their skills, we need to find the right balance between the needs of the organisation on the one hand, and performance and motivation on the other. This balance can be influenced by various factors on both sides: On the organisational side, the general optimisation of processes is the main reason for a continuous change in requirements. The half-life of knowledge is getting shorter and shorter, especially in technology-driven companies, and keeping up with these changes requires an enormous effort from the workforce. On the employees' side, motivation is the biggest element of uncertainty. Despite great performance capability, the highly qualified mechanical engineer, for example, may not be interested in taking the next career step and earning a higher salary or the benefit of a company car if this means that he has to give up his plan to travel around the world.

Top performers now expect to be able to adapt their career planning to their individual life stages, both in terms of maintaining employability (with their current employer and on the labour market), and in terms of their (often unpredictable) willingness to commit.

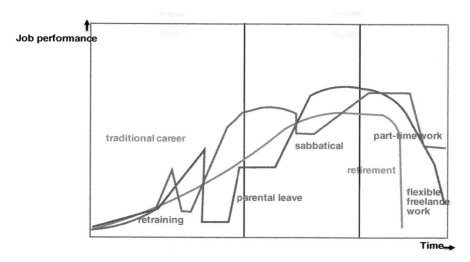

Fig. 3.1 Individual career paths

Individual career planning based on life planning is very challenging, given the diversity and volatility of employees' interests. It is often difficult to reconcile this with the long-term development objectives of the organisation. An example of what a personal development plan looks like is given below (Fig. 3.1) and will be examined in more detail in Chap. 9.

3.4   The Coronavirus-Effect

How do employees feel personally affected by the pandemic? The '*360 Well-Being Survey*' from CIGNA (2020), which includes the study '*Covid-19 Global Impact*', attempts to answer this question.

Cigna's *360 Well-Being Survey* captures perceptions of health and well-being, including an index that tracks physical, family, social, financial and professional well-being. The study involved 10,204 people in China, Hong Kong, Singapore, Spain, Thailand, the United Arab Emirates, the United Kingdom and the USA between January and April 2020.

It aimed to show the changes in attitude during the crisis and focused on four areas:

- The Cigna Well-Being Index.
- The health and wellness scorecard.
- The virtual health assessment tracker.
- People's opinions on what the new normal will look like.

Not surprisingly, with regard to family life, people felt that they are now better able than before to support their partners/spouse and their children and that they now spend more time with them than before.

3.4.1 Decline in Loneliness

The study showed a general decline in loneliness, despite lockdowns across most markets. Only 8% of respondents indicated that they 'always felt isolated from others' in April, compared to 11% at the beginning of January. The lockdowns also appear to have had a positive impact on relationships in some cases. When asked whether they felt closer to other people, 73% said they did in April, compared to 69% in January.

People also stated that they felt closer to their colleagues than before the crisis. 64% of respondents said that working from home and using technology had made it easier to communicate with colleagues, and 76% felt that their working day was more flexible. In the USA, this proportion rose to 93%, in Thailand to 91% and in Spain and the UAE to 90%, suggesting that working routines may change permanently once lockdowns have ended.

3.4.1.1 More Flexibility: Longer Working Hours
A key finding of the study was that working from home had improved the working lives of those surveyed—despite often longer working hours. Globally, 76% said that their working day had become more flexible, with Thailand (90%) and Spain (80%) leading the way. However, the downside of this flexibility is that more and more people are finding it difficult to switch off. Some 79% of respondents admitted that they were stuck in an 'always-on' mode, which shows an increase in most regions. In addition, uncertainty about job stability has also increased during the crisis.

3.4.1.2 Decline in Stress
Stress remains a global health problem, although levels seem to have dropped. For instance, 82% of respondents said that they currently felt stressed, which is 5% less than at the beginning of the year. The study also confirmed that the perceived causes of stress varied widely in nature and prevalence, ranging from personal, financial and work-related developments to health and relationships.

'The shift to *working* remotely has been *one of the most significant changes brought* on by the Covid-*19* lockdown', *said Arjan Toor*, CEO, Cigna Europe. 'There are some clear signs that working from home has contributed to an overall improvement in working life. This suggests that working routines may change permanently once the lockdowns are over. There is no doubt that the pandemic has brought considerable stress for all of us, but it is encouraging to see examples of people feeling that their well-being at work has improved during these times'.

3.4.1.3 Feel-Good Management as a Unique Selling Point

In the past, the health of employees was not a top priority for most companies. But Covid-19 has shifted the priorities. The importance of health and safety at work has been highlighted like never before since countries across the globe prepared to go into lockdowns. In the future, the way a company takes care of the health and well-being of their workforce will become a central USP in the battle for employees. While the so-called feel-good management style was not always taken seriously in the past, Covid-19 has shown us that it can lead the way. Feel-good management means that the company not only takes care of their employees' health, but that it supports an entire range of life-decisions. It means supporting employees in finding accommodation, covering public transport costs, subsidising childcare, providing coaches for professional and private matters, serving nutritionally balanced meals in work canteens, and offering gym memberships. The futurologist Sven Gabor Janszky (2020) anticipates the development of a multitude of apps and much discussion on the subject of health checks, which companies could harness to enhance employee engagement and commitment.

References

Ashkenas, R. (2012). *Forget work-life balance: It's time for work-life-blend. Forbes online.* Retrieved August 17, 2020, from https://www.forbes.com/sites/ronashkenas/2012/10/19/forget-work-life-balance-its-time-for-work-life-blend/?sh=2f9a2ad67e22.

Bialek, C. (2016). *Mit flipflops am sandstrand. Handelsblatt online.* Retrieved August 17, 2020, from https://www.handelsblatt.com/unternehmen/it-medien/xing-chef-thomas-vollmoeller-mit-flipflops-am-sandstrand/14859420.html?ticket=ST-8495273-MU2xy1FtSwhPyXurmUxMap2.

Cingna. (2020). *Covid-19 global impact study.* Retrieved August 17, 2020, from https://www.cignaglobal.com/static/pdf/globalversion-cignacovid-19globalimapctstudy-report.pdf.

Dimensional Research. (2012). *HR beat: A survey on the pulse of today's global workforce.* Retrieved August 16, 2020, from https://www.personalradar.ch/wp-content/uploads/2012/10/2012-HR-Beat-A-Survey-on-the-Pulse-of-Todays-Global-Workforce.pdf.

OECD. (2019). *Better life index.* Retrieved August 16, 2020, from http://www.oecdbetterlifeindex.org/de/#/11111111111.

PwC. (2013). *Dealing with disruption. 16th Annual Global CEO Survey.* Retrieved August 17, 2020, from https://www.pwc.com/cl/es/publicaciones/assets/16th-annual-global-ceo-survey.pdf.

Sven Gabor Janszky. (2020). *Handelsblatt 27.05.2020.* Retrieved August 16, 2020, from https://www.handelsblatt.com/unternehmen/beruf-und-buero/buero-special/buerotrends-digitaler-traditioneller-gruener-corona-koennte-die-arbeitswelt-nachhaltig-veraendern/25865016.html?ticket=ST-9814856-OuWzmcKbe9FIJXcdhz1b-ap2.

Troger, H. (2019). Management von Interessen und Erwartungen. In H. Troger (Ed.), *7 Erfolgsfaktoren für wirksames Personalmanagement* (2nd ed., pp. 169–187). Heidelberg: Springer Gabler.

Part II

Expectations of Good Work Opportunities— and the Sobering Reality

Expectations of a Good Job

4

4.1 What Is a 'Good Work Opportunity' Today?

4.1.1 Increased Expectations

The mutual expectations of employees and employers have increased significantly in recent years (Troger 2019). In view of the challenges that arise from competition in an international market, the demands placed on potential employees are becoming greater than ever—meanwhile, the chances of finding the right candidate for a position are shrinking. Not only are the numbers of candidates declining, their expectations for what they want in a job have been rising as well. This suggests that it will become increasingly difficult for entrepreneurs, HR departments and managers to respond to both, the expectations and needs of their existing employees and to those of potential employees. Creating attractive working conditions used to be much easier for HR managers of previous generations—for them, it was foremost and quite simply a question of having the right budget.

These increased expectations on the part of employees can be viewed from three angles: Firstly, people today have higher expectations overall, not only with regard to work but also to life in general. Secondly, employees' expectations have become much more diverse. And thirdly, the balance of power between employees and employers has very clearly begun to shift.

The extent to which employees' expectations and demands depend on their generation was investigated in a survey conducted by SAP (2012). The responses from 1500 HR managers in Australia, Germany, France, the UK, the Netherlands and the USA showed clear differences between baby boomers, Gen X and Gen Y. Overall, Gen X was the least satisfied with their current situation and made the most demands. According to the survey, they asked, in particular, for a more attractive job title and higher pay. The millennials were more interested in personal development than any other generation: 41% stated that education and additional leisure time were important for them. The baby boomers were the most satisfied. All they wanted was a little more free time.

© The Author(s), under exclusive license to Springer Nature Switzerland AG 2021   69
H. Troger, *Human Resource Management in a Post COVID-19 World*, Future of Business and Finance, https://doi.org/10.1007/978-3-030-67470-0_4

However, another study by PwC (2013) shows that not only millennials and Gen Z have high job expectations and want to make full use of their market power. While 'stereotypical' differences between the generations were noticeable in their general behaviour, there was a surprising amount of agreement between all cohorts in terms of the expectations they place on their employers. For example, all respondents insisted on more flexibility and freedom in choosing their working hours and place of work. Employees across all generations also had clear ideas about leadership: an authoritarian leadership style with one-sided communication will no longer work. The old motto 'silence is praise enough' needs to be discarded by today's managers.

According to PwC, the survey as a whole and across all generations highlighted one thing in particular: the self-confidence of today's employees when it comes to asserting their demands. This applies not only to the demands about the job itself, but in equal measure to the balance between work and private life. All age groups unequivocally demanded more leisure time, among other things, in line with this general desire to achieve a healthy work–life balance.

4.1.1.1 The Wishes of Employees

What do employees really want? What would they change if they could? Some revealing answers to these questions are provided in *The Employee Voice*, a study by Peakon (2019), a provider of online surveys. It analysed more than eleven million anonymous contributions from employees around the world.

One question that they were asked was: *'If you had a magic wand, what is the one thing you would change about your organisation?'*

There were no predetermined response options—the participants were allowed to answer freely. Would they want a 3-day week on a full salary? Or 60 paid holidays per year? The following is a list of the ten areas where they most wanted to see changes in their companies—in order of priority (cf. Peakon 2019):

– Rank 1: Pay
– Rank 2: Communication
– Rank 3: Management
– Rank 4: Colleagues
– Rank 5: Office
– Rank 6: Processes/workflows
– Rank 7: Department
– Rank 8: Salary
– Rank 9: Product
– Rank 10: Customers

Strikingly, these employees did not want anything 'magical' or impossible. On the contrary: they described very real issues and demanded very real solutions.

As expected, issues relating to salary were high on the agenda, while other important comments focused on workplace relations, such as those between management and employees. The participating employees also used the question to comment on their working environment, business strategy and internal processes.

They mentioned 'communication' within the company as another significant area of concern.

The study also breaks down how the needs and perspectives of employees change in the course of their employment. During their first year in a company, employees were particularly interested in issues such as the working atmosphere, motivation and objectives, or the role they play in the team.

Between 1 and 2 years of employment, the focus shifted to further development and training. For those who had been employed between 2 and 5 years, work–life balance and opportunities for advancement were of central importance.

Employees who had been with their company between 5 and 10 years thought more about the strategy and goals of the company. In comments made by these respondents, keywords such as 'company decisions' or 'customer experience' were more frequent. Finally, those who stayed with the same company beyond 10 years paid primary attention to *appreciation* and *personal satisfaction*, as reflected in the use of keywords such as 'pride' and 'mission'.

4.1.1.2 Generational Differences

The study also revealed that it is not just the length of service that influences the way employees view their situation within the company, but that the generation they belong to can have a bearing on it as well. An exception to this rule was 'work–life balance,' which was similarly important to all generations. For other areas of concern, clear differences were visible. The following topics mattered most to individuals across generations:

Baby boomers: security, pride, respect, family
Gen X: a possible role as mentor, good cooperation
Gen Y: leadership position, promotion opportunities, changing to other offices or
    roles, new opportunities
Gen Z: salary, overtime

The way in which members of different generations communicated with each other also varied. Older employees, for example, appreciated e-mail, while millennials prefered the instant messaging service *Slack*.

4.1.2 Diversity of Interests and Values

The diversity of the workforce in terms of age, origin, education, religion and other factors has previously been mentioned. Due to their increased bargaining power, employees are able to communicate and assert their wishes much more confidently. Naturally, we all want a healthy and a meaningful balance between our professional and private life.

The shortage of skilled workers in particular explains the large number of surveys—with young people as the primary target group—that examine people's criteria for choosing a job. The following factors are often cited as significant: a new challenge, a well-blended team, personal advancement.

After that follow salary, company car and bonuses. Despite similarities at a certain level, the interests and ideas of employees diverge according to age, personal goals and current life situation. An international study by PwC (2013) with the aim to examine job expectations of millennials compared to those of non-millennials (baby boomers and Gen X) surveyed approximately 44,000 PwC employees and revealed clear generational differences. For example, in relation to company loyalty, where the results showed that around 60% of millennials expected to work for the same employer for 9 years or more, while it was 70% for non-millennials.

Another difference was the desire for direct and timely feedback on performance, which was much more pronounced among younger workers (41% vs. 30%). Not surprisingly, 'mobility' was also a factor: 37% of millennials would regard a job transfer abroad as a pivotal moment in their career, while only 28% of older employees showed an interest.

We should not, however, think that the different ideas and interests of employees can easily fit into four simple 'generational pigeon holes'. By living and working together, the generations learn from each other and recognise the value and strengths of their older and younger colleagues. This mutual enrichment across the generations makes generalisations difficult or even counterproductive. We feel like individuals and we want to be treated as such (Troger 2019).

4.1.2.1 Values

The expectations we have for a 'good' employer, as well as our interests, are not only based on a number of existential factors, but also on our values (Veldsman and Pauw 2018). Interestingly, many of these values cannot clearly be attributed to socio-demographic factors, such as age, income or education. While trends are discernible, most sociologists consider these to be negligible. The Bremen-based research and consultancy firm *nextpractice* (2016) investigated the prerequisites of a 'good job' in its study 'Wertewelten Arbeiten 4.0' (translated from German: 'work 4.0 in a world of values'). To this end, they interviewed 1200 employees across all age groups and all levels of education and hierarchy. Cluster analysis of these interviews revealed seven value systems ('value worlds') that can be clearly distinguished and categorised. Each category represents a clear and consistent view of the world of work shared by the respective employee group. Each of the seven groups was characterised by the interests and attitudes that influenced the decision-making of the group members, as well as by their deeply rooted values in relation to the world of work. The survey produced the following breakdown:

Value system 1 'ability to live free from work-related worries:' Around 30% of respondents fitted into this value system. They identify with the desire to work in order to be able to live a carefree life. They feel that the increasing competition is a burden and struggle with the pressure of having to work more and more and still face an uncertain future. Not surprisingly, this group particularly laments the growing discrepancy between the realities of work and their ideal.

Value system 2 'working in a strongly united community marked by solidarity:'
About 9% of the workers interviewed subscribed to value system 2. They feel that values such as solidarity, loyalty, respect and social cohesion are becoming less important. They are struggling with increasing pressures and risks, but also with a lack of purpose and growing divisions within society.

Value system 3 'working hard for prosperity:' About 14% of respondents were assigned to this group. Like the previous groups, they also complain about the general deterioration of working conditions since the 1990s. However, in contrast to the other two value systems, they also see some positives aspects in today's world of work. Work may not always be fun, but hard work will pay off sooner or later.

Value system 4 'commitment to excellence:' 11% of respondents felt responsibility and leadership positions were more of a motivation than a pressure. Employees who subscribe to this value system strive for excellence. Overall they believe that recent developments in the world of work have been positive and that this will continue to be the case, albeit to a lesser extent.

Value system 5 'realising one's full potential:' For the 10% of workers who fitted into this category, today's world of work offers almost unlimited opportunities. For this group it is important that they maintain and improve their labour market value through continuous education and training. These workers want diverse and above all flexible work opportunities that help them to reach their full potential. Security and recognition are of secondary importance for them.

Value system 6 'finding a good balance between work and private life:' This value system, to which around 14% of respondents subscribed, is characterised by an optimistic view of the future. However, they take a critical view of today's working conditions because their own wishes to reconcile family and career have not yet been realised. Work–life balance is important for this group and they expect companies to find ways to adapt to the wishes of their employees.

Value system 7: 'in search for meaning outside work:' A good 12% of those surveyed were assigned to this value system. The people in this group are interested in social justice, meaning and personal development opportunities. Life outside work is just as important as job satisfaction. Recent developments in the world of work are viewed critically. Instead of living to work, these workers want to turn things around: Work should first and foremost serve to support quality of life.

4.1.3 The Attractive Employer

After these considerations about the expectations, values and wishes of employees, the question of what makes the 'perfect employer' remains. Or, to put it another way: what makes an employer attractive in the labour market? In Germany, the answer seems clear: You should build cars! For many years, the top ten most attractive employers have consistently included the five big names of the German automotive industry (Daimler, BMW, Audi, VW, Porsche). The study 'Attractive Employers' by

Berufsstart.de (2020), which included 4300 university students, graduates and young professionals across Germany, provides another example. The study's authors first looked for the 'most attractive' companies and then—in an open-ended question—asked about the characteristics that made these companies more attractive than others. A distinction was made between 'primary attributes' (e.g., salary) and 'secondary attributes' (e.g., working atmosphere). The evaluation focused largely on a comparison between economists and engineers (together they represented over 60% of all participants). A distinction was also made between male and female respondents, although no significant differences were found.

With regard to the **primary attracive attributes** of a company, almost all participants, regardless of their field of study, agreed: attracive factor no. 1 refers to the company's *continuing education and training* offering. Only among engineers was *salary* in first place and CET in third place. For economists it was the exact opposite. However, both groups were in agreement about *promotion prospects* and put this primary factor in second place. Engineers attached greater importance to *industry*. Further significant differences were also evident in terms of *image*, which was rated much higher by the economists. For engineers, on the other hand, *job security* was particularly important. Among the **secondary attractive attributes**, *working atmosphere, work–life balance, variety* and *family friendliness* were mentioned most frequently. In this area there were almost no significant differences between engineers and economists. However, these attributes were somewhat more important for female participants than for male participants.

In 2019, the employment website StepStone also conducted a study on the characteristics of an attractive employer—and called on employers to meet the expectations of their employees. Nationwide, 19,000 highly skilled workers and managers took part in this survey. The attractiveness factors that emerged from the survey were no great surprise—however, the wide gap between wish and reality was (see StepStone 2020). The attractiveness factors according to the StepStone survey:

1. **Attractive salary:** 96% of respondents said that they would like to be well paid for their services. However, only four out of ten people actually rated their current salary as good. The evaluation of their own salary depended strongly on the industry in which the person worked; the most satisfied employees were in the pharmaceutical industry (58%).
2. **Career and training opportunities:** The majority of all employees surveyed had specific career goals and indicated that they wanted to achieve them through training opportunities. Despite this, nowhere was the gap between aspiration and reality greater than here: 91% of respondents attached importance to this factor, but only 17% stated that these opportunities were offered by their current employer. The employees who were most often offered career and training opportunities worked in the aforementioned automotive industry.
3. **Flexible working:** 90% of all respondents said that flexibility in the job was important to them. However, the reality of the working world—at least before the pandemic—did not meet this expectation. Only half of those surveyed said that

they had flexible working opportunities. The StepStone survey showed that companies in the insurance sector offered more flexibility than others (66%).

4. **Company culture:** This is a question of how communication and leadership are handled in the company, and to what extend employees are involved in decision-making. For 90% of respondents, this factor played a significant role, but only 18% gave a positive testimonial about their current employer in this regard.

5. **Meaningful tasks:** 89% of respondents wanted to see the meaning behind what they do and to know that they contribute to the overall success of the company. However, only about one-third (33%) recognised the purpose of their work (see StepStone 2020).

4.2   Survey: Employee Expectations of a Good Job

In collaboration with an employment agency that specialises in analysing employee satisfaction, I conducted a quantitative survey of 4560 employees in 2019/2020. The aim was to determine what they expected of their employer in order to achieve job satisfaction.

For this purpose, 18 characteristics (from 'A' to 'R', see Table 4.1)—we could also call them 'values'—were divided into the six categories of strategy, organisation, management, team, company image and health:

1. **Strategy:** Common goal (A)—Customer orientation (B)—Mission (C)
2. **Organisation:** Market flexibility (D)—Innovation capability (E)—Equal treatment (F)
3. **Management:** Communication (G)—Competence of superiors (H)—Sincerity (I)—Fairness (J)—Individual promotion and development (K)
4. **Team:** Working atmosphere (L)—Team spirit (M)
5. **Company Image:** Attractive image (N)—Identification (O)
6. **Health:** Occupational safety (P)—Workload (Q)—Autonomous work(time) organisation (R)

Table 4.1   18 characteristics/values

A	Common goal	J	Fairness
B	Customer orientation	K	Individual promotion and development
C	Mission	L	Working atmosphere
D	Market flexibility	M	Team spirit
E	Innovation capability	N	Attractive image
F	Equality	O	Commitment and engagement
G	Communication	P	Occupational health and safety
H	Competence of superiors	Q	Workload
I	Honesty and openness	R	Autonomous work (time) organisation

4.2.1   The Research Question

To represent the 18 characteristics, a number of statements and/or expectations were devised and participants were asked to choose those that applied to them and to rate them in order of priority. A maximum of five statements could be selected.

They were asked to perform the following task:

Please write a number from 1 to 5, depending on importance (1 for the most important), next to the letters that relate to the five most important characteristics for you personally.

It's important to me that …

A … we all work towards common company goals.

B … we align our work with the needs of our customers.

C … we have and live a common mission statement.

D … our company adapts flexibly to changes in the market.

E … our company constantly scrutinises and improves products, processes and technologies.

F … all employees, regardless of age, gender, language, etc., are treated equal.

G … I can ask questions and obtain necessary information at any time.

H … my manager works conscientiously and competently.

I … my manager is honest with me and acknowledges his or her mistakes.

J … all employees are valued and fairly treated and remunerated.

K … I am promoted and developed in my work.

L … we have a good working atmosphere.

M … we can rely on each other and have a feeling of togetherness.

N … my employer has an attractive image.

O … I feel that I belong in my company.

P … occupational safety is guaranteed.

Q … my workload is balanced.

R … my work and working hours can be arranged individually.

4.2.2   Survey and Method

The survey took place from 2 September 2019 to 28 February 2020 in the so-called *Euroregion Tyrol—South Tyrol—Trentino* (this includes areas from Northern Italy and south-western Austria). This prosperous region is characterised by a high number of internationally active, mainly small and medium-sized enterprises. The regional economy is operating at full employment. Due to the size of the survey, it can be considered as representative for the whole economic area of Northern and Central Europe.

35 companies from the following sectors of the economy took part in the survey: industry (13), trade/services (18) and hospitality (4).

The following enterprise sizes were represented: 21 small, 11 medium-sized and 3 large enterprises.

A total of 4560 employees were invited and 3648 of them took part in this voluntary and anonymous survey, representing a response rate of 80%.

4.2.2.1 Clusters

The 3648 participants were allocated to seven clusters; four of them related to employees and the remaining three clusters to their respective employers.

Employees
(a) Generation: 'baby boomers' (>55 years old), 'X' (45–54), 'Y' (25–44), 'Z' ($\leq$24)
(b) Gender: male/female
(c) Education level: compulsory education/apprenticeship and vocational secondary school/university graduate
(d) Hierarchy level: Employees without management responsibility/middle management/senior management

Companies
(a) Sector: industry/trade/hospitality
(b) Company size (number of employees):: <100/101–500/>500
(c) Department: administration—production/technology—sales/customer services

4.2.2.2 Evaluation Method

The method chosen for evaluation was analysis according to frequency distribution. The raw data were cleansed and questionnaires with missing or invalid answers were removed. Next, descriptive statistical analysis was performed to compare the normalised frequency of each statement at each priority level. The analysis was performed using the common statistical programming language R.

4.2.3 The Results

An evaluation of the results showed the following distribution of characteristics (Fig. 4.1):

4.2.3.1 General Findings from the Survey

(a) Overall, the characteristics could be divided into three categories with regard to their relevance for the employees questioned (see Table 4.2): the three very important characteristics were: *Fairness* (J)—*Working atmosphere* (L)—*Common goal* (A).

This was followed by seven important characteristics: *Equality* (F)—*Team spirit* (M)—*Autonomous work (time) organisation* (R)—*Honesty and Openness* (I)—*Individual promotion and development* (K)—*Customer orientation* (B)—*Communication* (G).

Finally, there were eight less important aspects: *Competence of superiors* (H)—*Mission* (C)—*Innovation capability* (E)—*Commitment and engagement*

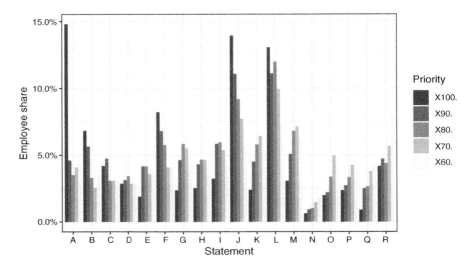

Fig. 4.1 Distribution of the 18 characteristics

(O)—*Health and safety* (P)—*Market flexibility* (D)—*Workload* (Q)—*Attractive image* (N), the latter being by far the least chosen.

(b) The six categories were relatively evenly represented, with the exception of company image.

(c) It is not easy to determine which of the characteristics was seen as the most important: If the most frequently chosen characteristic is seen as the most important, then common goal (A) comes first, followed by fairness (J) and working atmosphere (L). If, however, the most frequently named characteristic among the five allowed choices is considered the most important, a different picture emerges: 44% of all respondents rated working atmosphere (L) among their top 5, fairness (J) was chosen by 40% and 'only' 28% considered a common goal worthy of inclusion in their top 5. This leads to the conclusion that for most of those who ticked A, it was also top of the list, while a significant group did not mention it at all. L and J, however, were chosen by a high number of employees, albeit not in first place.

The same applies to team spirit (M): it was frequently among the top 5 (22% chose this), but rarely in first place.

4.2.3.2 Generational Differences

With regard to generational cohorts, it can generally be observed that (Fig. 4.2):

(a) The older the employees, the more importance was given to working towards a *common goal* (A). While this characteristic was by far the most important for baby boomers, it was only in fourth place for Gen Z.

Table 4.2 Importance of the characteristics (rounded values)

Characteristic	% Top 5	% No. 1	Characteristic	% Top 5	% No. 1
L = Working atmosphere	44	13	G = Communication	18	2
J = Fairness	40	14	H = Competence of superiors	16	2
A = Common goal	28	15	C = Mission	15	4
F = Equality	24	8	E = Innovation capability	14	2
M = Team spirit	22	3	O = Commitment and engagement	13	2
R = Autonomous work (time) organisation	21	4	P = Occupational health and safety	13	2
I = Honesty and openness	20	3	D = Market flexibility	12	3
K = Individual promotion and development	19	2	Q = Workload	11	1
B = Customer orientation	18	7	N = Attractive image	4	<1

(b) In contrast, the two values *fairness* (J) and *working atmosphere* (L) were clearly prioritised by younger employees (Gen Y and Gen Z).

(c) *Equal treatment* (F) emerged as a major concern, especially for the youngest generation.

(d) The generational difference is particularly noticeable in two other aspects: *customer orientation* (B) had more significance for the two older generations than for young employees, while the opposite was the case with *autonomous work (time) organisation* (R)—it was heavily demanded by young employees, but was of little importance to older colleagues.

(e) Finally, a comparison of the different priorities reflected in the answers of baby boomers and Gen Z employees:

Babyboomer: *Common goal* (A)—*Fairness* (J)—*Equality* (F)—*Working atmosphere* (L)—*Customer orientation* (B)—*Mission* (C)

Generation Z: *Fairness* (J)—*Working atmosphere* (L)—*Equality* (F)—*Communication* (G)—*Common goal* (A)—*Autonomous work (time) organisation* (R)

4.2.3.3 Gender

(a) *Common goal* (A), *fairness* (J) and *working atmosphere* (L) were the most important values for both men and women (see Fig. 4.3), with men more often than women giving priority to a *common goal*.

(b) Women most often named *fairness* (J) as the most important characteristic, followed by *working atmosphere* (L) and *common goal* (A).

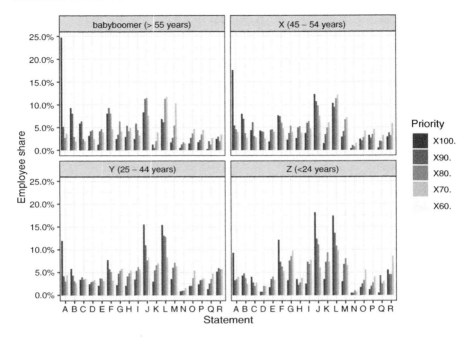

Fig. 4.2 Generation-based distribution

(c) *Equal treatment* (F) also played a very important role for women (it was the third most frequently selected characteristic in the top 5).

(d) A striking, but perhaps not entirely surprising difference was that *autonomous work (time) organisation* (R) was rated significantly higher by female employees than by their male colleagues.

4.2.3.4 Education

(a) The central finding from this cluster (Fig. 4.4) may seem surprising at first: the lower the level of formal education, the more emphasis was placed on a clearly defined *common goal* (A). This might be explained by the supposition that employees with lower levels of education may be less confident in this area and therefore place more trust in the leadership of the 'informed manager'.

(b) For the cohort of graduates, the most important characteristic by far was *working atmosphere* (L), followed by *fairness* (J), *common goal* (A) and *autonomous work (time) organisation* (R).

(c) The distribution is similar for the other two groups, but there are some differences: While many employees who fall into the category 'compulsory education only,' as mentioned above, selected *common goal* (A) as their first priority, they almost never considered *autonomous work (time) organisation*

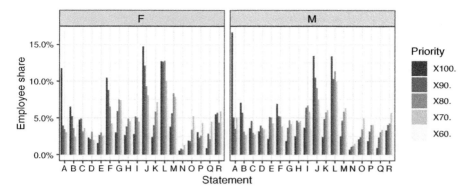

Fig. 4.3 Gender distribution

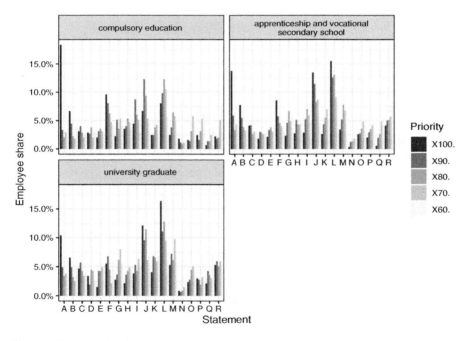

Fig. 4.4 Education level

(R) important enough to be in the top 5. The most balanced distribution of priorities can be found in the group 'apprenticeships and vocational secondary school'.

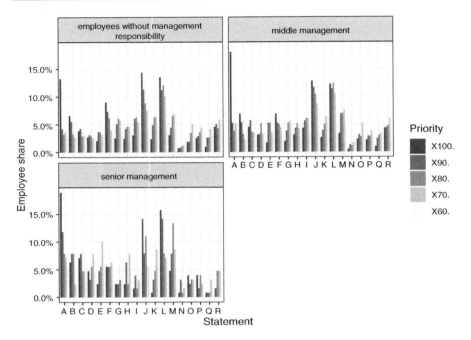

Fig. 4.5 Hierarchy level

4.2.3.5 Hierarchy Level

(a) With regard to the hierarchical level of the respondents (Fig. 4.5), the relatively balanced distribution in middle management is striking. An exception was the *common goal* (A), which was given top priority by many of the managers.

(b) In the category 'senior management,' apart from an expected high level of agreement with the *common goal* (A), the omission of *attractive image* (N) was particularly notable: Although all respondents rated this by far least important, one could have assumed that this would be different for senior managers. In addition, two further characteristics emerged which are less important to employees at this level: *workload* (Q) and *autonomous work (time) organisation* (R). The latter may seem surprising at first, but could be explained by the fact that the autonomous organisation of one's own workload is already theoretically possible for executives, but is of no practical relevance to them because of their heavy workload.

4.2.3.6 Economic Sector

(a) The vast majority of employees in the industrial or according to Fig. 4.6 chose the *common goal* (A) first—before *fairness* (J) and *working atmosphere* (L).

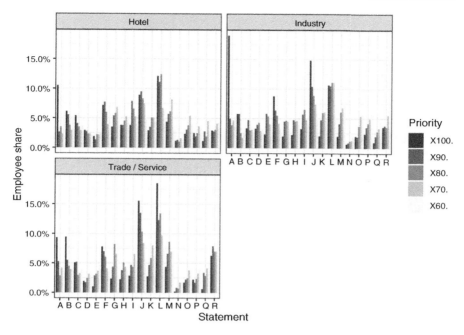

Fig. 4.6 Sector distribution

(b) Employees in the hospitality sector produced a relatively balanced spread of priorities, but they are the only cluster that did not attach much importance to the *attractive image* (N) of their employer.

(c) By contrast, the results from the trade/services sector stand out: By far the most important characteristic for them was the *working atmosphere* (L). This was followed by *fairness* (J) and—by a clear margin—*autonomous work (time) organisation* (R), *customer orientation* (B) and *equal treatment* (F). Only then, in sixth place, followed the *common goal* (A).

4.2.3.7 Company Size

(a) In principle, the larger the company, the more important it was for the employees to have a clearly defined *common goal* (A) (see Fig. 4.7). In smaller companies, employees are likely to be more aware of such a goal already. It is also noticeable that in larger companies the participants chose either the *common goal* (A) or *fairness* (J) when awarding the top position. *Working atmosphere* (L) and *equal treatment* (F) followed as choices, albeit with a considerable gap.

(b) In medium-sized companies, these four aforementioned characteristics were ranked relatively similar, whereas this was not the case in small companies

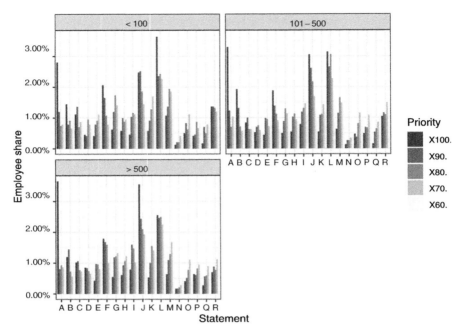

Fig. 4.7 Company size distribution

where *working atmosphere* (L) was considered the most important characteristic.

(c) Another finding that stood out (but perhaps not surprisingly) was that in small businesses the characteristic of *autonomous work (time) organisation* (R) was considered important by employees.

4.2.3.8 Department

(a) Generally, there are almost no differences between departments (Fig. 4.8): *working atmosphere* (L), *fairness* (J) and *common goal* (A) were the most frequently prioritised characteristics across all departments. However, one exception was notable: field staff stated *common goal* (A) as their top priority significantly more often than others.

(b) Employees in administrative departments, in particular, but also their colleagues from production and technology, selected *working atmosphere* (L) as their top priority.

(c) In addition to *fairness* (J), employees who belong to the field staff category also attached great importance to *equal treatment* (F), while *autonomous work (time) organisation* (R) was particularly important to their colleagues in administration.

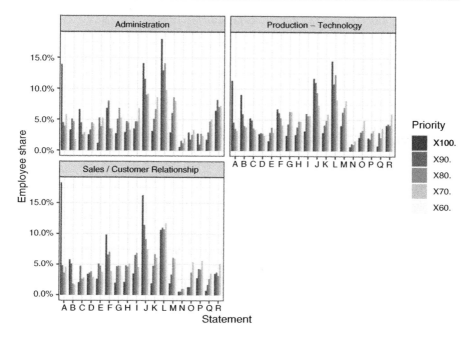

Fig. 4.8 Department distribution

4.2.4   Conclusions

It should be noted that the survey did not reveal any major surprises—at least not for those with HR experience. Perhaps the most surprising result was a noticeable indifference towards the *company image* (less than 4% found this important). Given the widespread emphasis on employer branding, this result is particularly interesting. If we combine it with the findings about the values that were highlighted as very important, we can see quite clearly that—certainly from the employees' point of view—employer branding must come from 'within the company' and should not be associated with an often artificially inflated 'brand attractiveness'.

Overall, for employees of all age groups, educational levels and fields of work, the values of *fairness*, *working atmosphere*, a *common goal*, *equality*, *honesty and openness*, *team spirit* and *autonomous work (time) organisation* play an important role in the evaluation of their workplace.

The crucial question is: How can these expectations best be met? Based on the developments described earlier, we can be fairly certain that employee expectations are becoming more and more important and that meeting them will increasingly be the decisive factor the success of a company.

The growing bargaining power of employees, on the one hand, and their highly differentiated expectations, on the other, mean that HRM departments will be ever less able to perform this crucial task of meeting employees' expectations successfully. Instead, it will be the responsibility of every manager or supervisor to meet the expectations of their employees as effectively as possible—if they want to keep employees motivated and retain them. In future, successful HRM will therefore be practised through the efficient and—as far as possible—clearly defined division of responsibilities between HR departments and managers.

4.3   The Coronavirus Effect

The Covid-19 pandemic has triggered the worst global economic crisis since World War II. The massive economic impact of the pandemic has far-reaching consequences for the labour market. The question that arises, therefore, is: How will the expectations of employees regarding their jobs or their employer be affected? In view of this crisis, which is affecting many economic sectors and industries, one could be tempted to think that workers might have lowered their expectations, especially if they are now on short-time contracts or have been made redundant. At the same time, an increase in the 'primary need' for job security could also be expected.

The latest Global Millennium Survey by Deloitte provides interesting information in this context: Within the last year, they conducted two surveys instead of one because of Covid-19. In addition to the primary survey, in which around 18,400 members of Gen Y (millennials) and Gen Z from 43 countries took part between 21 November 2019 and 8 January 2020, another survey was conducted between 28 April and 17 May 2020—a so-called pulse survey. For this purpose, about 9100 people of the same age group from 13 countries severely affected by the pandemic were interviewed. The aim was to find out what impact the changes brought about by Covid-19 had on the lives of younger generations and how their views on the economy, the environment and politics might have changed.

Both surveys started with a snapshot of the general mood among the two generation cohorts Y (born between 1983 and 1994) and Gen Z (1995 to 2003) using an 'optimism index' based on five questions on the economy, politics, finance and society. The results of this 'Millz Mood Monitor' (Deloitte) are both remarkable and hopeful: although the economic impact has hit these generations particularly hard—almost 30% of Gen Z respondents and 25% of millennials had lost their jobs or were on unpaid leave at the time, and another 25% were on short-time work—there were no signs of resignation or panic. On the contrary: These young people were showing great steadfastness and fighting spirit in this difficult situation.

For our purposes, only the results of the survey that are applicable to the world of work and employers are discussed here; for further findings, please refer to the original Deloitte report.

4.3.1   Stress and the Anxieties of Employees

Close to half (48%) of Gen Z and 44% of millennial respondents in the primary survey said that they were stressed all or most of the time. In the pulse survey, however, anxiety levels fell eight points for both generations, indicating a potential silver lining to the disruption caused by the pandemic.

In a world without Covid-19, the key point of the 2020 Millennium Survey may have been the concern expressed by Gen Z and millennials in the primary survey. Before the pandemic, almost half of Gen Z and more than four out of ten respondents said that they felt stressed all or most of the time. One could think that mental health would be an even greater concern in the pulse survey, but surprisingly, stress levels decreased. In pulse countries, the proportion of people who reported feeling stressed all or most of the time fell from 50%, before the pandemic, to 42% in the pulse survey. For Gen Z, the stress level fell from 52% to 44%.

After the outbreak of the pandemic, millennials and Gen Z were clearly more concerned about their health, the well-being of their families, their job prospects and their long-term financial future. But the crisis also forced life to slow down. Many employees were now working from home, were spending more time with their immediate family members and commuting less in traffic jams or on crowded trains and other public transport. And although their jobs were probably affected in some way, most of them stayed in work but spent less money.

4.3.2   Working from Home

In a reimagined, post-pandemic world, many jobs that once required physical presence in an office will instead be done remotely. Unsurprisingly, the number of people working from home has jumped significantly since the pandemic. In the pulse survey, 32% of all employed respondents said that they had worked remotely all or most of the time prior to the pandemic. At the peak of the pandemic, that percentage climbed to just above 50%. Conversely, about 45% of employed millennials and members of Gen Z said that they had never worked remotely before the pandemic; after the onset of the pandemic that was true for only a third.

About two-thirds of employees said that companies were prepared to manage a virtual workforce and gave them high marks for their actions. Over 60% said that their employers had taken measures to support them during the pandemic—for example, measures relating to flexible working hours or holidays. Half of the millennials surveyed said that their employers had offered them training, education and skills development to enable effective remote working. And a majority of almost two-thirds said that their employers trusted them to be productive outside the office; respondents seemed to appreciate the opportunity to work from home. More than 60% said that once the crisis was over, they would like to have the opportunity to work remotely more often because they felt able to bring their 'true self' to work by working from home. This figure is higher among parents (59%) than among people without children (43%), and it is also higher among people in management positions

(62%) than among people in junior roles (42%). In addition, almost seven out of ten millennials indicated that the option of working from home and avoiding commuting in the future would reduce stress for them.

4.3.3 The Deal: Loyalty in Return for Accommodations

The Deloitte study shows that employees are generally satisfied with the response of their employers to the coronavirus crisis. In the pulse survey, 66% of millennials and Gen Z said they were satisfied with the speed with which their employers responded to the pandemic and with the way they supported their employees. Respondents praised employers for helping them carry on with minimal disruption; guidelines and technology had enabled employees working from home to receive a consistent level of support. Almost two-thirds of all respondents also said that their employers had taken measures to support their mental well-being during the crisis. A majority of the millennials and Gen Z workers surveyed also believed that their employers had sacrificed profits to help their employees and their customers/clients.

4.3.3.1 A New Kind of Employee Loyalty?

Is the consideration for the needs of employees, which employers have shown so far during the coronavirus crisis, the reason for the noticeable increase in employee loyalty—or is this increase based on existential fears? The survey results on the question of employee loyalty to their current employer (which was only investigated in the primary survey) showed that for the first time since 2016, more millennials declared that they intended to stay with their employer for 5 or more years instead of leaving within the next 2 years. The proportion of those who intended to leave within 2 years or less dropped to 31% from 49% the year before, while the proportion of those who said they intended to stay long term jumped from 28% to 35%. Similarly, the proportion of Gen Z workers who were generally more interested in changing jobs fell from 61% in 2019 to 50% in May 2020.

It remains to be seen how the economic impact of the pandemic will affect long-term loyalty. Will job-hopping be reduced as people seek stability once the crisis has waned? There is evidence that the actions of employers during the pandemic may have boosted loyalty even higher among those who are still working. More than 60% of employed respondents in the pulse survey stated that their employers' actions made them want to stay with them for the long term.

4.3.3.2 The Rising Need to Support Mental Health

The results of the Deloitte survey indicate that Gen Y and Gen Z consider stress at work to be a greater problem than their older colleagues. They consider good mental health to be a very important asset. In fact, about half of all people interviewed in the primary survey stated that they considered stress as a legitimate reason for staying away from work, and almost one in three had done so the year before. However, mental stress is still stigmatised. For example, in the primary survey, only 44% of Gen Y workers and 38% of Gen Z workers who stayed away from work due to stress or anxiety had told their employer this reason. The majority—especially women—gave other reasons. More than half of those who spoke openly about their mental overload highlighted their employer's active commitment to mental health at work. Only 16% complained about a lack of support. All this points to the undeniable importance of this issue, especially among the younger generation and especially at this time of great uncertainty. The feeling of being overloaded at work (whether real or perceived) is not the only cause of stress among workers; fears about the economic future of the company or one's own job security can also play a large part. Stress not only manifests itself as absenteeism from work, but also affects work performance and commitment and thus employee loyalty.

4.3.4 Conclusions

The cursory assumption that the uncertainty caused by the pandemic could reduce workers' confidence and bargaining power is therefore not tenable in the medium and long term. The shortage of skilled workers so often deplored by employers will surely not disappear with the coronavirus crisis. And even if the balance of power could temporarily shift back in favour of employers, such a development would be short-lived and would probably only affect those who fall into the category of average to low performers. High performers will continue to be in high demand—if not even more so—during a pandemic.

Loyalty is a core value that develops slowly and over time, and it is precisely in such times of crisis where it counts. However, an employer's appropriate response in moments of uncertainty can also be very conducive to improving employee loyalty. Good employers will take special care of their employees in these challenging times—not least because their employees' expectations of them will be particularly high.

References

Berufsstart.de. (2020). *Studie Attraktive Arbeitgeber*. Retrieved September 21, 2020, from https://www.berufsstart.de/karriere/attraktive-arbeitgeber/2020/index.php.

Bundesministerium für Arbeit. (2016). *Nextpractice. Wertewelten Arbeiten 4.0, Bremen.*

Dimensional Research. (2012). *HR beat: A survey on the pulse of today's global workforce.* Retrieved March 6, 2020, from https://www.personalradar.ch/wp-content/uploads/2012/10/2012-HR-Beat-A-Survey-on-the-Pulse-of-Todays-Global-Workforce.pdf.

Peakon. (2019). *The employee voice.* Retrieved September 20, 2020, from https://peakon.com/heartbeat/reports/the-employee-voice/.

PwC. (2013). *Dealing with disruption. 16th Annual Global CEO Survey.* Retrieved March 6, 2020, from https://www.pwc.com/cl/es/publicaciones/assets/16th-annual-global-ceo-survey.pdf.

StepStone. (2020). *Attraktiver Arbeitgeber? Was sich Mitarbeiter von Unternehmen wünschen—und was sie bekommen*. Retrieved September 21, 2020, from https://www.stepstone.de/Ueber-StepStone/press/attraktiver-arbeitgeber/.

Troger, H. (2019). Management von Interessen und Erwartungen. In H. Troger (Ed.), *7 Erfolgsfaktoren für wirksames personalmanagement* (2nd ed., pp. 169–187). Heidelberg: Springer Gabler.

Veldsman, D., & Pauw, D. (2018). The relevance of the employee value proposition for retention in the VUCA world of work. In M. Coetzee, I. Potgieter, & N. Ferreira (Eds.), *Psychology of retention*. Cham: Springer.

Taking Stock: Multiple and Complex Challenges, But No Effective Solutions

5

The challenges of the world of work are greater than ever,
HRM has never been more needed—yet the solutions
proposed have never looked less convincing.

5.1 Stakeholder Dissatisfaction

We are experiencing a world of work that is changing at an alarming pace under the influence of the megatrends of globalisation and digitalisation, as well as demographic changes. The challenges arise both at the macroeconomic and socio-political level and in the microcosm of individual companies. In economic, social, technological and socio-political terms, we are experiencing a fascinating era of transformation. Never before have HR professionals had more room for manoeuvre, never before have there been so many paths that point in completely different directions. The famous saying 'never before has HR work been as important as today' is still true, but should probably be complemented with 'and never before has it been so difficult and complex'. As if this alone were not enough, almost overnight we were faced with a new challenge: a coronavirus pandemic. When Covid-19 took over the world, it put everything else in the shade. It took our already VUCA working world to a new level, making it even more difficult to influence.

5.1.1 Role Conflicts

It is by no means an exaggeration to say that in recent years no other operational area has seen such an increase in complexity and variety of tasks as that of Human Resources. In addition, in no other operational area are employees expected to play as many different roles as in the HR department. Depending on the situation and who they are addressing, HR managers have to slip into a variety of different roles. Due to the variety of issues they deal with, it is not unusual for role conflicts to occur.

© The Author(s), under exclusive license to Springer Nature Switzerland AG 2021
H. Troger, *Human Resource Management in a Post COVID-19 World*, Future of Business and Finance, https://doi.org/10.1007/978-3-030-67470-0_5

Firstly, there are the traditional and explicitly mentioned roles of the HR professional, which HR pioneer Dave Ulrich (1997) described well in his 'HR Business Partner Model'. In addition to the roles of the 'management expert' and the 'employee champion' he also mentioned the roles of the 'change agent' and the 'strategic partner' for top management. In Ulrich's concept of transformational HR, HR professionals and top management must become business partners and work closely together to create value for the company. This model is still considered the benchmark for HR experts and has lost none of its relevance over the last 20 years, not least because of the simplicity with which it covers the entire spectrum of HR activities. Secondly, alongside these explicit roles of the HR manager, there are various unspoken but implicit roles, such as that of the 'scape goat' or the 'marketer' (see Troger 2018). Good HR managers are expected to fulfil these roles and the expectations placed in them, as well as prepare the monthly payroll in a competent manner.

The above-mentioned phenomena, trends and challenges are not without consequences for the activities of HR departments and their cooperation with management and employees. A wide variety of stakeholder expectations arise, which naturally leads to tension and dissatisfaction, especially as these expectations are diametrically opposed: Due to the different roles in HR work, the actors are often caught in a double bind. In a streamlining project, for example, the HR manager cannot be the employee champion or even the trusted confidant of the employees and at the same time be the strategic partner of top management and unconditionally implement their requirements. One of the main reasons why the role of the HR manager is questioned, therefore, is the lack of clarity about this role. With the growing complexity of the world of work, it is increasingly difficult for the HR department to meet the challenge posed by the variety of these roles.

5.1.2 Cost Pressure

Another reason why the top management of companies may criticise HR departments is the general cost pressure. This applies in particular to the so-called indirect area to which the HR department belongs. The services provided by a HR department—apart from the customary costs of payroll accounting—are often not easy to evaluate and their quality is difficult to measure. Good HR management is assumed to be a simple 'hygiene factor' because it does not manifest itself through particularly motivated employees. (It almost goes without saying, however, that deficiencies in HR departments would have a visibly negative effect). These invisible activities, which are taken for granted, are particularly vulnerable to attack as demands for savings, automation and outsourcing grow louder. The question of return on investment for various HR activities, such as employee champion or change agent, is also frequently raised. When and for whom are the relevant HR and organisational development initiatives worthwhile?

5.1.3 Self-Image/External Image

The dissatisfaction with the HR department, which is felt by many company leaderships, is often reflected in a reluctance to involve the head of HR as an equal partner at the highest decision-making level. Although they expect the HR department to take on the role of a business partner, top executives are often reluctant to relinquish control and share their decision-making powers.

The ambivalence of this situation is perhaps nowhere more evident than when a small, insignificant HR department is left alone to lead an isolated and frustrated existence, as it deals with decisions at the lowest management level, while the 'big' decisions—according to the mantra 'anyone can do HR'—are made without their involvement.

Finally, criticism of the HR department also stems from a frequently encountered divergence between the self-image of the various actors and their perception of the other. Most HR managers would confidently see themselves as valuable (discussion) partners for the employees, while the employees (and also the top management) see their competence more as being limited to the proper administration of employee data and, at best, to the organisation of further training events. Frequently, HR professionals also want to be seen as 'strategic business partners' and 'change agents' at the same time—i.e., they strive for maximum cooperation with both top management and the workforce. The failure to meet these expectations seems almost inevitable.

We can foresee that the expectations placed on HR will increase as the world of work becomes ever more complex, and this in turn is likely to lead to even greater dissatisfaction among the organisation's internal stakeholders. It is therefore not surprising that different sides want to see change and that this particular operational area has come under such criticism—in some cases there have even been calls for the dissolution of HR altogether (cf. Sect. 5.3).

5.2 Economic Science Approaches

The field of economic science provides different theoretical approaches for the economic evaluation of HR policies. The main focus here is on a cost-related examination of the exchange between companies and employees against the background of the legal and institutional framework. According to Holtbrügge (2015), the following three central assumptions form the theoretical basis for economic approaches to human behaviour:

The principle of **benefit maximisation** assumes that people fundamentally choose the action that promises them the greatest personal benefit according to their individual preferences.

The behavioural assumption of (**limited**) **rationality** presumes that people fundamentally want to take the decision that they assume to be the best. Since the information required to make this decision is usually incomplete or the ability to understand it is limited, which means that the consequences of a decision are therefore unpredictable, it is simply a wished-for rationality.

The third assumption refers to people's **opportunism** in the pursuit of their own goals. Opportunistic behaviour can be seen, for example, in the deliberate exchange of wrong or incomplete information between employee and HR manager.

The two best known economic approaches are the transaction cost theory and the principal agent theory.

5.2.1   Transaction Cost Theory

Transaction cost theory assumes that the exchange or settlement of transactions between different actors is not free of charge (Williamson 1981). Costs are incurred for the preparation, as well as for the execution, monitoring and adjustment of business relationships. In terms of human resources, such transaction costs are incurred throughout the entire working relationship between the company and its employees, although according to Williamson, the level of these costs depends on three environmental conditions:

(a) **The specific nature of a service:** The more specific a service, the higher the mutual dependence and therefore also the risk of opportunistic behaviour.
(b) **Uncertainty:** Contracts are basically imperfect and usually only reflect the current state of information. The higher the uncertainty and the complexity of possible future developments, the more scope there is for opportunistic behaviour.
(c) **Frequency:** The more often similar transactions take place, the more learning takes place and the less transaction costs incur. In the best case scenario, mutual trust develops and costs are eliminated.

Williamson distinguishes between costs that arise in the run-up to an employment relationship, such as information and agreement costs—so-called **ex ante transaction costs**—and those that may arise on both sides during an on-going employment relationship: monitoring costs, adjustment costs, termination costs—i.e., **ex post transaction costs**.

The aim is to ensure the lowest possible transaction costs through appropriate coordination of activities within the employment relationship. And this is exactly where various implications for effective HR management lie. With regard to recruitment, for example, the transaction cost theory makes it relatively easy to decide under which conditions temporary employment contracts are preferable to new hires.

5.2.2   The Principal Agent Theory

The second economic approach also focuses on the exchange between two actors in the economic process: An entrepreneur—the 'principal'—hires an employee—the 'agent'—to perform a certain task for which they are remunerated. The 'principal' is faced with the problem that the 'agent' will not only pursue the contractually agreed (company) goals, but also their own interests. When a contract is drafted, this has to be taken into account through defining the scope of action and remuneration on the one hand, and laying out the duties and control mechanisms on the other. Essentially, this is where the problem lies: Due to the frequently not openly expressed self-interests of the actors, there is an inherent information deficit on both sides. It is particularly difficult for the principals to get a clear picture of the performance and dedication of their agents. For this reason, we generally speak of information asymmetry in favour of the agent, although according to Picot et al. (2012), there are three common types of information asymmetry in business practice:

(a) **Hidden characteristics** are the characteristics and skills of the employee (agent) that are not known to management or the HR representative when the employment contract is signed. Even the most sophisticated selection and recruitment procedures have their limitations when it comes to assessing the qualities and potential of candidates. Consequently, there is a considerable risk that the most suitable candidate will not be selected in the end (adverse selection).

(b) **Hidden intentions** exist when the principal does not have a complete picture of the agent's interests and intentions. The same problem arises when the management suspects or indeed discovers the 'true' intentions of the agent, but cannot prevent them. Again, there is a risk of hiring the wrong candidate or of entering an undesirable dependency with subsequent salary demands.

(c) **Hidden actions** describe those situations in which the company management or the line manager cannot observe and evaluate the activities of an employee due to a lack of time or expertise. The agent might then feel inclined to reduce their work productivity. In teams, moreover, it is often not possible to extract the individual's productivity from the team result.

The principal agent theory suggests various governance mechanisms to reduce information asymmetries. The contractual stipulation of these mechanisms should ensure that the employee (agent) in question performs his or her task as instructed by their line manager. The choice of the right strategy in each case depends on the cost and the expected benefit.

As a theoretical approach, the principal agent model provides valuable insights into the behaviour of employees, especially in empirical HR research—for example, regarding the effects of variable forms of remuneration on the performance of managers. The connection between the provision of staff development and the productivity of employees or the negative consequences of hiring the wrong candidates can also be described well using this approach.

The advantages of these two purely economic approaches to HR policy decisions lie in their simplicity and transparency—because they quantify their impact. A comparison of different alternatives in a complex scenario can thus be greatly simplified. However, the limits of using economic theories to explain HR processes lie in a very reductionist view of human behaviour, as described above. It is a view that neither includes altruistic or charitable behaviours, nor does it take ethical considerations into account.

5.3   Behavioural Science Approaches

Whereas the economic models described above deal with the quantifiable effects of HR measures in terms of economic success, behavioural science approaches focus on people's psychological reactions and sensitivities to these measures. The literature distinguishes between two groups of behaviour models: One group is concerned with the exchanges between an organisation and its employees (social exchange theory), the other group deals with the motivational processes in the context of an employment relationship (motivational theory). Both groups will be outlined.

5.3.1   Social Exchange Theories

These approaches aim to explain the motivation behind why employees enter, remain in, or leave a company. The motivations of the two actors in this exchange are analysed and evaluated in terms of their levels of satisfaction and the fulfilment of personal expectations. The three best known theories of social exchange will be discussed in brief:

5.3.1.1 Organisational Equilibrium Theory

The Barnard-Simon theory of organisational equilibrium is about the inducements-contributions balance within an organisation. It looks at the decision-making behaviour of employees and distinguishes three types of decisions. Entry decisions are studied to understand the reasons why employees decide to enter into employment. The decisions to remain in employment reflect the commitment of employees, and the third category, the decisions to terminate an employment relationship, is about the reasons for doing so.

According to organisational equilibrium theory, these decisions arise when the people involved evaluate the working relationship (the exchange) by comparing the services they have provided (the contribution) with the reward they have received in return (the inducements). The inducements (and in theory the contribution) can be monetary or non-monetary.

The employees' assessment of the employment relationship depends mainly on two factors: their degree of commitment to the company and the opportunity cost, i.e., the potential benefits of alternative employment. According to organisational equilibrium theory, both of these factors depend on job satisfaction as well as the existence of alternatives.

The design of reward systems can also have its theoretical basis in this model because it explains how certain behaviour can be induced or avoided.

5.3.1.2 The Social Exchange Theory

Social exchange theory is based on the assumption that employees and companies enter into an exchange in order to achieve goals that they cannot achieve on their own. Both actors evaluate this exchange on the basis of the results achieved, which in turn reflect the difference between the perceived benefits and the required input. The exchange is maintained as long as the participants expect to benefit from it. Employees associate certain expectations with a working relationship (achievement of individual goals, satisfaction of material needs, etc.) and at the same time they compare their work situation with the alternatives available on the labour market. The result of this evaluation or comparison is expressed in the employee's satisfaction with the current exchange and his or her commitment to the company.

The aim of staff management must therefore be to ensure both a high level of satisfaction and a high level of employee commitment. Not only does this apply to the relationship between the company leadership and the employees; but the same logic also applies to the cooperation between employees and their line managers.

5.3.2 Motivational Theory Approaches

Motivational theories assume that human behaviour is determined by needs, which can be activated by incentives. Consequently, motivation is seen as the prerequisite for goal-oriented human behaviour, making it the focus of behavioural science. For an organisation, it is important to know how and through what incentives employees can be motivated in order to ensure the effectiveness of management strategies. Knowledge of how motivational processes work and how certain motivations affect the behaviour of employees is important for the design of company's incentive policies. The main difficulty in motivation research lies mainly in the fact that motivation is almost never visible through direct observation. Conclusions about individual behaviour and underlying motivations can only be drawn by analysing incentives and people's reaction to them.

With regard to the relationship between motivation and behaviour, the literature distinguishes between two approaches of motivation theory, based on either content or process. While content theories focus on the specific motives that control the behaviour of individuals, process theories concentrate on the motivational process and on internal laws.

Due to their great practical relevance—they provide HR experts with answers to the question of what motivates employees in the work context—two well-known content theories will be outlined.

5.3.2.1 The Maslow Pyramid of Needs

Maslow's pyramid of needs starts from the basic assumption that every person is motivated by the pursuit of specific needs. These needs vary in strength and are therefore arranged hierarchically. Maslow (1981) distinguishes between five categories of needs, starting with:

- **Basic physiological needs:** These are the basic necessities of life such as food and sleep. In terms of an employment relationship, a minimum income and a minimum amount of rest is established in this way.
- **Security needs:** This includes, for example, the need for a permanent contract of employment and a minimum level of security standards.
- **Social needs:** This refers to the need to belong and integrate into the team and, more generally, to the need for attention and consideration.
- **Appreciation needs:** This category of needs is about recognition by superiors and colleagues, which leads to higher self-esteem. Achieving goals and being given influence and power are particularly motivating at this level.
- **Self-actualization needs:** This is at the top of the human needs pyramid. It is about our desire to freely develop our talents and interests. Unlike the other four categories of needs, this is not about satisfying deficits, but about a need for growth. This need should never cease during the course of a working relationship.

Despite many weak points of this relatively simple motivation theory—vague boundaries between categories, no consideration of situational, individual or cultural factors—it is still the most frequently quoted and applied method when it comes to describing ways in which employees can be motivated.

5.3.2.2 Herzberg's Two-Factor Theory

In his Pittsburgh study, the motivation researcher Herzberg (1966) interviewed 200 technicians and accountants about pleasant and unpleasant work situations. He found that different people rarely mentioned the same causes. As a conclusion, Herzberg put forward his two-factor theory according to which job satisfaction and dissatisfaction do not represent the two ends of a continuum, but had to be seen as two separate phenomena. Accordingly, there are two categories of employee needs that must be satisfied: First, employee dissatisfaction must be eliminated by satisfying certain basic needs—Herzberg calls these hygiene factors. Then there are the motivators with which job satisfaction can be achieved or increased.

Based on this, a HR policy must use both categories of incentives as appropriate. According to Herzberg, the following aspects would fall into the category of hygiene factors: job security, relationship with superiors, general working conditions, workplace equipment, the basic company policy, and the control and monitoring instruments of the organisation. Insufficient fulfilment of these needs leads to frustration and dissatisfaction among workers. However, they are not sufficient for achieving the type of motivation that is needed in today's working world. According to Herzberg, this is where the following motivators are required: interesting work content, suitable responsibilities, promotion, bonuses, self-actualization.

The great merit of this motivation theory lies in challenging the benefit of purely monetary factors as motivational instruments and in doing so, to an extent, it achieved a move towards a more humanised way of looking at labour. However, the criticism of excessive generalisation also applies here, as does the neglect of situational and individual conditions.

5.4   Historical Development

When trying to trace the historical development of human resources, a rather blurred picture emerges with interruptions, overlaps and contradictions. What follows is a summary of the most significant developments of the last 80 years, with particular focus on three distinguishing features: Firstly, the tension between the purely administrative aspects of HR and the drive towards humanisation is looked at. Secondly, the role of HR management in relation to the entrepreneur—service provider versus strategic partner—will be discussed. And finally, there is the question of how HR management should be organised—whether it should be centralised or decentralised.

5.4.1   Scientific Management vs. Human Relations Movement

The eventful history of HR management theories began with the American engineer Frederick Winslow Taylor and his theory of 'scientific management' (cf. Taylor 1911). While working for a steelworks in Philadelphia, Taylor was the first to systematically investigate work processes with the help of scientific methods. His call for a radical division of labour was based on his insight that the less demanding the activities of workers were, the greater the learning effects for them. One of Taylor's findings was that labour productivity increases with the degree of specialisation at each workstation. The strict division of the work stages also results in a clear separation between performance and execution. This resulted, among other things, in the criticism that Taylor advocated absolute control and the dumbing-down of the workforce through the use of piecework. Critics regarded him as the epitome of inhumane work design. It was precisely this way of working, nonetheless, that contributed significantly to the spread of mass production in general. Above all, the worldwide upswing in the automotive industry—starting in the USA—would not have been possible without Taylor's insights. Management according to basic Taylorist principles was expressed above all in a centralist and hierarchical, discipline-oriented bureaucracy. The main task of 'personnel departments' was to use employees as a means of production and to integrate them into the production process, taking into account all technical and economic requirements.

During this administrative phase, personnel work was primarily seen as the punctual payment of wages and salaries and the 'personnel administrator' was in charge of administering the personnel files. Their low status within the organisation was also reflected in the fact that they were almost never involved in strategic processes. Personnel selection was also generally reserved for senior management.

From an organisational point of view, personnel work was generally subordinate to the commercial side of the business and the personnel department had only limited authority to issue instructions. Consequently, matters relating to staff were frequently only dealt with at the lowest management level.

5.4.1.1 Integration: Humanisation of Work

At the beginning of the 1960s, large companies in particular began to make adjustments in order to increase the ability of their employees to meet the growing organisational requirements. As a result, the importance of personnel work increased rapidly and started to be of strategic interest to the company. In 1965, the term 'personnel management' appeared for the first time in economics literature. The first personnel departments were created and became an autonomous entrepreneurial subdivision with the relevant decision-making powers. The scope of the new departments' activity was also significantly expanded: in addition to the familiar tasks of payroll administration and the administration of personnel files, came the new task of **personnel support**. Given the emerging need for organisational adjustments, the new personnel officers were now important points of contact for training, retraining and rotation programmes. In the recruitment process, too, the personnel department began to assume more responsibility. Last but not least, the company's remuneration system moved into the domain of the personnel experts— and with it, naturally, all aspects of personnel appraisal.

In terms of organisational structure and procedures, the Taylorist system with its clear division of tasks and centralised management continued to dominate the personnel department. The hierarchical structure with a clear functional division continued, and all decision-making, communication and information processes remained firmly centralised.

The growing profile and importance of personnel work for an organisation, as described above, continued into the 1970s. With widespread economic upturn, there was increasing pressure on employers to align working conditions and employment relationships more closely with the skills and needs of employees. The 'human relations approach', which had originally begun in the late 1920s with the Hawthorne experiments of psychologists Mayo and Roethlisberger,[1] eventually gained ground as a counter-movement to the Taylor model. The latter had long been seen as the epitome of inhumane work design. The fundamentally social character of human beings and their needs beyond income maximisation increasingly became the new focus of the personnel experts. Criticism for the limitations of Tayloristic methods also emerged from the field of business studies, as the most important prerequisites for this model—the sameness and repeatability of activities—were no longer fulfilled within the context of new production and service concepts.

The role of '**director of personnel**' was created and personnel policy was finally discussed at the highest decision-making level. At the same time, there was an increased professionalisation of the personnel department, especially in terms of

---

[1] At the Hawthorne plants of the Western Electric Company in Chicago, the two researchers wanted to demonstrate the effects of improvements in working conditions (e.g., better lighting) on worker productivity. However, when productivity continued to increase after returning to the original poorer conditions, this effect (the Hawthorne Effect) was attributed to the mere presence of the researchers. The social contact with the workers and the efforts made for their welfare had resulted in an improvement of the working climate.

staff development. This meant that, for the first time, the personnel department was seen as an important service provider in both administrative and support terms—by staff and management alike. The democratisation of personnel policy and the decentralisation of responsibility subsequently began to take hold more and more.

5.4.2   The Current HRM Controversy

Since the 1970s, Human Resources have been viewed as an autonomous business division responsible for the procurement, deployment and development of employees and have been integrated into the overall strategic processes. Meanwhile, the concept of **value creation** had become the main indicator for the meaningfulness of all activities in a company. Applied to operational HR work, services to both internal and external customers can be value added, enabling the HR department to charge internally for its internal services. As with every value chain, key personnel processes were now examined for their internal contributions and continuously optimised.

The almost unrestricted access to knowledge and the increased demands that companies place on their HR staff, as well as their own self-imposed high standards, have led to an altogether very high degree of professionalisation in the area of HR. And although the scope of activities of HR departments and their strategic influence has continued to increase in recent years in the course of the ever-increasing complexity of entrepreneurial processes, the **role** of HR and its process-related and organisational positioning has been the subject of highly controversial discussion among business economists for some years now. The spectrum of opinions in the business science debate ranges from the view of the **HR department as a strategic partner** for achieving competitive advantages and thus contributing to the creation of value, to the belief that it is a **redundant cost driver** serving mostly an end in itself and should therefore be **abolished**.

The latest addition to HRM, **agile management**, is currently being glorified as a panacea. With reference to increasingly complex markets and Industry 4.0 with all its drivers, everything is somehow supposed to become 'agile'. The basic principle of agility—taken from ideas in evolutionary theory—is the flexible adaptation of processes, structures and management models to continuously changing market and environmental conditions. Novotny (2017), for example, proposes the introduction of 'iterative process landscapes' instead of conventional waterfall processes, as well as customer-oriented dynamic organisational structures with 'serving' managers in flat hierarchies.

A very mixed picture also emerges with regard to the question of the **organisational structure** of HRM: the proponents of a decentralised model point to the increased complexity due to dynamic market and environmental conditions. This could only be countered with appropriately flexible organisational structures that are adapted to the situation. The increased density of rules and a strictly hierarchical control function of a central HR department would not be customer-oriented, but rather obstructive and far removed from any problems (cf., e.g.,

Drumm 2008). A decentralised organisation, according to Deeg et al. (2010), would extend the individual scope of action of employees, which would strengthen the self-regulation and personal responsibility of employees.

Proponents of a centralised approach to HR management point in particular to the self-serving needs of decentralised units and their special interests, which require a considerable effort to be coordinated, especially in times of limited resources. Moreover, centrally structured HR departments would focus much more on the overall company task than decentralised units because the need for integration and coordination would be eliminated (cf. in particular Nienhüser 1999).

In summary, the debate among academics and practitioners on the strategic orientation, tasks and organisation of HR is far from over. What seems certain is that factors such as industry sector, company size, economic situation, but also legal and socio-political aspects will continue to play a decisive role in determining the right approach in individual cases.

5.4.3   Reorganisation or Dissolution of the HR Department?

The obvious response to the dissatisfaction of the most important customers with the performance of the HR department is a critical questioning of the department and the necessary adjustments. Ultimately, the HR department should be ideally suited for this kind of reorientation and restructuring—despite the typical blinkered attitude often found in the analysis of one's own department. In practice, however, the exact opposite is often the case: HR staff tend to feel comfortable in their own world of administration or staff development.

5.4.3.1 Shadow Agenda

When HR experts are not involved in the strategic decision-making processes of the organisation, their reaction is often to establish a 'shadow agenda', involving, for example, the introduction of new time recording systems, the organisation of training courses or the schedule for the next HR management meeting. Hostile voices may imply that HR professionals have a distinct ability to tolerate silence and to sit out any ugly situations at length.

However, if the focus of the HR department's response should be to improve performance, which usually means developing competencies, then this would normally involve the allocation of additional resources. Yet it is precisely this aspect of the cost-benefit ratio that often gives rise to criticism of the HR department. In times of tight budgets, how many company leaderships will accept additional costs in a (supposedly) unproductive area such as HR?

5.4.3.2 Revamping and Outsourcing

A different approach may involve the revamping of HR or the outsourcing of certain services. In any case, many companies have been outsourcing payroll accounting to specialised external service providers for some time now. Even employer branding, which is gaining more and more importance, is in some cases no longer handled by

HR professionals but by the marketing experts in the marketing department. There are, moreover, specialised organisations coming forward offering training and further education—the very core of HR work—and they are reportedly just as good and certainly much more cost-effective.

Taking into consideration the four-tiered nature of HR tasks according to Ulrich, a more consistent separation between services of various kinds for company leadership, managers and staff on the one hand, and the role as a strategic business partner for the company leadership on the other, would seem to emerge as a solution. A general division into operational and strategic tasks may also be an option.

5.4.3.3 Division into an Employee-Oriented and a Business-Oriented HR Department

Last but not least, one could also be inspired by the popular concept of employee-oriented HR and divide the HR department into employee-oriented HR work versus business-oriented HR work. Particularly in larger organisations, some interesting possibilities might arise against the hybrid of centralisation and decentralisation.

In my opinion, however, all this is theoretical; in practice, the following points speak against a reorganisation in terms of a division of HR:

(a) It would result in a 'two-tier system' within the department: on the one hand, it would have the smart, strategic and respected business partners; on the other hand, it would have the jaded, less informed, operational workers. Not only would the attractiveness of such a 'second class' of HR be severely affected by such a division, but the lack of mutual exchange and cross-fertilisation would also lead to a decline in quality.

(b) It is likely that a qualitative problem would also arise if certain operational HR tasks were divided between other parts of the company (finance, marketing, etc.) Who should ensure quality in HR processes? The finance director may lack the expertise to monitor performance over time. After all, we are not talking about merely reviewing sub-steps or time tracking tools, but about comprehensive HR processes.

(c) Finally, the fundamental question of the company's HR policy and its strategic approach in terms of human resources is at stake. HR management must be seen as **one** big process—from recruitment to exit interviews—within the organisation, and consequently it requires a clear strategy and a transparent executive structure. Any kind of division of the HR department will make it more difficult to define a strategy, implement it and coordinate all of the processes involved.

5.4.3.4 The Dissolution of the HR Department

The renowned business expert and visionary Ram Charan (2014) proposes a radical response to the dissatisfaction with the HR department's performance: the complete dissolution of the department. For him, this is not about the activities as such—these would largely be taken over by other areas—but rather about the department as an institution and, above all, about its head. He justifies his provocative proposition with three specific criticisms:

Firstly, he accuses HR managers of being too far removed from real business activities to understand how decisions and performance targets are reached. Secondly, he argues that HR professionals have lost the ability to connect people with metrics in order to identify the strengths and weaknesses within the organisation. And thirdly, he suggests that they are no longer able to effectively match the skills of employees with the requirements set out in the business strategy.

Charan regards most HR managers as process-oriented generalists, well versed on everything relating to pay roll or trade unions, and primarily interested in internal matters such as motivation and employee retention. In his view, they lack operational experience as plant managers, sales executives or finance officers. For this reason, Charan says, most HR managers do not provide CEOs with enough added value, which makes them redundant.

Charan would eliminate the role of head of HR and split the department into two new departments under different leadership: Firstly, a HR-A group (for administration) would take care of salaries and employee benefits and report to the finance director. Secondly, a HR-LO (for leadership and organisation) would be responsible for employee competencies and continuing professional development and report directly to the CEO. HR-LOs should be headed by promising talents from operational departments or finance, who could use such a role for their professional advancement.

Apart from a noticeable mild disregard for HR tasks in general, Charan is fundamentally right both in his criticisms and in his call for a change of direction. However, I believe that his conclusion amounts to throwing out the baby with the bath water simply because the water in the bath needs changing.

I would counter Charan's provocative approach with the following:

(a) The CEO he references is only one of several stakeholders—albeit a central one. If the HR manager 'only' fails to deliver enough added value to this stakeholder, there seems to be little justification for such a radical step. Perhaps the company's employees find that it is precisely the role of the HR leader that provides them with significant added value.

(b) The very fact that HR professionals are primarily concerned with issues of motivation and staff retention, as Charan points out in his criticism, makes their role all the more important, especially in times of high staff turnover and instability, and the general shortage of skilled workers. HR work therefore belongs in the hands of true experts in this field and should not be used merely as a 'stepping stone' on the career ladder.

(c) The quite sensible outsourcing of certain administrative services to external providers should not be carried out with the purpose of dissolving the department, but instead create scope for an even more in-depth and comprehensive service for employees.

Not surprisingly, Ram Charan's proposal has met with a great deal of opposition from international industry experts. A positive side-effect of this, however, has been the critical examination of the role and tasks of HRM and its contribution to value creation within the company.

5.4.3.5 Conclusion

In summary, the proposed solutions—a retreat into the 'HR shell', organisational restructuring, or the dissolution of the HR department—are not going to achieve the desired goal: to provide an effective response to the increasingly complex challenges of the world of work.

The following chapters of this book present an alternative, but also very obvious solution. Although this approach is easy to describe and understand logically, it is certainly not always easy to put into practice. It requires neither major organisational changes nor an increase in resources. It neither calls for decentralisation nor for hierarchical subordination. What we need is simply a new, clearly defined concept of cooperation between the actors in the HR department and the leaders of other departments. It is therefore an idea that must first be anchored in the minds of the individual stakeholders, and it begins with a new way of thinking about the HRM process.

References

Charan, R. (2014). Und Tschüss, HR. *Harvard Business Manager, 9,* 3–5.

Deeg, J., Küpers, W., & Weibler, J. (2010). *Integrale steuerung von organisationen.* München: Oldenbourg.

Drumm, H. J. (2008). *Personalwirtschaft* (6th ed.). Berlin: Springer.

Herzberg, F. (1966). *Work and the Nature of Man.* New York: Ty Crowell Co.

Holtbrügge, D. (2015). *Personal management* (6th ed.). Berlin: Springer.

Maslow, A. H. (1981). *Motivation and personality.* Longman: Pearson.

Nienhüser, W. (1999). Zentrale personalarbeit. In C. Scholz (Ed.), *Innovative personalorganisation* (pp. 158–167). Luchterhand, Neuwied: Center-Modelle für Wertschöpfung, Strategie, Intelligenz und Virtualisierung.

Novotny, V. (2017). *Agile Unternehmen: Fokussiert, schnell, flexibel.* Göttingen: Business Village.

Picot, A., Dietl, et al. (2012). *Organisation. Theorie und praxis aus ökonomischer Sicht* (6th ed., p. 92). Stuttgart: Schäffer-Poeschel.

Taylor, F. W. (1911). *The principles of scientific management.* New York: Harper.

Troger, H. (2018). *Die führungskraft als personalmanager* (pp. 93–102). Wiesbaden: Springer Gabler.

Ulrich, D. (1997). *Human resource champions—The next agenda for adding value and delivering results.* London: Harvard Business School Press.

Williamson, O. E. (1981). The economics of organization: The transaction cost approach. *The American Journal of Sociology, 87*(3), 548–577.

Part III

Effective HRM in an Individualized and Fragile Working Environment

Rethinking Human Resources Management

6

6.1 Personnel Management vs. Human Resources Management

The previous chapter aimed to demonstrate that the current proposals and approaches to HR management are only of limited use when it comes to effectively influencing and shaping the new world of work. What is needed is a fundamentally new way of thinking and of operating. For this purpose, it is first necessary to provide a definition of the relevant concepts and to clarify the context within which they are used.

6.1.1 Leadership Is Relationship

The management of employees could be defined as the goal-oriented influencing of behaviour through communication processes used by supervisors within the hierarchical structure of an organisation. The goal, generally, is the pursuit of business objectives. This definition implies a number of facts and interconnections, both within sociological theory and in business practice, and these are briefly described below (cf. Troger 2018).

Generally speaking, leadership can be described very simply as someone influencing the behaviour of another person through their own behaviour (cf., e.g., Wunderer and Grundwald 1980). This book focuses on leadership within an organisation and in this context, it must be seen as the direct influence of a person on the behaviour of employees. While the generic concept of leadership—defined as direction—can also be applied to technical matters, the focus of staff leadership is to provide purposeful guidance and to influence the actions of other people through social interaction. Therefore, the leadership of employees is a social process between at least two people; it is an interactive relationship between the leader and the led. In addition to the individuality of the two main actors, this relationship consists of two further components: the structure of the organisation overall and the specific

H. Troger, *Human Resource Management in a Post COVID-19 World*, Future of Business and Finance, https://doi.org/10.1007/978-3-030-67470-0_6

situation. Weibler (2012) characterises this leadership relationship as reciprocal and asymmetrical because the two sides exhibit different expectations and behaviours according to the individuality of the participants—although the behaviour of the leader generally has a stronger influence on the employee than the other way round.

6.1.1.1 Leadership Situations and Leadership Goals

The relationship between leader and employee will always exist under specific, sometimes unforeseen, environmental conditions and is, therefore, situational in nature. Such situations can arise from a wide variety of factors and they can have a significant influence on the relationship between managers and employees. Examples of factors include the work content, the equipment used, the situation in the market; they may even involve the personal relationships between co-workers at any given time. In practice, there are many influencing factors from the immediate organisational environment to the economic or socio-political context that can be taken into account to achieve one's goals. With every situation that involves leadership, the leaders and the led usually have one or more goals in their sights. These can be business goals or technical/material goals—beyond the standard revenue and profit targets. Non-monetary management goals, such as societal influence or social security, can also play a role. In addition to this, there are personal leadership goals. These are often found in target agreements and, ideally, they should help to ensure leadership success for both parties.

6.1.1.2 Leadership Tools and Leadership Success

The tools and methods that are used by leaders in their managerial activities are referred to as management tools. While in practice this is understood to mean traditional management tools such as target agreements, bonuses and control systems, the field of management science differentiates between management tools, management techniques and management styles. In this context, management tools are understood to be those tools that are used directly by the manager in order to be successful in a specific situation.

Management techniques, in contrast, refer to the basic procedures and behaviours of managers. The focus is, therefore, on how the management tools are used. Frequently, the relevant management principles are anchored in the company vision papers and policies. Examples include approaches such as 'Management by Objectives' or 'Management by Results'.

The third element, leadership style, should also be seen as another factor that does not depend on the situation in question. It is a term used to describe the general way in which a leader influences behaviour in order to achieve his or her goals. This aspect relates primarily to the individual leader and less to the external conditions or the tools available. The spectrum of these recurring patterns of leadership behaviour can range anywhere from laissez-faire to participative or to authoritarian.

This theoretical discussion on human resources management should not detract from the two simple and essential facts mentioned at the beginning: firstly, that leadership has always been a fact of life and is not tied to particular areas or circumstances; secondly, that ultimately it is always about a relationship between two people. Therefore, the management of people is neither an invention of the business world nor limited to the workplace. The latter has merely provided us with a differentiated understanding of the term over the last 70 years.

6.1.2 Human Resources Management

While the management of workers has existed for as long as people have employed others to do work for them, the concept and discipline of 'personnel management' is relatively new. At the beginning of the twentieth century, the first assembly lines were built in the United States and later in England, and soon the first personnel departments were established. This was the birth of personnel management as a distinct business function. It had to fulfil two central tasks: First of all, it aimed to achieve the highest possible labour productivity. For this purpose, the work processes were broken down into individual components, time was recorded and the sequence of activities was analysed. The American engineer Frederick Taylor is regarded as the founder of this *Scientific Management*, which aimed to determine the optimal sequence for each and every step of human activity (see Chap. 5). His approach was not only based on studies of the precise time taken, the skills involved and their implementation in workflow processes, but also the meticulous selection of the right people for each task. Put simply, personnel management has its origins in the streamlining of the first conveyor belt processes and was mainly the brainchild of engineers.

In addition to workforce productivity, the second key area of responsibility for the first personnel departments was to ensure legal compliance for personnel related activities. The close ties between HR work and the field of law, or rather the development of employment law as an independent discipline, explains the importance and the influence of the legal professions on HR work, which—unlike that of engineering—has remained unchanged to this day.

6.1.2.1 A Change of Perspective

These two aspects from the early days of staff management set the tone until the early 1980s. Although the 'human relations movement' soon developed as a reaction to what many considered to be an inhumane way of organising work based on a Taylorian approach, its representatives nevertheless focused on the same two goals—only from a different perspective. They sought to replace the technocratic Taylor model with a welfare approach. However, the main focus, as always, was labour productivity. When the term 'personnel management' first appeared in the mid-1960s, it involved bureaucratic and administrative tasks, as well as providing assistance to employees. The workforce was still seen as a means of production in Gutenberg's sense, whose characteristics and needs had to be taken into account— but always with the intention of optimising work performance.

Tellingly, a shift in perspective began to take hold during the economic crisis at the beginning of the 1980s. On the one hand, staff cost had massively increased in the years before and was the main target of streamlining efforts. On the other, the globalisation of markets and the increased complexity of the economic and working world led to calls for additional HR-related services.

From today's perspective, it is clear that the concept of 'Human Resources Management' as opposed to 'personnel management' has become established and that it has come to be seen as an integrated part of business management. This does not mean, however, that the discussions among academics and practitioners about the strategic orientation, the tasks and responsibilities and the structure of HR management are over (cf. Chap. 5). In this respect, it is not even possible to speak of a common understanding of the term.

6.1.2.2 Tasks and Responsibilities

For a definition of the tasks and responsibilities of HR management, however, such a uniform understanding or underlying perspective is essential. Stock-Homburg (2013) provides an excellent overview and distinguishes ten different perspectives for HR management, based on four dimensions: time, objective, content and scope (as shown in Fig. 6.1).

With regard to time, a distinction is made between strategic, operational and tactical perspectives of HR management. According to Stock-Homburg, all three perspectives result in a set of tasks and responsibilities for HR management.

In relation to setting goals in HR management, the author focuses on the competition-oriented perspective, as this aligns staff activities with market demands and thereby secures the long-term competitiveness of a company.

From a content point of view, Stock-Homburg favours the integrated perspective over the systemic one, as the former includes not only those activities that preserve the (business) system, but also involves individual elements and encompasses the actual management of employees.

Lastly, the concept of HR management is also defined in terms of its scope, i.e., who within the company is responsible for the various staff management activities? While the traditional, function-oriented perspective places the main responsibility for staff-related management activities with the HR department, the overarching perspective, according to Stock-Homburg, sees the responsibility for staff management as being shared by all parts of the company in equal measure. This means that all of the managers within an organisation are responsible for managing the staff in their particular division.

6.2   A Single Process with a Single Aim

In line with the perspectives described above, two broad areas of activity for HR management can be distinguished: One is at the level of the employees, where the focus is on their behaviour and cooperation within the team as well as their interaction with their supervisors. It is, therefore, about the immediate leadership relationships within the organisation. Stock-Homburg refers to this as the **micro-level** of HR management.

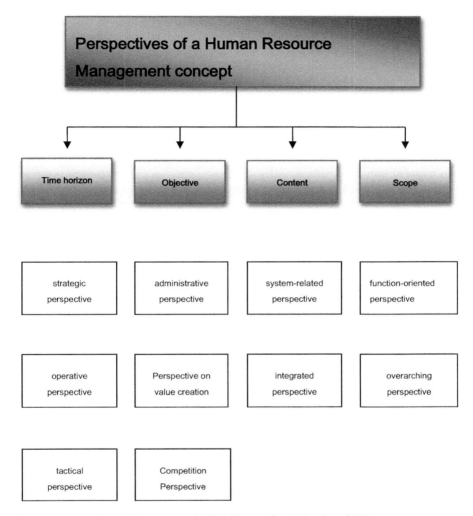

Fig. 6.1 Perspectives of the concept of HRM (Source: Stock-Homburg 2013)

These micro-level activities are embedded in a HR management strategy that applies to the entire company. The **macro-level**, in turn, encompasses the actual instruments and areas of responsibility of a HR department. With reference to the Harvard approach, Stock-Homburg distinguishes between the employee flow systems of workforce planning, staff acquisition, staff development and staff release—i.e., HR activities that deal with the fluctuations in the employee structure—and the reward systems. The latter include a company's employee appraisal and remuneration systems. Stock-Homburg believes that these two levels of HR management complement each other and that all areas within an organisation should be aware of them.

No matter whether we are talking about HR management, personnel management or staff leadership today: we are talking about working with and leading people. And regardless of whether we are talking about the recruitment process, the development process or the employee management/leadership process: it is all about ONE key operational process: the effective management of people as a human resource.

This single key process 'HR' or, the management of the workforce, gives equal weight to the concept of direct people management at a micro-level and to the supportive and overarching work of the HR management department at the macro-level—and it pursues ONE single goal: to increase the overall success of the company through the effective management of employees in terms of economic and social efficiency (cf. Troger 2018). Economic efficiency is hereby defined as the highest possible work productivity of employees, while social efficiency refers to their satisfaction with the work situation or the meeting of their expectations. It is the dualism of these objectives that makes their achievement so challenging for the 'process owner'.

This leads up to the crucial question: Who is the process owner? Without meaning to jump ahead to the next chapter, it is worth noting: There can only be ONE process owner—the respective line manager. This is not to say that HR professionals are no longer needed, quite the contrary: precisely because the management of the most valuable resource is increasingly becoming the management of the most difficult resource, it needs the support of the HR professional. However, the direct supervisor must remain the process owner, because only he or she can respond appropriately to the individual needs within the leadership relationship.

It is worth remembering that staff management as an independent business function emerged in the USA about a 100 years ago because the increasingly complex means of production that is human labour was to be made more efficient. It was no longer left to individual leaders to set their own staffing policies.

Fifty years later it was again a matter of reducing complexity: the globalisation of markets and the resulting competitive pressure demanded downsizing, centralisation and streamlining of operational processes by means of new (HR) management methods. Personnel administration transformed into personnel management as a functional area of business management and provided assistance with the help of tools to automate and reduce complexity and to systemise.

Summing up, we can, therefore, conclude that the HR function has arisen, on the one hand, due to the complexity of the interpersonal relationship between leaders and those led, and on the other, due to external circumstances—i.e., organisations are complex entities in a complex world. And it is precisely against this backdrop that a return to the original concept is necessary: HR management must once again become a much more integral part of the real leadership process.

6.3   The HR Actors

Based on personal experience in various management teams (both as head of HR and as CEO), I was given reason to believe that there are two functions that most of my executive colleagues—at least by their own admission—could perform equally as well as the respective department leader: purchasing and HR. Everyone had 'good personal contacts' to some supplier or other and viewed themselves as having excellent price negotiation skills—i.e., was a purchaser. And even on pressing issues of HR management, colleagues were always on hand with more or less forthright criticism and a wealth of well-meant advice. The many 'you should' and 'why don't you' comments still echo in my ears and at times they made me doubt my own judgement. Particularly among older executives, everyone seemed to be a HR expert.

I believe there are three explanations for this widespread attitude among management colleagues and also for why HR management has always faced difficulties in being taken seriously as a profession in its own right:

(a) As described earlier, HR functions have over time been taken on by engineers, then by lawyers, later by psychologists, pedagogues, sociologists and business economists. It would seem, therefore, that there is no clear link between the role of HR manager and a chosen academic qualification. Surprisingly, it has only been a recent development that the possibility of taking a higher education course with a focus on HR has become available.

(b) The (concealed) disregard for the work of HR professionals: 'What could possibly be so difficult about keeping staff records, sending out pay slips and organising training courses? In interviews, there is always an additional need for us technical experts anyway'. Such is the attitude of many colleagues from other departments.

(c) Staffing decisions tend to be seen as a manifestation of power. Which manager would not like to choose their own employees, decide freely on pay rises for their staff, and, if necessary, arrange a replacement when they can no longer tolerate somebody in their team? They could gladly dispense with the intervention of a neutral third party.

Everyone *Should* Do HR!
Can anyone do HR? I wish they could. At the very least, every manager should be able to do more of it in the future. Given that the most fundamental expression of HR management is to be found in the relationship between the supervisor and their direct reports, and that this relationship has become much more complex, it is high time that this supervisor, i.e., the line managers, took the reins again.

A century ago, workforce management was needed to optimise the workflow through empirical methods, but today this approach simply no longer works. At the beginning, you only had business owners and employees, then came the managers. With increasing size, other actors on both sides were added, such as personnel departments or employee representatives and trade unions. Ultimately, however, the management of staff has always been about one thing: the immediate and direct leadership relationship between two people.

6.3.1 The Top Management

At the top management level, namely the strategic level, management pioneer Ram Charan believes that there are three main stakeholders (G3) that should decide on the cornerstones of effective HR management: the Chief Executive Officer (CEO), the Chief Financial Officer (CFO) and the Chief Human Resources Officer (CHRO). Together with Dominic Barton (Managing Director of McKinsey) and Dennis Carey (Vice Chairman of Korn Ferry), Charan et al. (2015) suggest that the G3 should meet once a week to discuss internal and external early warning signs relating to what he calls the company's 'people engine'—its employees. In doing so, the HR manager, as an equal partner within this leadership team, could optimise their contribution. In these experts' opinion, this would be the best way to link the financial figures with the people who are ultimately behind them. The following three strategic areas of responsibility would then be assigned to the head of HR:

(a) **Forecasting results:** First, the CHRO should assess the chances of a business plan's success with regard to the managers or employees directly involved. He or she will identify the staffing requirements of any given project and determine whether the candidate in question meets these requirements. Together with the CFO, they will also compare the relevant budgets and key performance indicators (KPIs) with the objectives and adjust the former if necessary. The HR expert's assessment of the competitors or of their staff resources should also be taken into account.

(b) **Diagnosing problems:** According to the authors of this model, the head of HR is better placed than anyone else (external consultants included) to identify the reasons why targets are not being met. Apart from dealing with external factors, this is a matter of relating business figures to the performance of individual managers and to the cooperation within teams.

(c) **Initiating staffing measures:** In accordance with the results obtained, the HR leader will support the responsible managers and employees in overcoming deficits or acquiring new skills. He or she will look for new potential employees and propose staff reassignments.

Dave Ulrich (2016), the founder of the 'HR Business Partner Modells' (cf. Chap. 5) also emphasises the importance of the role of the HR manager at the top decision-making level, but suggests a team of four instead of three stakeholders. In his opinion, the head of IT (CIO) should also be part of the team, due to the growing role of digital data processing.

6.3.2   The Line Managers

At the **operational level**, the focus is on the work of HR professionals on one side, and managers, or rather line managers, on the other.

Line managers, as actors in HR management, have the fundamental task of representing the interests of the company management in all HRM decisions. Regardless of whether this concerns work instructions to an employee, organisational matters or the allocation of bonuses: the manager performs a HRM task. These tasks are not administrative, but instead have a shaping purpose. They requires a high level of knowledge about the work content, the situation and above all about the employees involved. The formal employment contract, which is usually drawn up by the HR department, is less useful here, and the so-called psychological contract takes precedence, alongside the job description. As discussed in Chap. 2, the psychological contract relates to the mutual expectations and promises between the supervisor and the employee that go beyond the legal employment contract. This can include verbal agreements, or be derived from the behaviour of the two parties (cf. Troger 2019).

The challenge of the psychological contract lies in its continuously changing nature and in the diversity and unpredictability of the employees' interests. The psychological contract will become even more significant in the future because the focus will continue to shift towards the assessment of each respective situation, and most notably, it will be on the expectations and the needs of the employee. This growing focus on employees' needs will be the consequence of an increasingly employee-driven labour market. Only the respective line manager of an employee will then be able to respond to the employee's expectations and to enter into agreements with them—some of which may even be implicit—in order to ensure that employees are able to make the best possible contribution towards the achievement of the company's objectives.

6.3.3   The HR Professionals

HR professionals will continue to perform their administrative and systematising tasks on behalf of the business owners or the top leaders of the company. Most of these tasks are characterised by a high degree of standardisation and do not require detailed knowledge of the employee's specific field of work. Above all, detailed knowledge of the individual employee is usually neither necessary nor can it be expected in larger companies, and only these tend to have their own HR department.

In addition to the routine management of personnel files and the punctual payment of salaries, the experts from the HR department will continue in their efforts to fulfil their role as business partners and to increase their influence on the company's top management. With regard to the HR department's contribution to the attractiveness of a company, Benedikt Hackl and Fabiola Gerpott (2017) surveyed 662 HR professionals and managers on the role of HR as a partner of the leaders within the organisation and as a strategic impulse generator for the organisation. The researchers defined 'employee recruitment' and 'employee retention' as the criteria for an attractive company or successful HR management. Subsequently, four types of departments were identified, depending on the characteristics of the two dimensions 'influence on corporate strategy' and 'influence on managers': the HR department as **executor** (little influence on corporate strategy and executives), as **coach** (strong influence on executives, but little influence on strategy), as **strategist** (strong influence on strategy, but little influence on executives) or as **impulse generator** (strong influence on executives and corporate strategy). Only those HR departments that are impulse generators rate equally as high in attractiveness to both external applicants and employees alike.

The study shows that the much-lauded strategic partnership of HR and top management is not enough, although it does succeed in increasing attractiveness on the labour market to new recruits. In terms of 'employee retention', this type of department produced the worst results of the study. What is needed, therefore, is the influence of managers and their close cooperation with the HR department so that the right measures can be implemented to increase the company's internal attractiveness, in other words, to increase 'employee retention'.

6.4   The Shoulder-to-Shoulder Approach

Following these observations, two points stand out: First, effective HRM at strategic and operational level requires both HR professionals and direct supervisors, i.e., line managers. Second, neither of the two actors can achieve the goal on their own. What is needed instead is a high level of cooperation between them. For this reason, I suggest that a shoulder-to-shoulder approach is indispensable.

The goal of effective HR management, which is to increase the success of the company through the management of employees according to economic and social efficiency, requires constructive cooperation between HR professionals and managers at all stages of the HRM process, especially at the operational level.

Using a shoulder-to-shoulder approach means that the HR professionals must, or rather are permitted, to leave their potential comfort zone as consultants and administrators, but also their potential danger zones as exposed decision-makers and scapegoats. What we need is a new model of task sharing between the HR experts and the direct managers of those employees that are affected by the respective HR decisions.

This emphasis on working shoulder-to-shoulder also has the effect of rendering the usual questions and discussions about the role, participation or the internal inclusion of HR staff redundant and standard excuses, such as 'We were informed too late', etc., no longer apply.

In future, neither the theoretical discussion of transformational versus transactional HRM, nor the conflict between the roles of service provider and strategic partner will be given the same attention.

The question of *centralised* versus *decentralised* HR policy resolves itself naturally as a result of line managers taking on a key role, and the location of HR within the organisation also loses importance: What matters is that decisions are reached on an equal footing, whether in person or virtually—given that we live in the global digital age.

The blame game between different line functions and HR should also be a thing of the past, as they will work closely together in the future. They are mutually dependent on each other to achieve their common goal: to ensure that the management of employees contributes as much value as possible.

What this new cooperation between the two actors can look like in the day-to-day running of a company will be described in the following chapters. To this end, everything that falls under HRM is divided into three key processes: The **recruitment process**, from HR marketing to the signing of the employment contract; the **staff management process**, with a focus on staff deployment, the agreement on goals and evaluation; and the **staff development process**, which includes the important elements of education and training, as well as career planning.

References

Charan, R., Barton, D., & Carey, D. (2015). People before strategy: A new role for the CHRO. *Harvard Business Review, 7–8*, 16–21.

Hackl, B., & Gerpott, F. (2017). Was machen eigentlich Ihre Personaler? *Harvard Business Manager, 2*, 43–47.

Stock-Homburg, R. (2013). *Personalmanagement. Theorien, Konzepte, Instrumente* (3rd ed.). Wiesbaden: Springer Gabler.

Troger, H. (2018). *Die Führungskraft als Personalmanager*. Wiesbaden: Springer Gabler.

Troger, H. (2019). Management von Interessen und Erwartungen. In H. Troger (Ed.), *7 Erfolgsfaktoren für wirksames Personalmanagement* (2nd ed., pp. 131–146). Wiesbaden: Springer Gabler.

Weibler, J. (2012). *Personalführung* (2nd ed.). Munich: Vahlen.

Wunderer, R., & Grundwald, W. (1980). *Führungslehre* (Grundlagen der Führung) (Vol. 1). Berlin: De Gruyter.

The Recruitment Process

From Staff Planning to Hiring

7

7.1 Staff Planning

7.1.1 Quantitative and Qualitative Staffing Needs

The staffing needs of an organisation express how many employees with what qualifications are needed in a workplace at a given time to achieve the organisation's objective. The planning of the required staff capacities can therefore be seen either as a starting point for all other areas of HR work or as an essential part of a company's operations planning, such as production, procurement, financial and sales planning.

Following the above definition, four dimensions can be distinguished when determining the required staffing needs:

(a) **Quantitative dimension** indicates the number of staff required, usually expressed in FTE (full-time equivalent).
(b) **Qualitative dimension** indicates the required qualifications.
(c) **Time dimension** specifies from when to when the people are needed.
(d) **Location dimension** indicates the workplace or department.

The primary objective of HR planning is economic in nature—to use the smallest amount of human resources possible in achieving the highest value for the company. In addition, it is also about ensuring that the workload of employees is distributed as evenly as it can be and that a certain flexibility and adaptability in response to unplanned customer fluctuations and changing environmental conditions is provided.

Staffing needs can be determined by various methods and a rough distinction between **quantitative** and **qualitative** approaches can be made. The former are strictly summary in nature and can either be past-oriented (e.g., regression method or trend extrapolation) or future-oriented (e.g., Delphi method).

Qualitative procedures are much more complex and include task and time studies for individual vacancies. The results are detailed job descriptions and specifications.

© The Author(s), under exclusive license to Springer Nature Switzerland AG 2021   121
H. Troger, *Human Resource Management in a Post COVID-19 World*, Future of
Business and Finance, https://doi.org/10.1007/978-3-030-67470-0_7

Firstly, the aim is to determine the character and intensity of every type of requirement associated with the various positions in an organisation—with an eye to the future. Secondly, the existing or potential qualifications of the employees must also be recorded with regard to their type and specifications. The subsequent comparison of job requirements and employee qualifications forms the basis for (qualitative) staff planning.

A detailed description of the different methods of staff planning will not be given here—especially since most HR managers are not too fond of these tools and tend to neglect them, with the exception of standard labour cost planning. Instead, some particular challenges relating to this aspect that have arisen as a result of changes in the labour market will be highlighted.

7.1.2   Challenges Within the New World of Work

The manifold changes in the parameters of the world of business and work were described in detail in Part One of this book. What follows are some of the problems that these changes have brought about for the reliable planning of staffing needs (cf. Troger 2018):

(a) In light of the overall dynamic nature of markets, it is becoming increasingly difficult to make reliable predictions about the economic development of a company and to draw up appropriate staffing plans.
(b) Due to the coronavirus pandemic, human resources planning has been taken to a level of volatility previously unthinkable; reliability has almost become a matter of luck.
(c) Given the cost transparency in most markets and the resulting narrow calculations, it is virtually impossible to plan for reserve staff. In many cases, replacements cannot even be planned for confirmed departures.
(d) The shortage of qualified workers can often make a qualitative staff plan seem like a futile wish lists.
(e) The short-lived nature of many decisions on both the employee's and the employer's side means that the carefully and meticulously prepared staff plans can become out of date and meaningless after only a few weeks.
(f) Line managers, who tend to be sceptical about top-down staff planning, complain even more about the futility of elaborate analyses of staffing needs and fear that their flexibility will be restricted by 'pseudo-precision planning'.
(g) Estimates of the quantitative capabilities of employees are increasingly turning out too high. This can result in unplanned absences caused by excessive workloads, and eventually can lead to difficulties in finding a replacement.
(h) In the technical areas in particular, the industry 4.0 related boom in automation makes reliable predictions about qualitative and quantitative staffing requirements almost impossible.

(i) The diversity and variability of employees' interests, talents and competencies beyond those that are evident from their CV and job interview make staff planning more challenging because they cannot be planned for in advance.
(j) Based on the experience gained during the first wave of Covid-19, decision makers will need to be even more cautious and HR professionals are expected to be even more vigilant and able to react quickly.

7.1.3   Long-Term Planning Under Uncertainty

In view of the above-mentioned changes in the labour market, it does not seem easy to achieve meaningful quantitative and qualitative staff planning. Nevertheless, the fact that the economic future (and the future HRM) involves many uncertainties, making the only constant the continuing shortage of skilled workers, is precisely the reason why long-term planning of the organisation's most important resource is all the more important. The planning process, however, has to change.

Some of the key steps in this process are listed below; the fundamental premise being the close and mutually trusting, shoulder-to-shoulder cooperation between line managers and HR professionals.

(a) It starts with the regular exchange of information regarding the skills, interests and attributes of employees—especially of those with relevant key competencies for the company.
(b) Flexible reactions to unplanned departures can only be ensured through the timely planning of diversity in the composition of the team and the workforce as a whole. The universally advocated concept of diversity management must therefore start with staffing needs planning and take into account not only factors such as ethnicity, gender and age, but also the interests and hidden skills of employees.
(c) Knowledge and competencies have never before become obsolete as quickly as they are today. Yet at the same time, it has never been easier to acquire new knowledge. For the planning of long-term staffing needs, this means that it is possible to consider unskilled workers for certain positions, thanks to targeted on-the-job training. The age of the person hardly plays a role anymore—except perhaps in terms of the greater level of experience that may come with age.

As far as the creation of qualification profiles is concerned, multi-annual staffing plans are very useful, despite the uncertainty and volatility mentioned above. However, this can only be done in conjunction with an internal rotation system for key positions and with the consistent involvement of the existing staff. Due to the diversity of interests among (not just the younger) employees (cf. Chaps. 2 and 3), and the ease with which knowledge and skills can be acquired today, when drawing up staffing plans we can assume that there is much more hidden potential among the existing staff than we know of from their administrative records. The task, therefore, is to identify this untapped potential of competencies in close cooperation with the respective line managers and to harness it for the company.

7.1.4   Practical Tips and the Division of Responsibilities in Staff Planning

The following diagram illustrates the cooperation between line managers and HR professionals as a continuum (Fig. 7.1). Several practical suggestions and recommendations with regard to staff planning conclude this chapter.

Practical Tips
1. For the day-to-day running of the organisation—especially during the pandemic—the short-term 'dynamic' planning of staffing needs is more important than multi-annual planning, which is largely speculative.
2. Nevertheless, long-term staffing plans are very important indeed during these times of great volatility, albeit for different reasons: the continual exchange of

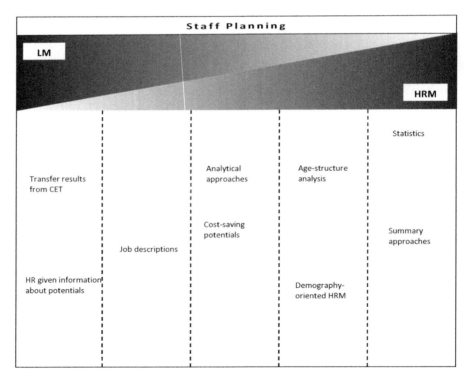

Fig. 7.1 Distribution of tasks and cooperation between line managers and HR professionals in relation to human resources planning

information between HR and the company's managers coupled with an internal rotation system.

3. Do not overestimate the quantitative capabilities of your employees—or underestimate their qualitative capacity.
4. Making sure that the composition of teams is as diverse as it can be will make it easier for you to react to unplanned changes later on.
5. Do not rely on pre-existing skills profiles and CVs for qualitative staff planning—both can change very quickly.
6. The growing shortage of skilled workers on the free market calls for a greater focus on staff development in staff planning.

7.2 HR Marketing

Given that employees are seen as a an organisation's most important resource, yet their numbers are dwindling and they are becoming increasingly unpredictable and reluctant to commit, the job of the HR marketing expert is clear: to do everything that can be done to increase the company's attractiveness in order to recruit new employees and retain existing ones. For this reason, HR professionals and entrepreneurs alike consider HR marketing—as a tool for attracting skilled employees—to be one of the main tasks of modern HRM. It is, therefore, all the more astonishing that the HR team is left to deal with this task alone—with the possible exception of the half-hearted support from in-house marketing experts. For the following suggestions, the shoulder-to-shoulder cooperation between HR professionals and line managers is once again of crucial importance.

7.2.1 Informing, Encouraging Action—and Brand Building!

The **informative function** of HR marketing is plain to see. The aim is to provide target groups with all the relevant information about the company—its mission, values, products and markets—as well as the information about the job vacancies. It means addressing the highest possible number of potentially suitable people and **encouraging them to apply**. At the same time, the existing employees should also be kept informed about what is happening inside and outside of the company in order to foster a sense of belonging and to increase their level of engagement, organisational identification and motivation. From a marketing perspective, the (potential) employee is not seen as an important resource but rather as an important customer. He or she should be won over to the organisation, convinced of its merits and opportunities and encouraged to make a long-term commitment to it. None of this is new and most companies or HR experts are already doing it. Yet, this in itself is often not enough to win new recruits and can sometimes even lead to the loss of existing employees. Glossy brochures, interactive websites and well-designed job advertisements alone are no longer sufficient. What matters is how your company is positioned as a unique brand on the market. The method for this is:

7.2.1.1 Employer Branding

The branding of a company is no longer based solely on the distinguishing features of its products, but increasingly also on its appeal as an employer. If the company is to win the competition for sought-after employees on the labour market or retain its own people in the long term, it needs to stand out positively from the competition as a brand. Employer branding is used to define the identity of an organisation as an employer. In addition to the mission and the objectives of the organisation, its driving values and, above all, its merits and the opportunities it can offer are communicated, in order to inspire and win over existing and potential employees.

Employer branding is not just about promoting a company, but also about a more integrated view of marketing, which involves aligning the company with the needs of employees as a customer segment.

In addition to informing and encouraging action, HR marketing therefore also has to be involved in designing and building an effective employer brand. To be clear, this is less about designing marketing measures than it is about designing the company's HR policies in accordance with the (known and anticipated) needs of existing and potential employees, who are the key target groups.

7.2.2   Target Groups

As indicated above, we can distinguish between internal and external HR marketing depending on the respective target group. The two target groups influence each other and jointly determine the brand image of an organisation.

7.2.2.1 External HR Marketing

A 'best employer' award, or at least a top position in an employer ranking, is very popular and makes the recruiter's work in the recruitment process much easier. However, such an award can also score points in negotiations for a bank loan, help to secure public funding, or impress in various advisory boards or stockholders' meetings. Company evaluations by its employees have now become one of the most important indicators of a company's social status within society. The main focus of external HR marketing, however, is the attraction of potential new recruits. In this context, Rowold (2015) mentions five goals:

- Creating a positive employer image.
- Raising public awareness of the company.
- Attracting a sufficient number of applicants.
- Reducing recruitment costs.
- Ensuring smooth transitions for replacements and new appointments.

In order to achieve these goals, it is necessary to know the target group and their needs thoroughly so that they can be addressed as effectively as possible. The effort invested by companies to achieve this still varies considerably. Google, for example, recruits an average of 7000 people worldwide each year and employs one recruiter for every 64 employees. Companies of a comparable size in Europe employ one recruiter for every 577 employees (see Buchheim 2017).

In order to motivate an external applicant to join the company, I need to know his or her interests and expectations. Do not jump to the conclusion that the answer lies simply in the right salary. For highly sought-after candidates, money is hardly ever the only incentive for joining a company. The critical question, therefore, is not just how I communicate my incentives to potential employees, but also what I have to offer—what are the unique selling points of my company in relation to the diverse range of interests of the applicants.

The *HOW*

In this age of the Internet, the classic **AIDA** formula (Attention-Interest-Desire-Action) from the field of marketing is increasingly being supplemented or replaced by the so-called **CUBE** formula, which focuses on the effective online promotion of the organisation's vacancies as well as their general online presence: The 'C' stands for content, for example, the informative value any vacancy that is advertised online should have. 'U' stands for usability, in other words, the ease of use. The HR marketing expert must position the message in such a way that the relevant information is immediately apparent to the visitor and ensure that visitors can navigate intuitively 'within the company' online. 'B' stands for branding, which is at the centre of all online marketing activities. The goal is to create an unmistakable visual identity—a brand—using colours, typeface and images.

Last but not least, perhaps the most difficult task: to convey and evoke emotions ('E') via the emotionless computer screen. Emotions are playing an increasingly important role for today's young applicants and employers expect their employees to show passionate commitment and to engage with their company.

The *WHAT*

The things people look for in a job are fulfilment, power, money, recognition, security (in times of crisis, such as the one we are currently experiencing, especially so) and more. It would not be helpful to discuss the latest motivation and attractiveness factors at this point. For one thing, they cannot be generalised, and secondly, such attempts at generalisations would result in the loss of one of the company's unique selling points in terms of employer branding. The task of HR marketing is to recognise the interests and needs of potential applicants through their continuous interactions with them, and to reflect these effectively in the company's incentive structure through the relevant offers.

Yet again, the HR marketing expert is dependent on the help of line managers to achieve this. Given the day-to-day interaction with the applicant's prospective colleagues, the line manager is best suited to know their 'typical' general preferences and behaviours. With this valuable information, he or she can help the HR professional to design a target group-oriented approach.

7.2.2.2 Internal HR Marketing

While the line manager already fulfils an important advisory and informative role in external HR marketing, he or she is all the more indispensable for effective employer branding within the organisation. Long-term employee retention, which is the primary goal of internal HR marketing, can be achieved with the help of three specific goals:

– An increase in loyalty and commitment to the organisation.
– A reduction in the rates of both staff turnover and sickness absence.
– The establishment of a pool of young talents in management.

The strategy for achieving this could be summed up with the following words: *Do good (to the employees) and talk about it*. This does not mean that HR staff must become the social reformers described in Chap. 5. In the same way that the sales professional, despite being customer-oriented, ultimately represents the interests of the company, the HR professionals, in their role as employee champions (cf. Chap. 5), will support the employees and focus his or her attention on them. The ultimate goal, however, is to optimise the employees' skills within the company for as long as possible.

Internal marketing, naturally, requires knowledge of the interests and needs of the employees. Despite all their soft skills and knowledge of human nature, it is unlikely that the HR professional will be able to know and understand all employees equally. As described in detail in Chap. 3, it is precisely the diversity and changing nature of their interests, or rather the growing desire to put them into practice, which makes the management of employees (and the managers among them) so complex. This task can therefore only be entrusted to the individual's direct supervisor.

When applied to employer branding, this means that good company advertising is even less relevant than in external HR marketing (and can sometimes prove counterproductive if there is no relation to reality). Instead, what matters most are the actual realities and actions behind the brand.

It is precisely this **brand building task** of HR marketing that poses the biggest challenge for HR professionals and managers. The responsibilities and the roles are clearly assigned: The managers get to know their employees, or rather their interests and needs, and compare these with what is possible within the company, while the HR professionals develop a suitably variable and diverse incentive system. Together they decide on the suitability, implementation and communication of the incentives.

In this context, we should take note that a global crisis, such as the one brought about by Covid-19, does not only bring challenges but opportunities as well: Companies that are sensitive to the needs and anxieties of their workforce are not exploiting their regained power in the labour market because employees fear for their jobs, but are now even more aware of their responsibilities towards their employees. With a jointly created sense of unity, it is not only possible to overcome the crisis more easily, but also to enhance the effectiveness of the marketing impact on the labour market.

7.2.3 Employer Branding: Methods and Channels

With regard to the cooperation between HR professionals and line managers in developing and implementing a suitable employer branding package, a number of channels are outlined below.

7.2.3.1 Internet Branding and Recruiting

The rapid spread of the Internet in recent years has made it an attractive platform for HR marketing. There is probably no longer any company in the industrialised world that does not have its own website to promote itself on the Internet and, if required, uses it to recruit potential employees. **Social recruiting** has become the universally recognised generic term for recruitment and HR marketing activities in social networks. By distributing the right content in a targeted manner online, it is possible to create a strong and sustainable employer brand at relatively low cost. The participants of the various social networks can serve as multipliers who willingly disseminate interesting content.

Active sourcing, which means the targeted contacting of potential candidates online, is an excellent tool, especially for hard-to-fill positions, because it allows you to reach 'passive candidates', i.e., those who were not looking for a change of jobs. In this way, the number of potential applicants can be increased many times over. Social business networks such as LinkedIn are most frequently used for this purpose. The advantages of targeting people via online job portals, social networks and the company's own website speak for themselves:

- Time and cost savings.
- Wide range of options for addressing the relevant target group.
- Near unlimited possibilities of a multimedia approach to presenting information.
- The opportunity for interactive dialogue (e.g., filling in applications, aptitude tests, etc.).

The ease with which potential applicants can contact a company and the opportunity for spontaneous feedback have made the Internet an indispensable tool for interactive communication between a business and its environment.

But it need not always be the PR professional's nifty new infotainment platform; even the simple company homepage provides a basic tool that can be used to present a company's services, USPs or basic online job board effectively, and thereby help to create an authentic brand in the employee market.

The motto 'the more, the better' does not necessarily apply here. Instead, effective online HR marketing should use its key components—the company website, job portals and social communities—in a combined and coordinated effort.

7.2.3.2 Recruitment Fairs

As a contrast to the online world of virtual and often anonymous communication, the classic recruitment fairs continue to enjoy great popularity. Globally successful corporations as well as local family businesses use them to find potential applicants and, above all, to meet them face to face. Although recruitment fairs achieve two strategic marketing goals by increasing the company's visibility and offering the possibility to conduct targeted on-site interviews (if the interest is there), their comparatively high costs must be taken into account. Some of the most extreme examples in this context include various international consulting firms that strive to outshine each other with their exclusive recruitment events in the most prestigious and expensive locations around the world. Assessment sessions alternate with spa treatments—IQ testing in the morning followed by glacier skiing or windsurfing in the afternoon. Only the best will do to attract the best—it would seem. The (online) advertising for such an event alone would go beyond the marketing budget of any 'normal' company.

In comparison to such extreme examples, **recruitment events at universities** offer reasonably cheap alternatives. This type of company promotion and early recruitment of graduates directly from the universities and institutes of higher education has a long tradition in the USA and is now becoming increasingly popular also in Europe—mainly due to the shortage of skilled workers. In addition to traditional graduate recruitment and career fairs, company tours, internships, or dissertation support can all be part of an organisation's HR marketing concept. The particular advantage of such activities lies in the wide-reaching societal impact of 'supporting young people in their education and career development'.

Due to the pandemic, recruitment fairs have taken a back seat and their significance, naturally, has diminished considerably. I expect this downward trend to continue even after the coronavirus-related restrictions. It is very likely that people will have become too attached to the convenience and efficiency of the many different opportunities for networking and meeting each other online.

7.2.3.3 Employees as Headhunters

The shortage of skilled workers and executive staff is the reason why HR consultants and headhunters are currently experiencing increasing revenues, since many companies are happy (or forced) to use them despite high commissions, especially for top executives. In addition, more and more organisations have been relying on their employees for headhunting in recent years. So-called employee referral programmes are increasingly proving successful in marketing and recruitment.

There is nothing new about employees informing a friend about a vacancy in their company. What is new, however, is the organised approach taken by companies and HR departments. Employee referral programmes apply the principles of active sourcing and social recruiting and use their employees' contacts to fill vacancies. In 2017, the German study 'Recruiting Strategies' identified employee referral programmes for small and medium-sized companies as their strongest recruitment channel—especially for trainees and professions that do not require higher levels of qualifications. Leni Reichmann (2017) conducted a survey of several hundred respondents (published in several social networks) as part of her master's thesis. It showed that the approval rate for employee referral programmes as a useful recruitment channel was over 95%. Interestingly, only half of the respondents stated that an incentive was an important factor for them.

A study conducted by the Technical Universität of München and the HR software developer Talentry (2017) highlights the key role played by employees and the many possibilities offered by social networks in terms of employer branding and recruiting. The Munich-based company was one of the first in its industry to develop a digitised employee referral programme with an integrated incentive system and cites the following advantages, along with others:

(a) **Innovation:** the development of new recruitment channels, including the integration of various social media channels (i.e., LinkedIn, Facebook, Twitter, Google+, WhatsApp, etc.) into the referral process.
(b) **Wide reach:** the establishment of a network of 133 potential candidates, on average, using employees' social connections.
(c) **Above-average suitability:** suggestions of suitably skilled candidates via the employees' technical networks that are relevant.
(d) **Tracking:** ensuring the clear identification of referrer and applicant via digital referral tracking.
(e) **Time saving:** reducing the time between advertising and filling the vacancy.
(f) **Flexibility:** recommendations can be made anywhere and anytime via smartphone.

In addition, several other advantages of employee referrals in the recruitment process can be noted:

The pool of applicants is likely to be of a **higher quality** as a result personal recommendations from employee contacts. Employees act as an initial filter and will only recommend candidates if they are convinced that they meet the requirements and fit into the company.

The advantages of employee recommendations continue into the induction phase: Given the **information advantage** of the 'newcomer', initial disappointments are largely avoided—especially if the referrer acts as a mentor at the beginning. Another common view is that by involving colleagues in the selection process, the **integration** process will be more successful and the **working atmosphere** and **productivity** in the whole department will be improved.

Charges of **favouritism** or **over-homogenisation** (employees tend to recommend people with similar backgrounds to themselves) can be countered with the facts that a recommendation does not constitute a guarantee of employment and the HR professionals continue to remain in charge of the recruitment process.

Overall, the employer brand gains in credibility through employee recommendations because employees are viewed as highly credible brand ambassadors, not only by potential applicants, but also by suppliers, customers and other stakeholders.

Above all, employee recommendations build an effective bridge between managers, their direct reports and the HR experts, which can have a very positive impact on multiple aspects of the HR management process.

7.2.4   Practical Tips and the Division of Responsibilities in HR Marketing

In summary, *social recruiting, active sourcing, employee referral programmes* and all the other methods and tools of HR marketing help companies to compete in the increasingly competitive candidate-driven labour market. Besides providing information and encouraging prospective candidates into action, the main focus is on using the many different ways to build *employer branding*—and the effects of the latter are first seen within the organisation itself.

All these tools and channels are about relationships—ultimately, they are about the relationship between two people—one of whom is the line manager. Therefore, the line manager's role in the entire process cannot be overstated. His or her contribution or cooperation with the experts from the HR department is again shown on a continuum in Fig. 7.2.

The **employee value proposition**, meaning the company's overall offer to current and potential employees, depends on the content of the tasks and the incentives offered. However, it also depends on the right communication via the right channels and, ultimately, it is expressed through a distinctive employer brand. Employer branding can therefore be seen as a fully integrated HR management activity, whereby that which is unique to the company is explored, identified and communicated internally and externally.

Practical Tips
The following practical recommendations and the visually displayed division of tasks between managers and HR experts complement the above (cf. Troger 2018):

1. Think of HR marketing—besides having the function of informing and encouraging action—primarily as an internal design task/brand building task.
2. The brand building of a company is increasingly determined by its attractiveness as an employer.
3. The employees of a company are its most effective marketing channel on the candidate-driven labour market, because they are the most credible.
4. For effective HR marketing, I need to know my potential candidates' interests and expectations.
5. Whether through active social sourcing or university fairs: Recruit your employees to act as headhunters (use incentives, where applicable). They are reliable, affordable and effective.
6. In internal HR marketing, the line manager, being a key role model, is your most important marketing tool.

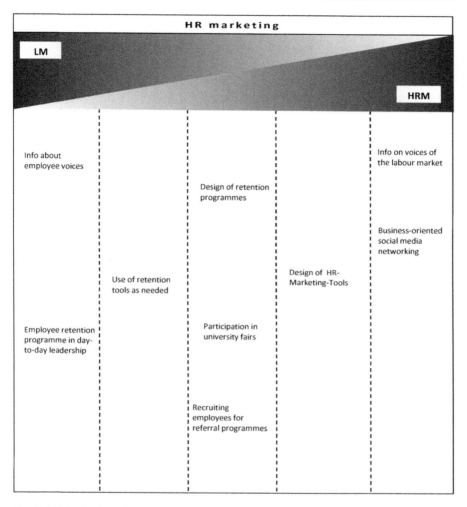

Fig. 7.2 Distribution of responsibilities and cooperation between line manager and HR professional in HR marketing

7.3   Staff Selection

Having successfully approached potential candidates with regard to a vacant position, we begin the selection process to find the optimal candidate. This process is not only considered to be the most important HR function overall, but it is also the most difficult, time-consuming and costly. Opinions among academics and practitioners on how best to carry it out are all the more divided. Do you need graphological reports, assessment centres and aptitude tests or can you simply rely on the gut feeling of an experienced HR professional? Will you prepare a stress test for the candidate or a friendly taster session with the team?

Since the main focus of this book is to highlight the need for HR professionals and line managers to work shoulder-to-shoulder, the selection process, too, will be considered from this perspective and divided into five phases; each starts by defining the course of action before describing it.

7.3.1   Phase 1: The Starting Situation

The first phase of the selection process involves clarifying a number of basic questions: Will the selection be made from external and/or internal applicants? Who is responsible for the selection? What criteria are used to make the decision?

The decision whether to recruit **internally or externally** is often not taken until the applications have been received, i.e., when we know what the job market has to offer. Arguments in favour of internal recruitment include the lower risk of appointing the wrong person, reduced induction period, time and cost savings, as well as the motivational effect (especially in relation to a management-level positions). The main drawback is the risk of 'organisational blindness' or rather the missed opportunity to bring new knowledge into the company.

For positions that require a high level of in-house knowledge or a long training period, internal candidates, if available, are more likely to be chosen. If, on the other hand, there is a lack of knowledge and experience in the company or if none of the internal candidates meet the requirements, external candidates must be used.

The first problems often arise when the **right composition of the selection team** is discussed: Should the line manager be involved? Does the HR professional have the necessary specialist knowledge? The first question can only be answered with a clear 'yes'—meaning the second question is unnecessary. The objection that the line manager could choose a 'more agreeable' candidate instead of the best candidate makes no sense: It is not the best, but the most suitable candidate who needs to be chosen. If the line manager does not yet have the skills to select employees, he or she will have to learn them—or be replaced. The role of HR professionals in this process is to supervise and to support the line manager in their management task. For important selection decisions, a second manager is often involved—especially when a second round of interviews is held.

What should be the procedure? The entire process must meet specific quality criteria, particularly in terms of validity (there is a proven link between the procedure itself and induced characteristics) and in terms of reliability (with regard to time and different assessors). In addition, the time and financial outlay must of course be kept within reasonable limits, and the legal parameters must be taken into account. As mentioned above, the line manager is not required to be objective and neutral in their decision, but this should be discussed in advance.

7.3.2   Phase 2: Candidate Screening

The selection process begins with the preparation of the job profile and person specification for the vacant position, together with the advertisement. The more precise and detailed the person specification, the easier it will be to compare the candidates, and the faster the next step can be taken: a pre-selection of the received applications using the classic ABC analysis as the decision-making tool. This could mean, for example, that C applicants who do not meet the mandatory criteria will be sent a rejection letter without delay. B candidates might not quite meet some of the desired criteria, but could still be considered for the second round. These candidates might also be eligible for an alternative position. Naturally, the better the ratio between the number of vacancies and the applications, the more inflexible the selection will be at this stage.

In order to avoid disagreements within the interview panel from the onset, it is best to prioritise the individual job requirements in advance. Especially when it comes to choosing between specialist and social competence, a suitably differentiated set of requirements will be helpful. In addition to the curriculum vitae, any enclosed educational and work qualifications, certificates, references, etc. are verified and evaluated (in particular the job references).

In larger companies it is now common practice to pre-select online. Candidates are asked to fill in online application forms containing the most important information. The in-house HR software then screens the entries and filters out the C applicants while also sending them a polite rejection.

The next step is usually also done online: the search for information and the 'digital footprint' of the candidates that are to be invite to an interview. Younger candidates, in particular, often publish personal details about their private lives, leisure activities, club memberships, etc. on social media networks. Social media screening is not yet fully covered by law, it can, however, provide revealing information about a candidate's personality.

7.3.3   Phase 3: Selection Interviews

After pre-selection, screening, and verification of the enclosed documents, the most interesting candidates are invited for an interview—preferably by telephone, in order to get a first impression and, if necessary, to check their language skills. For most recruiters, but especially for the future supervisor, the job interview is the most important source of information for the selection of the right candidate. The aim of the interview is to get a personal impression of the person and the mutual exchange of information. On the interviewer's side, anything raised in the application can be discussed, and the candidate has the opportunity to get to know the company and their potential future supervisor a bit better.

When choosing between a **structured or unstructured interview**, I generally favour the latter, as it is much better suited to getting to know each other. As an interviewer, you can expect that the applicant will be well prepared for the interview and will use 'textbook-style' answers, even for follow-up questions. Moreover, the unstructured interview enables you to better respond to the individual characteristics of the candidates and to react spontaneously to their answers. The more spontaneous and relaxed the conversation, the better the chance to get to know each other in an authentic way. However, in unstructured interviews, comparability between several candidates tends to be somewhat difficult and there is a risk that essential aspects of a future working relationship will not be addressed.

I therefore recommend a division of roles: The managers involved may ask their questions freely and address any topic they wish, while the HR professional pays attention to that the interview stays on track and ensures that there is structure in terms of content and form. Following the interview, the managers and HR experts will exchange their thoughts and impressions.

7.3.4   Phase 4: Recruitment Tests

There are still various popular tests for the selection of suitable candidates, despite the effort involved. They are usually carried out after the first interview and are based on the premise that certain characteristics of the candidates—which may not be observable during the interview—can be detected using the results, so that future behaviour can be predicted.

A rough distinction can be made between ability and personality tests. The former are intended to measure aspects such as memory performance or the ability to solve problems in certain situations. Personality tests, on the other hand, are designed to capture the applicant's character traits, values and attitudes, regardless of the situational circumstances.

Particularly elaborate and complex testing, which is often used when filling executive positions, can involve the use an assessment centre. These offer a combination of different methods for determining social and personal competencies. For this purpose, several trained observers monitor and assess a group of candidates in different situations (group work, individual exercises, interview, discussions and the like) over a longer period of time (1–2 days), in accordance with established rules.

Due to the structured multi-observations of a large number of characteristics carried out by several observers and the 'authenticity' of the situations for the candidates (who may prepare themselves theoretically but cannot control all of their reactions over such a long period of time), the assessment centre is generally considered to have a high degree of predictive validity.

Given the globalisation of the economy and the world of work, some striking differences between countries in the use of the various testing methods are noticeable. While intelligence and personality tests are the exception in Germany and Austria, for example, they are widely used in France, Spain, Italy and the United Kingdom. Similarly, while graphological reports are rarely used in German companies, they are widespread in countries with romance languages.

7.3.5   Phase 5: The Decision

As previously mentioned, the exchange between the interviewers following the interviews is of fundamental importance for the decision-making process. Based on observed behaviour and the candidates' replies, the interview panel must draw conclusions about the applicant's future behaviour within the team, with their supervisor, and in specific situations. The future line manager, in particular, has an important task here: Should they choose the candidate with the most technical expertise, even though they may have doubts about their people skills or how they would fit into the team? Or should they prefer the other candidate whose pleasant demeanour gave them a good impression right from the start, but whose CV shows multiple job changes in the past and raises questions about their commitment?

The HR professional with all their experience can be a valuable sparring partner here, who can help by bringing a certain objectivity to the interviewers' preferences and conclusions. As a general rule, the aim should not be to select the **best** candidate, but the **right** one, in other words the **most suitable** one. If, ultimately, a decision has to be made between two candidates, however, and the HR person and the line manager cannot reach an agreement, my suggestion is to leave the decision to the line manager—also to protect the HR staff from future blame. After all, it is the line manager who must work with the new employee and supervise him or her.

A decision in favour of one candidate equals a rejection of the other candidates. While the line manager can start to make plans for the new employee, it is up to HR staff to give those that have lost out a friendly rejection, without making them feel too rejected. Ideally, the rejected applicants should receive an explanation of why they did not go any further (this should be done in accordance with the respective equal opportunities regulations to avoid potential discrimination claims). Whatever the case, care should be taken to word the rejection in a way that shows respect and appreciation—despite the standard phrases that are unavoidable. Perhaps some of the candidates may even go on the company's database to be contacted again at the next opportunity. The professional and courteous handling of this phase makes an important contribution to the overall employer branding of the organisation.

7.3.6   Practical Tips and the Division of Responsibilities in Staff Selection

Figure 7.3 shows the distribution of the most important responsibilities between HR and line managers in the selection process. To conclude, some practical suggestions are listed below.

Practical Tips
1. Be as specific as possible in your job description and person specification and prepare yourself well for the interviews—the candidates will do the same.
2. Do not choose the best, but the most suitable candidate.

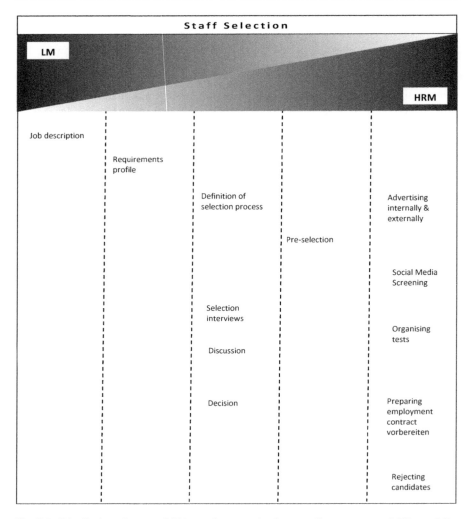

Fig. 7.3 Distribution of responsibilities and cooperation between line manager and HR specialist in the selection of staff

3. The future supervisor must be present at the interviews. A division of roles is advisable: While the line manager may choose their questions freely and on any topic they deem relevant, the HR professional should pay attention to the formal structure.
4. Conduct at least two interviews with the potential recruits.
5. In the event of doubt, the decision should be left to the future line manager.

6. make sure that the rejections are worded respectfully and that the candidates receive an appropriate explanation for their rejection—but only after the future employee has signed the contract.

7.4   Staff Hiring

The final part of the recruitment process is the hiring of the new employee. For the HR department, this means drawing up an employment contract and planning the new recruit's integration into the company, while the person responsible for the department prepares the integration into the existing team and arranges the details of their induction period. The main steps of this last phase of the recruitment process are briefly described below.

7.4.1   The Formal Employment Contract

The employment relationship between employer and employee is usually formalised through a written contract. According to the principle of contractual freedom, the two parties are generally not bound by any conditions in terms of either form or content. Nevertheless, most employment contracts contain the following points as a standard:

- Start date, probationary period (if applicable), notice periods, working hours, holiday regulations
- Type of activity, pay-scale category/salary band, reporting lines, authorisations
- Fixed and performance-related remuneration, additional benefits, regulation of expenses
- Non-compete clauses, confidentiality clauses, ownership rights

Irrespective of the wording in the employment contract, the employment relationship entails various rights and obligations for both parties involved, which are usually regulated by law.

The employees' **primary obligation** is the personal performance of their job; the employers' duty is the obligation to pay remuneration. There are also a number of **secondary obligations** on both sides. In the case of the employees these are, for example, the duty of compliance, the duty of confidentiality or the duty of loyal and incorruptible service, while the employers have a duty of care towards their employees and must ensure their safety at work.

In most companies, when you sign an employment contract, you also sign a job description. In addition to the job title and a purpose statement, all the tasks associated with the job should be listed. Furthermore, the reporting lines and communications to other positions are usually mentioned. The more precisely the job description is worded, the easier it is to establish the (formal) relationship between the employee and the supervisor.

7.4.2   The Psychological Employment Contract

Despite the general freedom regarding the wording of employment agreements, many aspects of the future employment relationship are not recorded in writing. Certain aspects such as loyalty or the quality of work may be mentioned, and mutual expectations may be raised, but they are not formalised. Other needs, fears and expectations may be thought, feared or hoped for, but they are neither expressed verbally nor written down. This is how the contracting parties enter a mutually signed legal contract and a unilaterally conceived, so-called psychological contract'.

Psychological contracts are generally defined as the mutual expectations (Table 7.1) and obligations between an employer and an employee that exist beyond the legal employment contract. They are about the psychological relationship that is based on the social exchange between the parties (cf., e.g., Rousseau 2001). The subjectively perceived promises and obligations in this social trade-off can refer to verbal agreements or can even be implied from the behaviour of the contracting parties.

Core questions of the psychological contract on the part of the employee are, for example (cf. Troger 2019): How secure is my job? How much effort—such as overtime—is expected of me? How will this help me to develop my portfolio of competencies?

On the employer's side, the basis of the psychological contract is generally formed by all of the employee's statements and their behaviour. Initially, the line manager will discuss the resulting expectations with their colleague from HR, however, the judgment on whether or not the contract is being fulfilled will be made by the manager alone during the course of their working relationship with the employee.

7.4.2.1 Failure as a Foregone Conclusion?

The problem with this type of agreement is its non-binding nature and the different interpretations on both sides. It does not matter what the promising party means, it matters what the recipient of the promise understands and believes. This is why transparency of communication in the context of the psychological contract is vital. It is up to the line manager, above all, to address the expectations on both sides and to clarify possible misunderstandings at the outset.

Table 7.1 Typical expectations that arise from a working relationship

Employer expectations	Employee expectations
• Performance and goal-orientation • Loyalty • Flexibility • Alignment with the company's goals • Personal responsibility • Commitment to excellence • Acceptance of directions	• Opportunity for self-actualization • Training and development • Recognition • Employment security • Work autonomy • Participation in the decision-making process

Often, further challenges in fulfilling the psychological contract arise from the time lag between the performance and the reward. Especially when it comes to the popular promise of a pay rise 'in line with adequate performance progress' in the 'foreseeable future', a breach of contract is almost a foregone conclusion. Here too, clarity of communication is essential right from the start. The HR expert has the task, for one, to address these issues explicitly and clearly at the beginning of the employment relationship and, in addition, to draw the attention of the line manager to possible conflicts that may arise due to changing interests and expectations in the course of the employment relationship.

In my role as HR consultant, it is a constant challenge to align the world view and expectations of business owners with the interests and expectations of young potential employees. Rarely do thoughts and intentions deviate more from what is said than at such encounters: The entrepreneur speaks enthusiastically about their business and assumes that the candidate has no choice but to join them. The candidates in turn also present themselves from their best side, express their interest and demonstrate their desirability for the entrepreneur. In reality, however, they feel more and more sceptical if their counterpart only emphasises the positive aspects of their company.

For this reason, I always recommend that the more difficult aspects of the job should be addressed as well. This will feel authentic and it enhances credibility.

7.4.3   Employee Onboarding

With the induction programme in hand, the HR manager welcomes the new hire on his or her first day of work and accompanies them to their department, where they are received by the department leader or rather the line manager they report to. This is more or less what the operational start to a new job should look like. The 'onboarding', that is, the integration of a new employee into a company, can be divided into three phases, whereby the division of responsibilities between HR and line managers is clearly defined:

On the first day of work, the new employee receives detailed information about the company, such as products, structures and processes, from the HR representative. An official tour of the premises or an induction seminar are also common practice. In larger companies, there are usually manuals for new employees. The colleague from HR is generally also responsible for introducing the 'newcomer' to the other departments. The workstation, computer, telephone and, if applicable, the company car should all be ready for use so that the employee can see that they were expected. This phase of the integration process also involves HR administration, which is responsible for creating a staff file, notifying the relevant social security and taxation agencies, clarifying the employee's family situation with them, explaining the remuneration arrangements and for ensuring that the new employee feels overall reassured and confident.

A second phase of this onboarding process focuses on the **social integration** in the new company or rather in the team in which the employee will be working. Apart from the line manager, who may not have time for this task, a mentor would be an option here. Many companies use mentors in their departments to help new employees feel at ease in their new surroundings from the very first day. Mentors will help the newcomers to understand the informal rules and alert them to any 'no go's' and possible faux pas. Should the start of the job also involve a change of location for the new employee, the mentor will also help with the integration into local community?

Last but not least, the **operative or technical induction** into the new position is the third key aspect of the overall integration process. The line manager plays a central role in this. He or she must plan the first weeks and months in detail with the new employee, constantly check and, if necessary, adjust the pace and routine and, above all, provide continuous feedback.

The line manager will also let HR know how the induction phase is progressing—this should not be done on the last day of the probationary period, as is often the case in practice, but well before it.

Many working relationships fail within the first year—the reason can often be found in an inadequate induction or integration into the team during the first weeks. Role ambiguities and a lack of feedback from supervisors can result in disappointed expectations and frustration. The induction of a new employee involves a considerable extra effort for the line manager, and this must be taken into account in staff planning. It is not advisable to rush the operational induction with a view of using the new employee to their full potential as early as possible, as this may result in the loss of the employee altogether.

7.4.4 Practical Tips and the Division of Responsibilities in Staff Hiring

The most important steps or responsibilities for the HR professionals and the new employee's department leader (or line manager) are shown in Fig. 7.4. Some practical tips are also provided to make the process easier.

Practical Tips
1. If this has not been done already, now at the latest, you should provide the new employee with a job description that is as precise as possible—as the formal basis for the relationship between employee and line manager.
2. As the employee's line manager, make sure you clearly address the mutual expectations beyond the contract and the job description. In most cases, working relationships fail because the psychological contract of employment is not fulfilled.
3. Ensure that the interdepartmental induction programme is adhered to, even if the employee is urgently needed in your department.
4. Ensure the social integration of the new employee—ideally with the help of a mentor.

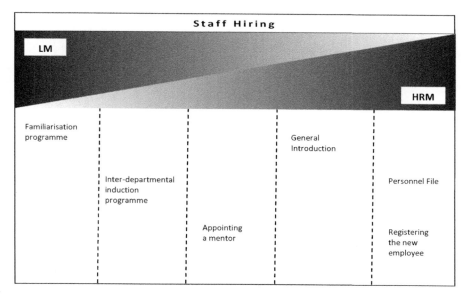

Fig. 7.4 Distribution of responsibilities and cooperation between line manager and HR professional in the hiring of a new employee

References

Buchheim, C. (2017). Wir brauchen Verkäufer. *Harvard Business Manager, 2*, 98–101.

Reichmann, L. (2017). Analyse und Bewertung der Incentivierung von Mitarbeiterempfehlungen. Thesis for obtaining a Master of Arts at the Universities of Amberg-Weiden, Deggendorf and Regensburg. Supervisor: Prof. Dr. Bernt Mayer

Rousseau, D. (2001). Schema, promise and mutuality: The building blocks of the psychological contract. *Journal of Occupational and Organizational Psychology, 74*(4), 511–541.

Rowold, J. (2015). *Human resource management* (2nd ed.). Heidelberg: Springer Gabler.

Technische Universität München, Talentry. (2017). *Social recruiting study*. Retrieved October 20, 2020, from https://www.talentry.com/wp-content/uploads/2017/07/SRS_Webversion_TUM.pdf.

Troger, H. (2018). *Die führungskraft als personalmanager*. Wiesbaden: Springer Gabler.

Troger, H. (2019). Management von interessen und erwartungen. In H. Troger (Ed.), *7 Erfolgsfaktoren für wirksames Personalmanagement* (2nd ed., pp. 131–146). Wiesbaden: Springer Gabler.

The Staff Management Process

8

Staff Deployment—Feedback—Remuneration—Diversity
Management—Individual Work-Life Balance—Employee
Well-Being

The management of staff can be understood as the direct, personal and individual relationship between an employee and their supervisor in daily business (cf. Troger 2019a, b). It is a key process in two respects: firstly, because of its significance for the company, and secondly, because of its inseparable position between the recruitment process and the professional development process—in relation to the employee's tenure with the company. The staff management process begins with the first day of work and covers all of the stages and aspects of the cooperation between the employee and their supervisor. This also underlines the fact that the role of the latter in this process clearly outweighs that of HR professionals. The HR specialist mainly has to communicate the right methods and develop and provide the appropriate management tools. And while I do not wish to detract from the importance of these tools, it should be highlighted that here, too, the line manager, who has to apply the tools he is given, is becoming more and more important: Individualised leadership also implies that the tools that are used will be less generic and, therefore, it means that they must be adapted to the individual and the context.

The following sections highlight the key moments in the management process and describe the roles of both supervisor and HR representative.

8.1 Staff Deployment

8.1.1 Delivery on a Promise

The recruitment and the selection process, which were described in the previous chapter, could also be seen as the basis of a broad mutual promise—whereby the risk of disappointment should not be underestimated (cf. Troger 2018). The stakes are high: for the company, every new employment relationship is a partial victory in the increasingly difficult battle for employees as a limited resource. For the candidate, a successful appointment means taking the right step on his or her chosen *career path*.

© The Author(s), under exclusive license to Springer Nature Switzerland AG 2021
H. Troger, *Human Resource Management in a Post COVID-19 World*, Future of Business and Finance, https://doi.org/10.1007/978-3-030-67470-0_8

At times it may happen, therefore, that people agree to take on too big a task or that claims relating to the *employer value proposition* turn out to be a little overblown.

The delivery on this promise, or rather the actual implementation of its contents, depends on the correct deployment of the employee and the development of the promised potentials. Staff deployment can be defined as the optimal allocation of employees to the various positions within the company. In this context, the term 'optimal' refers to the match between the requirements of the job and the skills and qualities of the jobholder. While the requirements of the job are expressed in the *job description*, which should be as detailed as possible, the skills and qualities of the jobholder can at least be guessed from the employee's *skills profile*. The job description is also used to compile a *person specification* which contains all the technical and personal requirements and attributes that are considered important for the position. The person specification can, therefore, be seen as a link between the position and the personal characteristics and forms the basis for the person-related aspect of the staff deployment process.

This subtask of staff deployment should be performed jointly by the head of the department, or the line manager, and the HR representative: The supervisor as an expert on the tasks and the challenges of the position, and the HR representative as an expert on the respective 'category' of employees. Working together, they can assess the individual suitability of each person for the job.

Once the individual suitability of the jobholder has been established, the main task of staff deployment is to answer some basic questions about the content, place and time of the work that is to be done.

8.1.2   *What* Work Should Be Done?

On the one hand, the totality of the tasks of the organisation or the department is used as the basis for defining the content of the job. On the other hand, there is the entirety of the workforce with all its skills and characteristics. These two totalities must be combined in the most optimal way possible with the help of job descriptions and skill profiles. Against this backdrop, the aim of the task design, for the head of the department, is the efficient creation of job roles. The key criterion here is the degree of *specialisation*. As we know from the theoretical understanding of business economics, a high degree of specialisation in a particular task leads to higher productivity and quality as a result of the learning effect. It also means that the induction period will be shorter and the allocation of tasks generally easier.

This rationale has resulted in three standard solutions for expanding the range of tasks:

Job rotation involves the exchange of workstations at a certain frequency, which may be hourly or half-yearly, depending on the task. The aim is to avoid repetitiveness and to aid the acquisition of multiple qualifications and skills.

Job enlargement describes a horizontal expansion of tasks, that is, the addition of qualitatively comparable tasks. The objective is the same as above.

Job enrichment is the most challenging way of increasing task variety, since it involves the addition of qualitatively more demanding activities and also increases the responsibilities and decision-making powers of the employee.

The primary responsibility for determining the diversity of tasks lies, of course, with the line manager. He or she knows the various roles in the department inside out and has probably developed a sense of which employees—including new ones—can best take on which tasks.

Job enrichment also constitutes an important staff development measure and is, therefore, one of the core tasks of HR. In addition, these types of measures also fulfil an important organisational development function in terms of flexibility and independence—this too is often the task of the HR professional in a company.

8.1.2.1 Impacts Due to Automation and Digitisation

In view of the widespread fear of job losses as a result of digitisation, any form of job expansion can have a significant impact: The wider the field of activity of the employees, the easier it is for them to grow into new fields of work. In addition to the employability of the employee, this also has an effect on the overall development of the organisation. It can effectively counteract the continuing shortage of skilled workers and make it easier to fill positions internally when employees leave the company.

8.1.3   *Where* Should Work Be Done?

'Ideally from home', will be the most likely response today, given the impact of the coronavirus pandemic (autumn 2020). The right workplace has long been a favourite topic in the field of ergonomics. What physiological, psychological and sociological criteria need to be considered to ensure that work can be carried out as smoothly as possible and to minimise the negative effects of one-sided physical and psychological stress? The answers were sought primarily in the fields of natural sciences and medicine.

Today, the optimal design of the workplace focuses mainly on three areas: ergonomics, virtualisation, control.

8.1.3.1 Ergonomics

Various laws on occupational safety require an employee's workplace to be designed according to ergonomic principles in order to ease work processes and prevent fatigue or even ill health. This includes limiting noise levels as well as the user-friendly design of handles and pedals. In the office, the aim is to create a computer workstation that is tailored to the individual employee and is as low-fatigue and stress-free as possible. Even the employee's personal reach zone should be organised accordingly. The strain on the individual employee results from his or her specific characteristics, abilities and needs, and, therefore, varies from employee to employee. It is the supervisor's responsibility to address these issues and to find individual solutions.

8.1.3.2 Virtualisation

Due to developments in information and communication technology, the role of location in the provision of a service is increasingly less significant. Especially when the activities do not require direct interaction with customers, suppliers or colleagues, various forms of remote working are available. Depending on the requirements, the work can take place in the home of the employee, in a mobile office or even directly at the customer's premises. It is quite clear that as a result of this, the management of staff takes on a new dimension for the supervisor.

8.1.3.3 Control

Since the coronavirus pandemic in particular, many employers have realised that employees can be as productive outside the company. Others, however, fear the loss of control and are looking for technical solutions to monitor the performance and behaviour of their staff. While in the past there were private investigators and surprise monitoring calls, today digital surveillance programmes of every kind, or the so-called monitoring tools, are rapidly gaining ground. The usefulness of such monitoring is questionable. In my view, it is more likely to jeopardise the mutual trust between employees and their line managers. In most circumstances, after all, the aim is to achieve a result within a certain time and not to work as long as possible.

8.1.4 *When* Should Work Be Done?

In the past, working hours were negotiated at trade union level—for individuals they were usually part of an unalterable general framework. Today, however, the issue of working time is at the centre of discussions and negotiations—and not only because of the pandemic. There are three reasons for this: Firstly, the ability to deploy employees flexibly has become a critical success factor for companies. Secondly, free time has become a highly sought-after commodity for people. And thirdly, employees' ideas and needs in terms of the allocation of working time and free time (*work-life balance*) are highly individual.

Given that the discussion in the 'World of work 4.0' and also in this book which repeatedly highlights the need for individualisation, the organisation of employee's working hours offers a tried and tested means of accomplishing this. There are three basic approaches to the individualisation of working time:

8.1.4.1 According to Volume (Chronometric)

The length and the amount of working hours is agreed in the employment contract, on the basis of legal provisions and collective agreements. Possible deviations from the standard working hours can be linked to operational necessities (short-time work or part-time work) or to the needs of the employees (part-time work, sabbatical).

8.1.4.2 According to Distribution (Chronological)

This division of working time is also regulated by law and refers to the distribution of working hours over a 24-h period, including regulated breaks. The spectrum ranges from the classic 9-5 model to some more extreme variations of working time arrangements on both sides. In the case of on-call work, for example, a working quota is agreed with the employee, which the company can fall back on whenever necessary. By contrast, with flexitime agreements or variable working hours, the scope of discretion lies with the employee.

8.1.4.3 According to Trust

This extremely flexible form of working time organisation is now being used in particular in the creative sector. There are neither chronometric nor chronological restrictions, it is simply a matter of completing the task or achieving the goal.

It is within the parameters of these three dimensions that the working time is agreed between employer and employee. The employer's aim is to optimise the deployment of labour in line with operational requirements and to react as flexibly as possible to market fluctuations. On the employee side, it is a matter of reconciling professional fulfilment, family obligations, leisure interests and economic goals. Given the current situation on the labour market, this poses the following challenge for entrepreneurs and their HR managers: Which working time model can we offer to meet the needs of customers and employees alike and still be economically successful?

Despite the comprehensive and detailed working time regulations of most countries, on the one hand, and the different interests and needs of workers on the other, there is usually sufficient scope for win-win agreements between companies and employees. However, the following three rules must be observed (cf. Troger 2018):

1. **Do not seek a one size fits all solution,** but look for a solution that could theoretically apply to everyone, i.e., one that is perceived as fair.
2. **Do not look for a solution by—general—administrative means, but by—individual—creative means.** In the past, the HR administrator was entrusted with the task of finding generally applicable and simple administrative solutions. Nowadays, the satisfaction of employees and managers—and, therefore, effective employer branding—can only be achieved through the creative implementation of tailor-made individual solutions.
3. **The line manager (not the HR manager) must find the solution with the employee.** They must identify individual needs or enquire about and respond to them. For example, if a flexitime model is to be agreed, only the line manager can know the employee's individual needs at any given time and reconcile them with the department's objectives. The (necessary) review of a trust-based working time solution can also only be carried out by the line manager and not by the HR manager. The latter will suggest possible solutions to the problems and make the tools available. They are also responsible for any cross-company reviews of the

effectiveness of the solutions and, if necessary, for suggesting the appropriate corrections.

8.1.5 Smart Working (from Home)

Smart working and **remote working** have been around long before Covid-19. Smart working describes an approach to work organisation that aims to increase efficiency and improve outcomes through a combination of flexibility, autonomy and cooperation, taking into account a range of different methods and, in particular, the use of technologies, but also the conditions under which people work and the satisfaction they obtain through their work. Remote working can play an important role in this. Even before the pandemic, some kinds of work were already carried out remotely and not within the office workplace, depending on the right circumstances. The technical requirements had to be met and, if necessary, solutions to legal issues could usually be found quickly and unbureaucratically—after all, it was mostly a question of exceptions to the rule. This technology-driven trend was suddenly accelerated rapidly due to the pandemic, and has now become a generally valid and accepted work concept. However, remote working has now almost exclusively turned into working from home, and what used to be an occasional request from a handful of employees has become either a recommended guideline or binding rule—for as many as possible.

As a result of the sudden and forceful impact of the coronavirus crisis on companies, many of them quickly and unbureaucratically implemented homeworking arrangements, whereby the main focus was on technical equipment and data protection rather than on the relevant employment legislation. Since then, the respective employer associations in various countries have been working with trade unions to develop a legal framework for remote working from home. From the provision of the necessary work equipment, to the recording of working hours and breaks, the procedures in case of sickness or work-related accidents—it is important to provide a new binding framework for the employment relationship between employees and the company.

In addition, working from home adds a new dimension to the relationship between employees and their managers. Leadership at a distance becomes a challenge. On the one hand, the freedom associated with homeworking makes it more difficult for managers to coordinate and control the work that is being done, and on the other hand, it also reduces employees' opportunities for consultation and discussion. In any case, working from home requires an unprecedented level of mutual trust from everyone involved.

8.1.5.1 Some Advantages of Working from Home
(a) No travel to and from work saves time and money.
(b) Autonomous time management means that employees are empowered and more motivated.
(c) Potential for undisturbed work and increased productivity (under the right conditions).

(d) Sickness absences could be reduced: a temporary indisposition or a slight cold should not deter many workers from carrying out certain activities.
(e) Satisfied employees mean less staff turnover.
(f) It becomes possible to employ highly skilled professionals beyond commuting distances.
(g) Less work journeys and business trips save resources.

8.1.5.2 The Right Conditions for Effective Working from Home

(a) Technical requirements: security measures that ensure data protection; a speedy, reliable and secure connection to the Internet; the relevant software.
(b) Fixed rules and deadlines for coordinating and reviewing work content and results.
(c) Competences of supervisors: technical competence, clarity of purpose (a helicopter view), empathy, relationship management, conflict resolution, confidence-building.
(d) Competences of employees: independence, receptivity to learning, openness, flexibility, self-management, results-orientation.
(e) A company culture based on trust and the promotion of employee autonomy.

8.1.5.3 IT and HRM

From these points it is clear that it is no longer simply the IT department that is important for the efficient implementation of remote working from home, but increasingly also the HR department. The challenge is twofold: on the one hand, it is a matter of imparting the skills described above and, on the other, it is about actively shaping the necessary company culture. The increased anonymity of virtual collaboration makes communication, relationship management and the promotion of team spirit more difficult. Virtual teams will have a less direct experience of the company culture and may show lower levels of engagement and commitment than those that are able to gather around the coffee machine on a daily basis.

In principle, the successful implementation of government-imposed remote working from home due to Covid-19 does not depend so much on the nature of the task, but rather on the attitude and competence of the actors. And the latter is very much linked to effective (HR) management.

8.1.6   Practical Tips and the Division of Responsibilities in Staff Deployment

So, *how* should work be done in future? In a nutshell: smart and agile. **Agility**, still a buzzword in the working world, stands for unlimited flexibility in terms of place, time, duration and depth of work. Staff deployment as an effective management tool is about more than the purely quantitative allocation of employees to positions and the ergonomically correct configuration of workstations. In the interplay between the

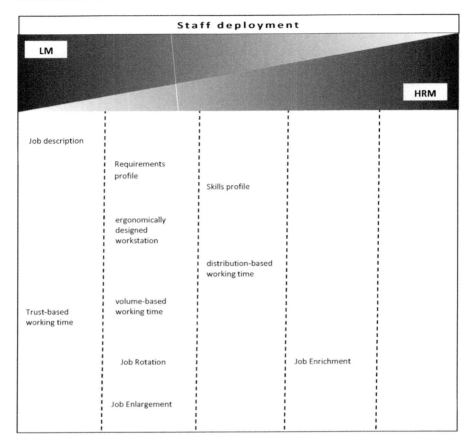

Fig. 8.1 Allocation of tasks and cooperation between line manager and HR professional in the correct deployment of staff

flexibility of the company and employee individualisation lies a great creative potential for effective staff management—tapping this potential lies in the hands of every leader within the company. Figure 8.1 illustrates what the cooperation with the HR department should look like in this context. A number of important aspects are highlighted again in the *practical tips*.

Practical Tips
1. Remember that the deployment of the employee is about the company's delivery on the promise made in the interviews.
2. A high degree of task specialisation can generally benefit the line manager, but is not in the overall interest of the organisation and certainly not in the interest of the employee, who usually seeks variety.

3. Efficient working, irrespective of the place of work, is in no small measure also a question of effective staff management.
4. The organisation of working time has become a hot topic: From the point of view of companies, flexible staff deployment is necessary; from the point of view of employees, it is about the desire to maximise their free time through a high degree of individualisation.
5. When designing the working time models, try finding a solution by individual means—instead of the general administrative route. Creating tailor-made individual solutions will generate employee and supervisor satisfaction.
6. The more agile and flexible the working relationship is, the more important it is to build mutual trust between employees and superiors.

8.2 Feedback Process

When I ask managers about the way they give feedback to their employees, I usually get one of the following two answers:

1. 'Of course I give feedback. It is what the appraisal review is for once a year. That is where we talk about everything in detail together'.
2. 'I talk to my employees every day. I do not need a special bureaucratic procedure for this at the end of the year'.

The feedback process, in general, and performance appraisal, in particular, play a crucial role in the working relationship between employee and organisation. While staff deployment can be seen as the company's first effort to deliver on its side of a promise, it is now a matter of mutually reviewing the implementation of this contract on both sides.

With regard to the company, the feedback process is the basis for systematic performance controlling, which in turn provides the foundation for planning and improving business results. Furthermore, the structured interaction between managers and employees provides a reliable distribution indicator for potential bonuses and basic information for the design of staff development programmes.

From the employee's point of view, feedback means first and foremost transparency of their performance. This typically increases their motivation and organisational identification. The following section describes various possibilities for systematic feedback and review. As far as the distribution of responsibilities between managers and HR is concerned, it is of course primarily up to the line manager to deal with this.

8.2.1 *Day-to-Day* Feedback

Regular dialogue with employees is perhaps the single most important task of a manager. Informal personal feedback given to employees about their ongoing performance is the basis of any leadership relationship. In addition to the completion of an assignment, the focus is also on the behaviour of employees towards co-workers, customers, managers and, last but not least, towards their respective supervisor.

Due to the excessive bureaucracy of the annual appraisal interview and its rigid and inflexible format, especially in the eyes of the younger generations, many large companies today are opting for structured feedback in real time. *General Electric*, for example, decided as early as 2014 to use a real-time peer feedback system named *performance development* (PD@GE), instead of conducting annual performance reviews. The approach is based on a series of ongoing conversations, the so-called touchpoints, which focus on the relationship between the employee and their supervisor. These touchpoints can be formal or informal, face-to-face or virtual, long or short, and they can be initiated by either side. Other large companies such as Microsoft, Accenture or Adobe have also been using structured day-to-day feedback procedures for some time, and they include different perspectives on their workers' performance (such as that of suppliers, clients and other stakeholders) as well. The diverse and easily implemented digital procedures today also make it possible for smaller companies to use this 'smart and agile' feedback method.

8.2.2   360-Grad-Feedback

The 360-degree feedback analysis is particularly popular when it comes to the evaluation of managers. It involves the manager's (or the employee's) own assessment of their behaviour. At the same time, he or she receives feedback—usually anonymous and in written form—from co-workers, customers, suppliers and, of course, from their direct supervisor. 360-degree feedback is, therefore, a multi-perspective assessment of competencies and behaviour and it is particularly well-suited for organisations with a management culture characterised by low-hierarchy power structures. What makes the dialogue between the person to be assessed and their superior particularly interesting is an open comparison of self- and third-party assessments—especially if there are major differences. This feedback process, which requires a relatively large amount of work and time, is mainly used in the selection and development of managers because it allows their leadership behaviour to be assessed from a variety of different angles.

For the company-wide use of this tool, the line manager must be the main contact person, but it is equally important that the HR professional plays a coordinating role. The latter is not only the expert for various feedback methods, but also has a control and monitoring function for the overall process. This is particularly useful here because 360-degree feedback is a relatively complex instrument of organisational and management development.

8.2.3 Annual Staff Appraisals

The annual appraisal interview is still the best-known HR management tool and exists—in whatever form—in almost every organisation. It is *the* classic instrument for the institutional communication between supervisor and employee. The aim of the interview is to assess performance and behaviour in the period under review and to look ahead to the next one. Usually, the employee's development perspective and relevant training measures are also addressed. In addition, there should be room for a discussion of the general work situation and the well-being of the employee.

After receiving detailed feedback, the employee is normally also given the opportunity to express his or her (dis)satisfaction with the manager's leadership. Although most experts advise against this, in practice the question of salary is often discussed or negotiated in the annual review meeting. Despite its widespread use, the annual staff appraisal is often viewed critically by line managers (who generally experience the same procedure with their supervisor) and employees alike.

Two aspects, in particular, are criticised, although in theory they should be mutually exclusive: on the one hand, the recurring uniformity of form and content and, on the other, poor preparation, especially on the part of the supervisor. Although it can be temptingly convenient and time saving to 'copy and paste', it also encourages you to accept the previous year's content uncritically and to conduct unprepared, superficial conversations. It is not without reason that preparation—both on the part of the supervisor and the employee—is generally seen as the most important aspect of the interview. And in this context, the involvement of HR experts can make all the difference. They are not only responsible for preparing and adapting the standardised forms, but also for monitoring and coordinating the entire process. They are, therefore, in charge of ensuring that the appraisal interview retains its purpose as a structured feedback and management tool over time and that it does not degenerate into nothing more than a yearly token action.

8.2.4 Management by Objectives

Although the annual appraisal interview is also used to discuss goals and the two are, therefore, similar, Management by Objectives (MBO) is more than just a feedback tool. It is a complex management approach in which goals are set for a defined period of time between supervisor and employee, and the degree to which these goals are achieved is then assessed. Depending on the degree of participation within the company, the objectives are either predefined or agreed together.

The great advantage of MBO is that all individual goals are aligned with the central company objectives in a downward cascading structure. In addition, the periodic reviews also involve structured feedback between employees and their line managers.

Here, too, the HR department has the methodological expertise and is responsible for coordinating the entire process—taking into account the needs of both top management and individual employees.

8.2.5 Performance Evaluation

Although, within the context of staff management, the feedback process should aim for much more, in the end it is mainly about one thing: the evaluation of the employee (in more ways than simply in relation to performance). The four methods of feedback described above all include an evaluation, among other aspects. To conclude this section on feedback, this evaluation process—as the core element of the entire spectrum of feedback options—will, therefore, be discussed again in its own right.

The supervisor's performance evaluation uses quantitative and qualitative criteria to make the employee's work results transparent and provides information about his or her potential for the future. Assessment can be conducted on three levels (cf. Troger 2018): While **outcome-based performance** reviews are about tangible, measurable results, assessment at the **behavioural level** focuses on the way performance is delivered. In contrast, an evaluation of the **level of potential** focuses on the employee's aptitude—in terms of behaviour and results—and in relation to future tasks.

In practical terms, performance evaluations form the basis for a number of decisions at both *individual* and *organisational* level. Applied to the individual, they provide indispensable input for remuneration decisions, promotions and individual development measures. They deliver the same information—in aggregated form—for an overall organisational perspective. Not least because of their documentation function, performance reviews can, therefore, be regarded as a tool for maintaining the system.

This makes a professional implementation of the process—the central task of HR professionals—seems all the more important. The definition of the evaluation criteria, in particular, must be very carefully considered with respect to their relevance. This refers to the contents that are to be evaluated, their strategic importance, their clarity and comparability and their suitability for use across companies. Furthermore, despite a high degree of objectivity in the criteria, the person who evaluates the performance is also an important factor in any performance review. Typical errors of judgement can of course distort the outcome here, if they occur. Once again, this is where HR has the task of providing appropriate support and, where necessary, training.

8.2.6 Practical Tips and the Division of Responsibilities in the Feedback Process

In summary, performance evaluations and the feedback process as a whole are part of the line manager's core responsibilities. The HR professional, on the other hand, is required to provide the appropriate methods and tools and, as an expert on procedure, is (co-)responsible for their professional execution. The practical tips and the diagram about the division of responsibilities (Fig. 8.2) aim to illustrate this process.

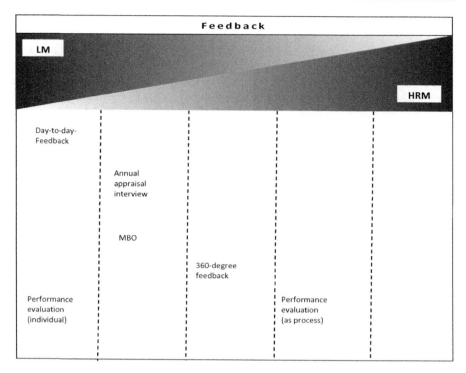

Fig. 8.2 Distribution of responsibilities and cooperation between line manager and HR professional in the feedback process

Practical Tips
1. While staff deployment is an attempt to deliver on a promise, the feedback process is a mutual review of how that promise is being met.
2. For the company, the feedback process forms the basis for systematic performance monitoring; for the employee, it means transparency of his or her performance and, therefore, it increases the employee's organisational identification in relation to their role, their supervisor and the company as a whole.
3. Instead of overly bureaucratic and rigid annual appraisal interviews, consider regular structured feedback in real time.
4. The most important aspect of the structured appraisal interview is a task- and person-oriented preparation on both sides.
5. Openly address the leadership relationship. The appraisal interview is about the quality of this relationship as a basis for cooperation and the joint achievement of objectives.

8.3   Remuneration

Only half of all permanently employed British people believe that they are fairly paid, according to a new report by the CIPD—the professional body for HR and people development (2019). The other 50% believe that they are underpaid. For its 'Reward Management report in 2019', CIPID surveyed 2031 employees and 465 HR professionals in British companies. Only 34% of respondents believed that everyone in their organisation was fairly paid. And only one in five employees believed that their CEO's pay was at least 'roughly right'.

The situation in Germany is even worse: More than three-quarters of workers there feel that they are not fairly paid. This was in any case the finding of an online survey launched by the public service broadcasting corporation ARD in 2016, following their broadcast of a debate on 'fair pay'.

In other words, most leaders and HR managers are surrounded by employees who perceive their pay as unfair and too low.

What is a fair reward, though? The question of distributional equity has been debated by countless thinkers for centuries, but none of them has come up with a convincing solution, except for the realisation that there is no justice. The role of equity in remuneration is a central and complex issue with moral, psychological and legal dimensions, and it can also be considered from a company policy perspective. In the following, an attempt will be made to get closer to the core of the matter.

8.3.1   Principles of Remuneration

In general, remuneration (or compensation, both terms are used synonymously here) refers to the sum of all material rewards received by the employee from the company in return for the work performed by the employee. But how is this work performance to be measured and how is it to be valuated? Should the focus be on input-oriented factors such as educational attainment, skills or working hours? Or is it only about measurable output, i.e., the results of work? Below, the classic indicators for determining the extent of remuneration are briefly outlined, followed by some new aspects (cf. Troger 2018).

8.3.1.1 Indicators

Working Time
Working time is still a key component of pay, especially for jobs related to manufacturing. The reason for this is arguably that it is relatively easy to measure. Qualitative aspects and effective deployment during working hours are not taken into account—if necessary, the shift supervisor will monitor the correct execution of work.

Broadly speaking, the importance of time as a factor in determining compensation declines with an increase in the level of qualification and hierarchy. With the exception of a night porter or similar occupations, there are fewer and fewer examples of pure time-based compensation in our western working world. Interestingly, HR managers like to remind people during job interviews that remuneration will not be time-based or—even less so—depend on attendance (and this was already the case before we entered the age of a digitalised *working world 4.0*). Nevertheless, the complaints about a general increase in working time, due to overtime, constant availability and working from home, are increasing.

Jobholder Qualifications
Another traditional method of determining remuneration is to take into account the skills and qualifications of the jobholder. These can be theoretical (school or higher education) and/or practical (work experience). In view of the general education and training situation in today's knowledge society, two things can be observed: Apart from the fact that a school leaving certificate is generally of limited value for determining competencies, the ever shorter half-life of knowledge means that theory-based qualifications can very quickly become obsolete and thus be worthless for the company. As a counter-argument, however, it can be stated that additional (theory-based) qualifications are very easy to acquire today because of the almost unlimited access to knowledge.

Requirements of the Job
The mental, physical and psychological demands that a job entails for the jobholder also represent an important factor in determining remuneration. This includes theoretical knowledge, operational tasks, decision-making and management responsibilities. Here too, the often complex job descriptions and ranges of responsibilities can make it difficult for many companies to define the particular requirements in detail and clearly. The consequence is vague definitions and overlaps.

Services Rendered
While the three valuation criteria mentioned so far are somewhat flawed by their sole reliance on input, this cannot be said of piecework wages or sales commissions. Neither the amount of working time, nor the qualification of the employee or the requirements of the position are the determining factors for payment, but only the service rendered. Despite the undeniable motivational effect of performance-related rewards, in practice there are virtually no purely performance-related remuneration systems. The main problem with such a system lies with the definition of performance indicators for more complex activities (e.g., management tasks).

8.3.1.2 Individualisation of Pay
As a consequence of this assessment logic, total remuneration is generally made up of a *fixed* and a *variable component*, both of which can include non-monetary elements. There are also the additional social benefits provided for by law. As a rule, the absolute amount of remuneration—defined by job categories—is usually decided by top management or the HR department on the basis of the applicable

contracts and regulations. The decision-making power of the supervisor is usually limited to a right of proposal regarding the amount of monetary remuneration.

The discussion is, therefore, primarily about the amount, or the variable part (*how much* compensation?), but hardly about the actual content (*what* compensation?). Given the individualisation of society (cf. Chap. 1) and the highly divergent interests and expectations of employees (cf. Chap. 3), I believe this is a major omission and a missed opportunity for HR marketing.

Cafeteria-style plans, which have been known in America for a long time and allow each employee to choose his or her individual compensation elements within a certain framework, seem to be very slow to establish themselves in our latitudes. Rigid legislation and inflexible collective agreements are often cited as justification for this, but it seems more likely that the reason is to avoid the administrative burden involved. Particularly with regard to the possibility of successful employer branding, the challenge will be to develop remuneration models in cooperation with line managers, which are tailored to the respective situation of the employees. To this end, it is necessary, firstly, to broaden the thinking behind the remuneration approach and, secondly, to return it to its origins.

8.3.2   The Goal: Work Delivered by Satisfied Employees

Beyond all philosophical, legal and social fundamental matters, the question of the right compensation is linked to an essential goal: ensuring that the work gets done by satisfied employees. In effect, they are actually two goals that are closely interlinked—and possibly even mutually dependent.

While the first part of this goal needs no further elaboration, the satisfaction of the employees deserves some clarification. When is an employee satisfied with his or her remuneration? The seemingly obvious linear relationship—the higher the remuneration, the higher the satisfaction—does not go far enough; the effect of remuneration on work output and job satisfaction is much more complex, as countless studies on this topic have shown. Firstly, job satisfaction is also influenced by factors other than those purely related to remuneration (intangible assets, job autonomy, supervisor, etc.) and secondly, their effect depends on many situational factors, such as the age and life situation of the person concerned, their personal values, the situation of the company and, last but not least, the absolute and relative level of remuneration.

In addition to the situational aspect, the motivational effect of the remuneration is, therefore, highly individual. Generalisation is only valid on one count: the dissatisfaction when the actual remuneration differs from the expected one. In the formation of these expectations, the assessment of one's own work performance is one factor. Even more important, however, is knowing how other people with comparable tasks are remunerated. The satisfaction with the remuneration for one's own work input is, therefore, primarily a question of the individually perceived **fairness** in the overall distribution of material remuneration by the company.

8.3.3 Remuneration Strategy

In addition to the aspects discussed above, the compensation of employees belongs to the core activities of HR management also from a cost perspective. In line with their overall strategic relevance, some strategic guidelines on remuneration policy should be established at company level. These guidelines should be regularly reviewed and, if necessary, adapted to the changing economic environment.

8.3.3.1 Remuneration Policy

What is the company's overall remuneration policy? What types of compensation are used? How are the fixed and variable components allocated? Especially with regard to an individualised approach to remuneration, such general guidelines are extremely helpful in order to avoid arbitrariness and a lack of transparency in daily business.

The remuneration policy should also make it clear whether the focus is placed on the strength of teams or on individual performance. The fundamental question to what extent employees should have a stake in the business results will also be evident from the policy. Finally, it should state whether, and to what extent, compensation should be used as a motivating factor. At a strategic level, the remuneration policy should also be discussed, where relevant, in view of its potential use in (external HR) marketing or as a retention factor for existing employees.

Finally, the relationship between the compensation of top managers and that of ordinary employees, which is a hot topic particularly in difficult economic times, should be mentioned: In order to avoid false rumours and speculation, a transparent remuneration policy is also advisable.

8.3.3.2 The Market

Of course, such deliberations on remuneration strategy cannot be done in isolation from market developments. In order to consider one's own strategy in relation to competitors on the labour market, the HR manager or the business owners consult colleagues from the industry or call upon the services of well-known providers of compensation studies. After clarifying the first issue of the market's remuneration strategy, the next step is to draw the appropriate conclusions: Would I, as a matter of principle, be willing to pay more because I believe that this would increase my chances in the battle for the best candidates? Or do I recognise my other strengths as an employer and deliberately pay less?

Of course, the available candidates and the special requirements of the company will also influence the decision: For a highly sought-after skills profile with strategic importance for my company, I will be prepared to pay more than the market.

8.3.3.3 Remuneration as a 'Shaping Tool' for HR Management

The last strategic aspect, which was touched on in the policy section, is this: the role of remuneration policy in the design of HR management strategies. This applies both to the more centralised influence of the HR manager and to the decision-making autonomy of individual managers. It can refer to the quantitative dimension, where either the line manager can decide directly on performance bonuses at individual or team level—or the decision can be taken by the HR manager after receiving the appropriate input from the line manager.

But in terms of qualitative aspects, too, there is an extensive range of benefits in kind, rights of use and services that reflect the diversity of employee interests. In addition to the direct motivational effect of these forms of remuneration, they generally also strengthen the employees' loyalty and commitment.

In view of the individual needs of employees and the diversity of material incentives, it would be advisable to grant line managers a wider margin of discretion for qualitative decisions. Firstly, they know the wishes and needs of their employees best, and secondly, they are also best placed to reconcile these with the requirements of their department (this includes, for example, treating time off as a non-monetary form of remuneration).

8.3.4   Personalisation Through Flexible Cafeteria-Style Plans

Cafeteria-style plans represent the best option for ensuring that the remuneration is tailored to the individual needs of the employees. This system, which came to Europe from the United States in the 1980s, allows each employee to determine part of their own remuneration, within a given budget, by choosing from a wide range of offers—similar to the way a menu is put together in a cafeteria. The range of offers can contain widely differing monetary and non-monetary material remuneration elements (cf. Table 8.1) and, therefore, it can take into account the diversity of interests and needs of the various employees at different stages of their lives.

This is gaining particular relevance in view of the increasing heterogeneity of the workforce and should, therefore, become an integral part of diversity management in every company. In this context, the flexibility of the cafeteria-style plans and their continuous adaptation to the changing needs of the employees are vital.

For the companies, or rather the HR department, this personalisation of the remuneration policy means a considerable amount of information processing and administrative work, but in return the value of the company incentives and thus employee satisfaction can be maximised in a cost-neutral way. From an external HR marketing perspective, the following applies: The more varied and extensive the cafeteria plan options, the more attractive the company's image as a future employer.

Managers, or rather line managers, are particularly important when it comes to the initial design of these flexible remuneration plans: They know the interests of their employees and know best which benefits belong in the 'menu plan' and which products will have the greatest motivating effect.

After that, the supervisor's task is mainly to advise the employee in putting together the ideal compensation package. It is also the line manager's task to provide the HR department with feedback about the employees' reaction and to make further suggestions based on the knowledge gained from the appraisal interviews.

Table 8.1 Possible benefits offered by a cafeteria-style plan

Monetary compensation	Working time	Benefits in kind	Insurance	Further Education and training	Consultations
Salary	Additional leave	Company car	Life Insurance	Language study trip	Career advice
Share of profits	Sabbatical	Company-provided living accommodation	Supplementary health insurance	Conference attendance	Tax and legal advice
Employer Loans	Early retirement	Shopping vouchers	Home contents insurance	MBA	Financial investment advice
Company shares	Reduced working hours	Travel vouchers	Legal expenses insurance	Specialisation	Real Estate Consulting
Investments	Educational leave	Parking space	Home Care Insurance	Research opportunities	Counselling

8.3.5   Practical Tips and the Division of Responsibilities in Remuneration

In summary, personalised employee compensation will become increasingly significant for companies in the future. This turns the once purely administrative task of payroll accounting into an innovative strategic HR marketing instrument and the supervisor into a kind of 'compensation manager'. Differentiation in the distribution of compensation will be based even more closely on the performance of the individual, and to this end the task of managing people will play a decisive role—a role that will itself be difficult to valuate and remunerate. Figure 8.3 shows the cooperation between line managers and HR with regard to employee remuneration, followed by some *practical tips*.

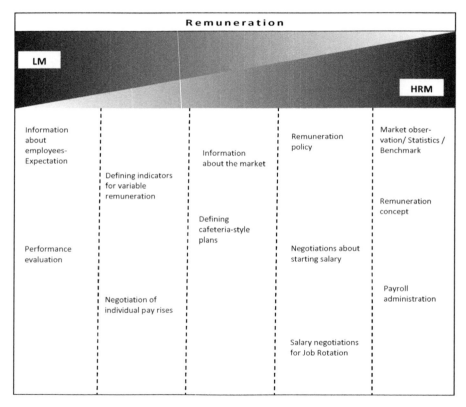

Fig. 8.3 Division of responsibilities and cooperation between line manager and HR professional in employee remuneration

Practical Tips

1. Neither the number of hours worked, nor the employee's qualifications, nor the requirements of the job should be the decisive factor in determining remuneration, but first and foremost the service rendered.
2. In view of the demand for individualisation and the diversity of interests among the workforce, do not limit yourself to the question of *how much* you should offer, but use this opportunity to create a motivational effect by increasing the diversity of *what you offer* in terms of (variable) remuneration.
3. Do not be put off by the administrative effort of a cafeteria-style system (this effort mainly applies to the initial implementation) but take advantage of the various designing possibilities it offers—also in terms of your diversity management.
4. The aim of the right remuneration is to ensure that the work gets done—by satisfied employees.
5. Avoid speculation among employees by using a transparent remuneration system—and accept the fact that 50% of your employees will still feel that they are not fairly paid.

8.4   Leadership Challenges of the Coronavirus Crisis

The previous sections of this chapter have outlined some key aspects of the staff management process. However, the everyday actions of a manager are also shaped by developments and phenomena in society as a whole and their effects on the world of work. This is especially true for such unexpected and far-reaching events as the Covid-19 pandemic. This chapter, therefore, concludes with a brief discussion of three particular leadership challenges in connection with this crisis.

8.4.1   Diversity Management

Diversity in the workforce refers to a wide range of individuals of different age, gender, religion, ethnic, cultural or social background, and other attributes. In particular, the age composition and cultural diversity of a workforce require new ways of thinking and approaches on the part of HR managers and supervisors.

8.4.1.1 A Diverse Mixture of Ages

As already mentioned on several occasions (cf. Chap. 1), we are currently experiencing slow, but unstoppable and dramatic demographic change across Europe. Due to rising life expectancy and falling birth rates, the world of work is facing an ageing workforce. Recruiters and staff developers, however, continue to focus primarily on young people, while the 55–60-year-olds almost tend to be seen as the 'reserve option'.

Most companies are not yet sufficiently prepared for this demographic change and its impact on the world of work. For one thing, everyday life in business as well as in society is characterised by a battle for distribution between the generations in terms of influence, money and security (cf. Troger 2019a, b). At the same time, the potential of older workers is still far too little recognised by companies. Despite various studies which clearly show the opposite, prejudices and stereotypes still prevail regarding the capabilities of older workers. As a result, far too little use is made of the opportunities for intergenerational learning and fruitful cooperation between age groups.

It is not my intention to insist on the merits of older workers for the sake of doing so, or to offer a strategy for getting out of this predicament, but instead I want to highlight the absolute necessity to make the best out of a (supposedly) bad situation. Sugar-coating and accepting the unavoidable is not an option and amounts to wasting a real opportunity. What is needed, by contrast, is the deliberate shaping of the teams and practices within the organisation according to demographic criteria. **Demography-oriented staff management** is, therefore, the only effective response to the challenges posed by demographic change. Such an approach is based on a respectful and non-judgmental company culture and the balanced distribution of resources. It begins with the job interview and has both the personal development of the employees and the social cohesion within the organisation as its objective.

The managing of mixed-age teams may pose particular challenges for leaders: Different patterns of perception, evaluation and behaviour can lead to negative attitudes, low spirits and group conflicts. This is where the support of psychologists and HR professionals, and particularly the sensitive handling of conflicts are needed.

8.4.1.2 Diverse Mix of Cultures

In the globalised working world, leaders are often faced with the challenge of managing people whose cultural backgrounds differ from their own. This bridging of intercultural gaps must be taken into account in the management process and in the use of the right tools. Stock-Homburg (2013) believes there are two dimensions to *intercultural leadership competence*: the *ability to lead* and the *will to lead* from an intercultural perspective. The ability to lead from an intercultural perspective is reflected in the professional and cultural knowledge and experience of a manager. This includes, for example, language skills and previous experience of working in a multicultural environment. The will to lead from an intercultural perspective, on the other hand, describes the manager's motivation to take the specific cultural characteristics of the people led into consideration during the leadership process. These two dimensions of *will* and *ability* should both be equally highly developed in order to lead intercultural teams successfully.

The advantages of multicultural teams—creativity and flexibility being the most frequently mentioned—are often matched by specific challenges: Misunderstandings, fears and mistrust hamper cooperation and create conflicts. For this reason, when leading intercultural teams, their composition or the selection of suitable employees is the first critical step. In addition to professional competence, the candidate's sensitivity for cultural differences and their communication skills are particularly important. This global mindset is a necessary prerequisite if cultural diversity is to develop its undoubted potential within the organisation.

Especially in an international context, it must be added that distances of time and place often have to be overcome as well, which can make cooperation within teams and their management much more difficult.

8.4.1.3 Diversity Management as Success Factor

Diversity management can be described as wide-ranging and socially relevant organisational approach based on intercultural awareness and inclusivity. Effective *diversity management* does not aim to eliminate differences within the workforce in terms of age, gender, education, ethnic origin, religious values, etc., but instead seeks to use these differences consciously within the company as strategic success factors. *Diversity management* as a strategic leadership approach is primarily relevant in the context of the company's recruitment policy and its participation in the labour market.

Thereafter, the efficient deployment of multi-generational and multicultural teams and their management in day-to-day business is based on a culture of awareness and respect for the diversity of society in all its dimensions.

8.4.2   Individual Work-Life Balance

This now almost hackneyed buzzword simply refers to a balanced relationship between professional and private life—rarely can such a complex matter be expressed in such a simple descriptive term. The complexity lies, on the one hand, in the variety of what can be packed into the 'two lives' and, on the other hand, in the multitude of individual combinations. Each person, or rather each employee, has his or her own personal 'two lives' and, of course, also his or her personal interpretation of what is 'balanced'. Therein lies the great challenge for supervisors: to meet the employees' individual expectations of a healthy work-life balance—while at the same time meeting company goals. In the following brief discussion, three aspects of this balance will be addressed.

8.4.2.1 Family and Free Time

According to periodically conducted studies by the Organisation for Economic Cooperation and Development (OECD), people throughout Europe are finding it increasingly difficult to balance work and private life. The *Better Life Index* (OECD 2020) examines how well people are able to reconcile work and family life, based on various questions. It shows that many people continue to worry about work-related problems after working hours. It also reveals that fewer and fewer people are able to switch off completely or take up leisure activities after work. Many respondents also felt that their heavy workload was affecting their families and friends.

We now know from numerous investigations that there are clear generational differences in attitudes towards work-life balance: While baby boomers have always seen this as a balancing act between professional and private needs, Gen X has consistently viewed it as two separate domains that had to be attended to alternately. Gen Y, on the other hand, no longer insists on a strict separation between work and private life, but rather focuses on maximising the latter. For the still young members of Gen Z, 'project life' consists of many little work projects and even more recreational projects. They have little interest in continuity and long-term work plans, but instead prioritise freedom and being able to personalise how they approach their work schedule.

Whether managers like it or not: If you want to have 'satisfied' employees—from whatever cohort—in your team, you will increasingly have to meet your employees' expectations about their life outside work.

8.4.2.2 Health

Health plays a vital role in the aforementioned OECD *Better Life Index*, which has the number of working hours in each country as its core criterion. When people talk about health at work, they are increasingly referring to mental health. This is reflected in a steady rise in absenteeism due to mental overload, while burnout has become a 'routine diagnosis' and will soon be the most common reason for early retirement. In all studies on this subject, employees complain about excessive workloads. This is an issue that should be of significant concern to both HR managers and line managers. The former should ensure the establishment of a company-wide approach to health care management, while the latter should focus on both the physical and mental health of their employees through mindful leadership in day-to-day business.

According to the OECD study, particular significance is attached to the regular use of buffer time—a lack of this seems to be one of the main explanations for conflicts and emotional exhaustion. And here, too, it is not only the HR administration's responsibility to develop the necessary system for taking breaks, but also the line manager's task to respond to the individual stress levels of his or her employees by organising their workload accordingly. The demands of work are not, of course, equally stressful for each individual employee, especially as our resources for coping with stress change according to age and phase of life.

The sensitive handling of different, life-stage-dependent needs is a critical prerequisite for a healthy work-life balance and depends heavily on the company and management culture that the employees experience within the organisation. In addition, various areas of a health-oriented HR policy can be identified which are the responsibility of both company-wide HR management and line managers: Active health promotion and company support services, information and awareness raising initiatives, staff development programmes for stress management and resilience are designed to provide employees with the necessary tools and resources for stress management and reduction.

8.4.2.3 Flexibility of Work

When the first workers demanded a better work-life balance from employers, they were mainly thinking of one thing: flexible working hours. While the entrepreneurial aim of making staff deployment more flexible is to make it more performance-oriented, at employee level it means a personalisation of both the working hours and the place of work. With the now-familiar approaches of working time flexibilisation and working from home, many of the employees' wishes for greater autonomy in terms of time and place can be satisfied. By adapting their working times to the individual needs of their employees, companies can improve the balance between work and private life.

The same applies to the choice of work location. Remote working is becoming increasingly easy due to advances in communication and information technologies. From simple flexitime arrangements with working time accounts to trust-based working time, from limited-term part-time models to sabbaticals lasting several months; from mobile to virtual workplaces: The most straightforward and practical way to individualise the employment relationship is to remove the boundaries of time and place and to make the deployment of staff more flexible. This means that employees themselves are increasingly playing a role in shaping their own working conditions.

This adds a whole new dimension to the management of staff deployment: it is now a matter of finding an efficient synergy between increasing flexibility—from the company's point of view—and individualisation in terms of time, place and content. The challenges for both actors involved in the effective management of staff are growing: HR professionals will have to come up with meaningful management and control mechanisms that are not tied to time and place and support staff in their ability to manage their own work. And line managers will increasingly have to rely on modern communication technologies to focus on goal-oriented leadership at a distance.

8.4.2.4 The Work-Life Blending Deception?

Two year ago, HR pioneer Christian Scholz, sadly deceased prematurely, published a highly critical review of the currently much vaunted concepts of flexibility, agility and mobility, and even went as far as calling the new buzzword *work-life blending* a sham (see Scholz 2018). He claimed that it could not be used to speak of a balance between professional and private life because the very concept of work-life-blending proposed to replace such a balance with the boundless interweaving of work and free time—comparable to the way cancerous growths take over a living organism.

Instead, Scholz proposed a '*work-life separation*', i.e., the clearest possible separation of the two domains. Much in the way that the youngest generation, Gen Z—which Scholz researched and described extensively—demonstrates: work from 9 to 5, and let your *real life* begin after that.

Given that a balance between work and private life is evidently no longer possible, because the latter is increasingly being taken over by the former (and the whole thing is presented to us as a harmonious union—i.e., blending), we should resist this form of exploitation and demand a clear separation. The reason for this 'exploitation'—foreign as well as self-exploitation—is seen in the technologisation or digitalisation of the working world—a fact recognised by both supporters and opponents of these trends. They have the effect that everyone is now accessible at all times and everywhere, and this generates the corresponding expectations (mostly with employers).

In addition, Scholz considers the aspect of **flexibilisation** to be particularly relevant to this ambivalence and he points to the *workplace 4.0*. There, flexibility stands only for the positive and the desirable: autonomous time management, time for family, friends and recreational activities—all of which is now reconcilable with the demands of the job. The difference between **flexibility as a possibility** for employees to personalise their working conditions, and **flexibility as a request** from employers only becomes clear on closer inspection. Are we talking about freedom of choice or round-the-clock employee availability? Although the one does not necessarily exclude the other, Scholz considers *work-life blending* to be the equivalent of 'deceptive packaging'—especially if an employer succeeds in presenting it as a major concession to their employees.

Whether it is ultimately a blessing or a curse will depend on the individual case and probably also on the market power of employers and employees. Either way, one thing seems certain: work-life blending means the dismantling of temporal and spatial boundaries. This makes clear agreements on mutual expectations all the more important, ideally through contractual arrangements. In order to maintain long-term performance, it is important to find the right balance between professional commitment and a fulfilled private life. For this reason, the *individual and sustainable work-life balance* of employees is an essential prerequisite for the 'delivery of work by satisfied employees'.

8.4.3 Employee Well-Being as Part of Company Culture

After the initial shock on the labour market due to the economic downturn caused by the pandemic and the inevitable introduction of short-time working, some isolated employers quietly rejoiced: 'It's about time that workers became more modest again and stopped making all these demands; at last we have the upper hand again and don't always have to back down in the negotiations'.

The vast majority of entrepreneurs, however, reacted differently: they saw the justified (existential) concerns of their employees and took responsibility. Together they looked for the best possible socially responsible solutions—and in most cases this was associated with considerable additional costs for the companies. It would have been easier to limit themselves to the statutory provisions for employee welfare and otherwise refer to government support measures.

From many conversations with entrepreneurs and HR managers in recent months, I have mainly observed three basic attitudes:

The first attitude, as already mentioned, was only taken by very few entrepreneurs. They saw the pandemic as a welcome opportunity to openly adopt a sharper stance towards their employees, to cut concessions and benefits and to get rid of (supposedly) low performers and unwelcome employees. Only the absolute minimum of the legally prescribed welfare measures was observed.

The second category of entrepreneurs behaved similarly, but tried to hide this behind legal requirements. They showed (outward) solidarity with their employees, complained about the situation and berated the inadequacy of government assistance.

8.4.3.1 Feel-Good Manager

The third category of entrepreneurs (and HR managers) considered not only the business perspective but also the interests of their employees and searched for ways to cushion the impact. In addition to the statutory provisions, these entrepreneurs worked with employee representatives and HR managers to find ways of supporting the employees and their families. In many instances, a Feel-good Manager was appointed to organise activities and measures that would make both cooperation within the company and the life of the employees outside the workplace easier. The measures ranged from financial support and advance payments to regular virtual meetings with workers at home (with or without a fixed agenda) and even the organisation of social activities after work, such as virtual games or 'Zoom parties'.

It remains to be seen whether a sense of social responsibility, philanthropy or economic calculation was behind these actions: The fact is that they were effective and brought social recognition to these companies—and motivated employees. These entrepreneurs practically wanted to do everything they could to create the best conditions for remote working with flexible working hours in order to keep the business going. On the other hand, they also wanted to keep the motivation of their employees as high as possible.

In these days of extreme crisis and existential anxiety, it is more important than ever to restore the self-motivation of employees. To achieve this, you have to listen to them, take their concerns seriously and work together to find solutions. No matter how independent your employees normally are: now they need an open ear and the support of their leaders.

8.4.3.2 Navigating the Coronavirus Crisis with the Right Company Culture

Every company wants motivated, loyal and flexible employees. In times of crisis, these three qualities are particularly valuable and form the basis for successfully overcoming the crisis. The companies that fall into the third category described above clearly have a good company culture. The right company culture is particularly helpful in conflict situations or times of crisis, such as the one caused by Covid-19, because it provides support and guidance.

The vast majority of entrepreneurs and HR experts today are eager to share their conviction that a company's most important resource is its people. A testament to this way of thinking was provided by a certain Italian entrepreneur who, at the beginning of the lockdown in March 2020, asked all his employees what they needed to be able to work well from home. Employees were given a document in which they could tick off whether they needed, for example, a comfortable desk chair, a larger screen or a houseplant. The item was delivered to them within 3 days. I cannot imagine a better example of employee appreciation and effective internal employer branding.

8.4.3.3 The Role of Leaders

Your company culture always depends on the people who shape it or have shaped it in the past. Leaders are the biggest factor in developing the culture of a company. Their role model effect is the most important part of this. In virtual meetings, as required by the pandemic, they should not limit their efforts to following procedures and task coordination, but create a positive atmosphere, encourage experimentation and new approaches, and of course share their own success stories. The bond between leaders and their staff is especially important in difficult moments—unfortunately, these days they can only rely on virtual communication to maintain it.

Today more than ever, the personal relationship—the person behind the employee—should be the focus of attention, and right now this personal relationship is made difficult by geographical distance. This situation requires a special kind of creativity and good will to keep morale high. For this reason, telephone calls and online meetings should always start with a focus on people's private lives and well-being, and only then move on to business matters. Efficiency-oriented managers first had to adjust to this personal touch. However, as we know from various surveys (see also Deloitte 2020 and StepStone 2020—Chap. 4), motivated employees reward it with flexibility, dedication and loyalty.

8.4.4   Practical Tips and the Division of Responsibilities in Dealing with Leadership Challenges

To conclude this section on special leadership challenges (regardless of the pandemic), some practical tips are given and the division of responsibilities between line managers and HR professionals is graphically illustrated (Fig. 8.4).

Practical Tips
Diversity Management

1. Start your demography-oriented HR management with a department-specific age structure analysis.
2. Avoid standardisation and 'generational pigeonholing' when it comes to understanding the attributes, skills and needs of your employees.
3. Focus on 50+ high performers. Make use of their experience, loyalty and people skills.
4. Diversity management as a success factor: Ensure a culture of non-judgemental cooperation and inclusivity within your company, regardless of age, gender, religion or ethnic background.

Individual Work-Life Balance

1. Do not dismiss 'work-life balance' as a hackneyed buzzword: It refers to a very complex and fragile balancing act—one that varies from person to person.

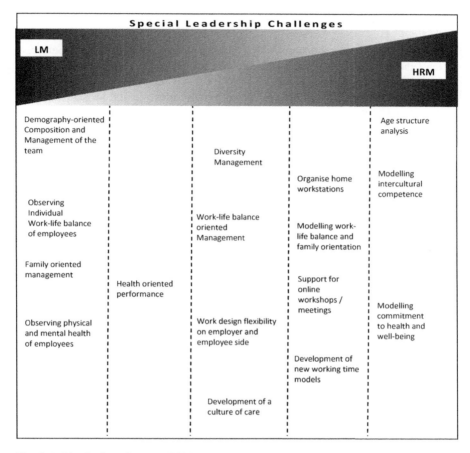

Fig. 8.4 Distribution of responsibilities and cooperation between line manager and HR professional in dealing with leadership challenges

2. Do not underestimate the negative sides of 'blended working': many people find it increasingly difficult to switch off, and this can sooner or later lead to burnout.

3. Mindful leadership in day-to-day business focuses on both the physical and mental health of employees. Regular breaks are of particular importance.

4. By making work assignments more flexible, the company can achieve greater performance orientation; employees associate this primarily with the personalisation of working time and place of work.

5. Give serious thought to how you can effectively support your employees in coping with high workloads and building up individual resilience.

Employee Well-Being

1. Even if you have never taken the idea of a feel-good manager seriously before, at least during the coronavirus pandemic you should either consider hiring one or assign an employee to this role.
2. Assess your company culture and be especially attentive and sensitive to your employees' concerns and complaints during this time of crisis.
3. Take special care of your direct reports during this time. Show interest in their personal and family lives.
4. Be flexible in adapting your employee welfare measures to the needs of your employees (and the company). Think about your employees' private lives as well.
5. Remember that the best companies are those that have satisfied, engaged and efficient employees.

References

Deloitte. (2020). *The Deloitte Global Millennial Survey 2020.*

DiversityQ. (2019). *Keeping staff in the dark about salaries feeds the perception of unfair pay, new research from the CIPD finds.* Retrieved October 24, 2020, from https://diversityq.com/49-of-staff-believe-they-are-a-victim-of-unfair-pay-says-cipd-report-1508354/.

OECD. (2020). Retrieved October 24, 2020, from http://www.oecdbetterlifeindex.org/topics/work-life-balance/.

Scholz, C. (2018). *Mogelpackung work-life-blending.* Weinheim: Wiley.

StepStone. (2020). *Attraktiver arbeitgeber? Was sich Mitarbeiter von Unternehmen wünschen—und was sie bekommen.* Retrieved September 21, 2020, from https://www.stepstone.de/Ueber-StepStone/press/attraktiver-arbeitgeber/.

Stock-Homburg, R. (2013). *Personalmanagement. Theorien, Konzepte, Instrumente* (3rd ed.). Wiesbaden: Springer Gabler.

Troger, H. (2018). *Die Führungskraft als Personalmanager.* Wiesbaden: Springer Gabler.

Troger, H. (2019a). Ein neuer generationenvertrag. In H. Troger (Ed.), *7 Erfolgsfaktoren für wirksames Personalmanagement* (2nd ed., pp. 117–134). Wiesbaden: Springer Gabler.

Troger, H. (2019b). Stärkenorientierter Personaleinsatz. In H. Troger (Ed.), *7 Erfolgsfaktoren für wirksames Personalmanagement* (2nd ed., pp. 81–95). Wiesbaden: Springer Gabler.

The Staff Development Process

The Renaissance of Staff Development—Life-Phase Oriented Staff Development—Staff Development from an Organisational Perspective

Staff development is not only the declared favourite activity of most HR professionals, but one of the few all-round positive terms in HR, indeed in the entire field of business administration. It involves the promotion and professional development of employees and thus aims to secure the future of the organisation. In the wake of far-reaching changes in the world of work, this topic has gained widespread attention, and within HR management it is the ultimate key task. In the following chapter, some central aspects of staff development will be examined, with particular reference to the distribution of roles between supervisors and HR experts. We start with a conceptual overview.

9.1 The Revival of Staff Development

Staff development is once again allowed to address people's well-being. This has not always been the case, as a brief look at the history of this still young branch of HR management shows. The term was first introduced in the United States in the 1960s as 'Human Resource Development' and encompassed company specific training and skills development activities. In the German-speaking countries, the first staff development departments were established in the 1970s. They, too, were mainly concerned with the development and organisation of vocational training programmes for employees. The educational gaps they aimed to fill were mostly of a technical nature. In the 1990s, even liberal economists began to talk openly about employees as the most important and scarce resource within a company, and suggested that companies should invest in their staff accordingly. Previously, such a view was the preserve of the so-called behaviourists or might have been expressed in the soapbox oratory of some exemplary entrepreneurs. Now, the focus of staff development, in terms of content, was on soft skills. The skills and qualities that fall into the category of social competence were regarded as particularly desirable. And since the work of Daniel Goleman (1996), even intelligence has been taught in staff development programmes—albeit emotional intelligence.

H. Troger, *Human Resource Management in a Post COVID-19 World*, Future of Business and Finance, https://doi.org/10.1007/978-3-030-67470-0_9

At the beginning of the new millennium and in the context of rationalisation efforts, people began to question the operational benefits of what had become an extremely diverse range of development activities. Employees had to take leave of absence for management seminars and sign contracts that provided for (partial) repayment of attendance fees in the event of premature termination of employment. The success of a course was no longer measured on the basis of ad hoc questionnaires at the end of the event, but was instead assessed by the supervisor in the course of the annual appraisal interview. Dedicated training control systems began to be established. A scattergun approach, which allowed practically every employee to participate in all the activities offered, gave way to a conscious and selective decision-making process between supervisors, HR managers and interested employees on the basis of individual career plans and competence portfolios.

At the same time, the efforts of staff developers in recent years have acquired an additional purpose, namely a marketing one. Personal development plans and training opportunities are important factors for *job attractiveness* (as described in Chap. 7) and a correspondingly effective *employer value proposition*, especially with regard to competition for the best young talent in the labour market. In the context of *new work* and the *world of work 4.0*, the budgets of staff developers are again as high as they were at their best. You might even say that the war chest has been filled to the brim in order to increase the odds in the battle for good employees.

9.1.1   How Did We Get Here?

I believe there are essentially seven reasons for this Revival of staff development as the ultimate HRM discipline (cf. Troger 2019):

(a) The Key Human Factor in a VUCA World
Growing complexity with increasing uncertainty in the markets, shrinking product life cycles, global competition and new forms of borderless collaboration mean that the importance of human labour in the value-added process is becoming ever more important despite increasing automation—or precisely because of it. Employees must constantly adapt and learn anew in order to maintain competitiveness in this complex and constantly changing world of work.

(b) Half-Life of Knowledge
The half-life of knowledge continues to shorten, while the demand for knowledge is increasing due to complexity and diversity. While it is still said to be an average of 10 years in terms of academic knowledge, the half-life of technological knowledge is sometimes less than 2 years. Fortunately, the technical possibilities and the offers available today make it easier for everyone to acquire knowledge. Nevertheless, in addition to the motivation of employees, on the company's side there is also a need to develop suitable concepts and programmes for the broad-based transfer of competencies.

(c) Maintaining Long-Term Performance

Employees will remain with companies for longer and longer, even if their health or efficiency may decline somewhat over time. A development programme for a newly recruited 55-year-old engineer is a good example of what will be normal and expected. The aim must be to maintain performance in general, and for older employees in particular, for as long as possible through suitable development measures.

(d) Diversity Within the Teams

The other two consequences of the demographic development, the lack of young professionals and the heterogeneity of the workforce, require a continuous transfer of knowledge and skills between employees of different ages, backgrounds and educations. The different educational approaches and learning techniques will be discussed in more detail later on.

(e) Staff Development as an Employer Value Proposition

Especially in the competition for the best people it is important to generate a strong and tangible competitive factor from all these aspects. The overstretched reference to 'individual development concepts' in job advertisements should manifest itself in corresponding development programmes and further training activities. It is not without reason that this aspect is at the top of the list of criteria for most job seekers when selecting a job.

(f) People Seek Diversity

Today, most companies rarely deny their employees the opportunity for further training, partly because the desire for variety and change is part of human nature, and partly because the shift in the balance of power in their favour means that employees are in a much better position to make such requests. At most, companies may expect the employee to make a contribution by taking leave. Incidentally, we are already talking about cases of 'bore-out' due to underchallenge.

(g) Helplessness of Employers

It should come as no surprise that the above-mentioned situation has led to a certain kind of helplessness among employers. The demand for good employees is growing, the supply is decreasing. As a result, staff developers get the green light, budgets are increased, and employers hope for a miracle.

9.1.1.1 The Coronavirus Effects

A crisis as far-reaching as the one caused by the novel coronavirus also has a direct impact on the budgets of staff developers. It is well known that most entrepreneurs begin to save money by cutting back on training. In addition to the financial effects, the coronavirus also brought about a change in methodology: For months now, the majority of training events have been held online. It is no exaggeration to call this a digital revolution in the education and training sector. While webinars were once considered an exception and were used mostly for dry administrative topics, today they are used even for online communication training. Due to the many advantages (including cost benefits) of this method and the expected further technical developments, it is likely that this type of training will remain popular even after the pandemic.

9.1.2 Employability

In addition to the benefits that the employee's supervisor and, as the case may be, the entrepreneur as the employer expect from staff development, the career and the *employability* of the employee are also at stake. The different types of education and training initiatives and various ways to impart learning are all intended to promote a range of competences that will ensure the long-term employability of the employee. The concept of employability goes beyond the individual company level and refers to the entire labour market of a country. The EU's 2000 Lisbon Strategy defines it as a person's continuing ability to gain and maintain employment in current and future labour markets.[1] Irrespective of any initiatives by public institutions in this regard, at the company level there are three factors that are relevant to promoting employability (cf. Richenhagen 2012):

(a) The **framework for the working conditions**, such as working time and work organisation: these can have a positive effect on the employability of employees or may even inhibit it.
(b) The specific **development of increased responsibilities** or, in a broader sense, their underlying training and qualifications. This refers not only to the employees' knowledge and skills, but also to their motivation.
(c) The **promotion of health** in the workplace as a basic prerequisite for the development of individual potential.

9.1.2.1 The Work Ability House Model
The **Work Ability Index**, developed in Finland in the 1980s, uses statistically determined values to describe the extent to which employees are able to do their jobs successfully (cf. Ilmarinen and Tuomi 2004). According to this index, there are two components that determine an employee's ability to work: firstly, his or her individual resources—i.e. physical, mental and social skills—and secondly, the work itself: content, work organisation, social environment, guidance. The Work Ability Index (WAI) consists of seven dimensions relating to the individually perceived work ability and is determined by means of a questionnaire. The result of the survey is a WAI value that lies between 7 ('no work ability') and 49 ('maximum work ability').

---

[1] A person may well be able to work, but not be employable. For example, consider a fully trained border police officer in the Schengen area after the borders were removed.

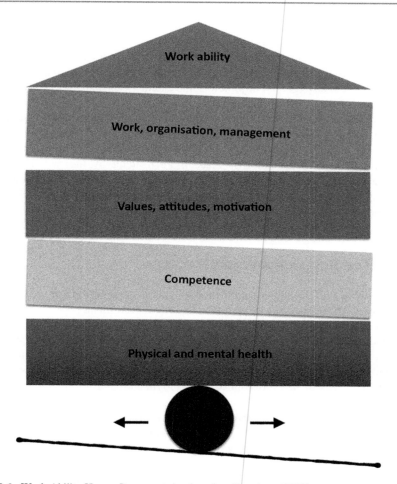

Fig. 9.1 Work Ability House. Representation based on Ilmarinen (2002)

The founder of the WAI, Juhani Ilmarinen (2002), suggests that the WAI value can be increased through the following four fields of action, which ideally should be worked on simultaneously. He presents them visually as the four floors of his *Work Ability House* (see Fig. 9.1).

The foundation of the house is formed by **physical and mental health**. Building on this is the **competence of the employee**. This is expressed in knowledge and skills. While these first two floors represent the employee's abilities and potential, the third floor describes the **individual attitudes and values** that motivate the employee. The last floor deals with **the work itself**, its contents, work organisation and, above all, the aspect of management.

All these aspects form the adjusting screws to promote and maintain the **work ability**, which is the roof of the house. In addition, external forces also have an effect on the stability and quality of the house: family, friends, society and the political environment. As in a real house, the individual factors build on each other and are in a functional relationship to each other. Disturbances on one level also affect the other floors and cause instability in the house. In recent years, the first three floors of the building seem to have got out of joint to some extent—especially if one is to believe the managers based on the fourth floor.

The question is: How do you build a house that is as robust and beautiful as possible, and how do you renovate it again and again when the passage of time and the regular 'climatic changes' can at times seriously affect the walls and the individual floors? The situation is made more difficult by the fact that houses today have to last even longer, and at the same time, environmental influences are becoming stronger and stronger. The answer to this question lies in an individually designed concept of staff development activities.

9.2 The Staff Development Process

Stock-Homburg (2013) defines staff development as the imparting of qualifications and training that enhance the current and future performance of managers and employees (education), as well as measures that support their professional development and advancement (promotion). This expanded understanding of staff development is, therefore, not only aimed at providing training and further education, but also at enhancing the career of employees. The focus is no longer just on responding to employees' lack of skills for immediate deployment, but also on targeted support and career planning.

This shift from a more reactive to a proactive approach is linked to the great importance that has been attached to staff development for the last 20 years. From the purely practical perspective of a line manager—who plays an important role in this context (cf. Sect. 9.4.4)—staff development encompasses all the measures aimed at acquiring, maintaining and improving the skills and competences of his or her employees.

9.2.1 The Seven Stages of the Staff Development

This section describes the different stages of the ideal staff development process, with particular reference to the respective responsibilities of the line manager and the HR specialists (cf. Troger 2018).

(a) Analysis of Staff Development Needs
Within the framework of the company's business strategy, top management and HR discuss the fundamental qualification and training needs. Based on a task analysis, the tasks and requirements are then identified, and the necessary skills defined in cooperation with the heads of the individual departments.

In the next step, staffing analysis is used to determine in which functional areas and on what content employees need to be trained. This analysis of staffing needs based on a classic target-performance comparison is primarily the responsibility of the respective line managers. They must, on the one hand, define the requirements of the positions and, on the other, identify the weak points as well as the development potential of their employees.

(b) Definition of Staff Development Objectives
Based on the development needs, it is the task of the staff developers to draw up an initial staff development concept. Initially, this is only a proposal for the desired development goals. Ideally, these are presented in a differentiated way in terms of knowledge, competences and behavioural goals. After approval by the departmental managers, follows the next stage.

(c) Planning of Staff Development Initiatives and Resources
This is done by the HR department. Companies have a wide variety of methods at their disposal for imparting the defined content and skills. These can be roughly divided into measures *on the job* (e.g., *job rotation* or *mentoring*), *off the job* (behavioural training, external training) and *near the job* (project work, quality circles).

When the interventions are planned, the costs are also calculated (in addition to the direct costs of training, there are also costs for the participants' absences from work, for example). While the HR expert selects the appropriate measures and trainer/coach—possibly with the involvement of the supervisors—the budget is usually approved by the company management.

(d) Definition of the Evaluation Criteria
Before the start of the training intervention, it is important to define the evaluation criteria according to the objectives of the measure. The staff developer should obtain a number of precise indicators from the supervisor, which can later be used to evaluate the staff development measure or to monitor its success on the participants' work behaviour.

(e) Implementation of Staff Development Measures
The HR manager is responsible for organising the implementation of the measures. The line manager only has to ensure that the employee is released from work, thus signalling that he or she takes the process seriously. As already mentioned, the majority of staff development measures are currently carried out virtually—which poses a particular challenge for providers.

(f) Securing the Transfer of the Education and Training Measures
Following the staff development measure, it is the line manager's responsibility to support the transfer of what has been learnt. Only when this transfer has taken place in everyday working life can one speak of a successful staff development intervention. If this does not succeed, either the wrong measures or the wrong trainers were

selected, or the employee was not sufficiently motivated for the intervention. Another reason could be the use of virtual training methods, which is particularly widespread at present because of the restrictions imposed by the ongoing pandemic. After all, not all content and topics can be conveyed through the use of webinars in such a way that the participants can apply them in practice.

(g) Evaluation of Staff Development Measures

The staff development process ends with the evaluation of the intervention. First, the basic quality of the intervention is evaluated by the participants and later, its medium- and long-term success, based on the above-mentioned transfer, is also evaluated.

Therefore, the ad hoc questionnaires at the end of the event are by no means sufficient for the positive evaluation of a staff development measure; what counts is the feedback from line managers after the next annual appraisal interview. In combination with staff development budgeting, this lays the foundation for the systematic monitoring and evaluation of the education and training interventions.

9.2.2 Education and Training

In short, education and training is about the need to fill either existing or future gaps between the job requirements and the skills profile of the employee. It is not surprising that education and training are at the heart of staff development and for many people are the sum of what constitutes staff development.

In terms of **content**, we can distinguish between three levels of education and training:

(a) Knowledge

The aim is to impart specialist knowledge, information about operational processes and technical functions and methods. It uses mostly frontal teaching methods, and the imparted knowledge is of a purely cognitive nature.

(b) Competence

This level is about acquiring skills. Simply knowing how a machine works or the grammatical rules of a language is not enough, what matters is the ability to apply them in practice. This is not usually learned at a desk, but through practical exercises at the workplace.

(c) Mindsets

Competence alone may not be sufficient to accomplish a task if there is a lack of motivation—for whatever reason. The communication of values also falls into this category. They are conveyed through discussions and persuasion processes. Ultimately, the aim of a continuing education measure is to impart a certain type of behaviour.

9.2.2.1 Competences

Competences refer to different dimensions of knowledge, skills and behaviour in the performance of a work task. Education and training measures serve to impart or update competences. A distinction is typically made between the following fields of competence:

(a) Technical Competence

This covers the skills and knowledge in a specific field.

(b) Methodological Competence

This competence includes basic systematic working approaches, the use of presentation techniques and other aids as well as the use of media.

(c) Social Competence

This refers to the ability to work in a team, i.e., the behaviour within the group and in dealing with superiors, customers and suppliers.

(d) Personal Competence

This relates to the personality profile of the employee. Qualities such as the ability to accept criticism, the ability to compromise, determination and self-discipline are seen as important competences in work behaviour.

9.2.2.2 Methods

There is a wide range of continuing education and training methods available to staff developers. Stock-Homburg (2013) provides a good overview. Accordingly, initial and continuing education and training methods can be divided into the following groups:

(a) Education-Based Methods

This refers to traditional methods, such as lectures and seminars in assembly halls. In combination with role play, group work or simulation games, this approach is still very popular. Education-based measures usually take place outside the company and outside normal working hours (and are, therefore, also referred to as off-the-job training). Due to a limited ability to absorb what is seen and heard (e.g., compared to what is experienced first-hand), frontal education-based methods usually lead to high transfer losses. Stock-Homburg also calls the theoretical knowledge generated in the seminars 'inert knowledge' because it is often difficult to apply in the workplace.

(b) Experience-Based Methods

With experience-based methods, which include practical exercises for the employee, a higher transfer to the real working environment is guaranteed. These realistic situations offer both a gain in knowledge and a transfer into practice, as the learning content is 'experienced' in a concrete way. The above-mentioned methods can be carried out either directly at the workplace (on-the-job training) or away from it (off-the-job training). On-the-job training includes the previously mentioned methods of job rotation, job enlargement and job enrichment (cf. explanations in Sect. 8.1.2), while, for example, quality circles and other cross-company projects refer to off-the-job training. The latter are also subject to a transfer problem, as there is no guarantee that the participants will apply the newly learned methods and skills when they return.

The so-called **action learning**, an experience-based off-the-job learning method in which an interdepartmental learning group under the leadership of a coach attempts to solve a concrete problem, increasingly uses virtual methods and e-learning elements in training and problem-solving processes.

(c) Feedback-Based Methods
This includes in particular the increasingly popular coaching and mentoring. Orientation assessments also fall into this category. While the two methods mentioned above mainly convey task-specific knowledge, the feedback-based methods focus on personal skills and attributes. The gain in knowledge or the change in behaviour is the result of an intensive personal interaction between the trainer (coach or mentor) and the learner.

Coaching is the guidance and support provided by an experienced (internal or external) expert to one or more people in specific professional situations, which can be either technical or personal.

Mentoring goes one step further by also supporting the periods between the specific operational situations. As a rule, the mentor is a 'neutral' expert who must never be positioned hierarchically above the mentee. In contrast to the more situation-related coaching, mentoring emphasises the process as such.

(d) E-Learning and Blended Learning
Regardless of the pandemic, e-learning has been gaining popularity—in the course of automation and virtualisation—for some years now. Strictly speaking, it is one of the education-based methods because it involves the transfer of knowledge—albeit personalised to individual time and location. E-learning creates virtual learning environments in which self-directed learning is possible. A frequently cited deficit, namely the lack of feedback, has now been largely eliminated through the use of interactive programmes.

The basic idea behind e-learning was, firstly, to find more efficient ways of providing education and training and, secondly, to make use of the diverse opportunities offered by information and communication technology.

Blended learning, i.e., the acquisition of knowledge and skills through a combination of e-learning and face-to-face sessions, attempts to combine the advantages of the various learning systems and thus ensure maximum learning transfer. First, internal and external experts are invited to present current specialist knowledge within the company at fixed dates. In self-study, each participant can then use electronic media to explore the topics in greater depth in a self-directed manner, independent of location, time and other people. The results can subsequently be discussed with the other participants in a workshop and tried out in the workplace.

9.3   Life-Phase Oriented Staff Development

9.3.1   A Question of Age (or Not)

In the coming years, demographic change will increasingly raise the question of age in connection with staff development, which in this context is primarily understood as training and further education measures. This is reflected in the fact that a person who is 55 today will still be of working age in 10 years' time, but without continuous training will no longer be able to work productively; or in the fact that the same 55-year-old cannot absorb new knowledge with the same ease as a younger person unless it has been adapted to suit his age.

When it comes to imparting competences in the context of staff development—and in a broader sense to maintaining employability—the *age* factor has several facets:

Which competences are to be imparted by which didactic means? Are age-homogeneous teams preferable to a mixed composition? And finally: are training measures for people above a certain age still worthwhile for an organisation?

Overall, these questions can be answered with two relatively new concepts: **age-appropriate** and **ageing-appropriate** learning. The premise, and at the same time the link between the two categories, will be the **motivation** to perform: and that is definitely not a question of age but rather of the attitude of the employee. It also forms the basis for any form of staff development.

9.3.1.1 Age-Appropriate Staff Development

Despite all the motivation in the world: It would be just as unrealistic to expect a 65-year-old employee to be equally productive in every respect as their 30-year old colleague, as it would be unrealistic to expect the same training programme to be equally successful for both. Does this mean that staff developers should set up special 'senior citizens services'? From a practical point of view, the answer could be yes: Today and in the coming years, the main task will be to make up for missed opportunities. After all, until recently, any form of investment in the training of staff over 50 was not considered worthwhile. Education and further training was reserved for the younger generation. The consequences of this can be seen when older workers are described in sweeping statements as one-sidedly qualified, not very flexible or not very motivated to learn.

In this respect, this type of age-appropriate staff development could be regarded as an immediate 'repair measure'. The idea is to give new skills to employees who have not received any further training for many years and for whom nothing was planned until retirement.

At a later stage, the model of **ageing-appropriate** staff development in the sense of lifelong learning should be applied (see subsequent section). Age-appropriate learning should then ideally be limited to teaching specific content to age-homogeneous groups or the use of certain didactic elements to reinforce the learning process.

Due to many organisations' reservations about training initiatives for older employees, these 'immediate measures'—in many companies they are bluntly called 'silver ageing' or '50+ programmes'—need to take some psychological principles into account (cf. Rump and Eilers 2014). There is not only a need to overcome prejudices on the part of colleagues, the self-image of older employees also needs to be altered on occasion. Confidence in oneself must be strengthened and the interest in lifelong learning (re)awakened. Especially in the early stages, it is important to avoid anxiety-inducing competitive situations and overload. Such moments can often occur in virtual training events. In the following, some aspects of an age-appropriate education and training policy are listed. However, it starts with a warning (Stöckl et al. 2002):

(a) No Ghettoisation Despite Age-Related Homogeneity
Who does not know the dread of having to go back to school? Generally speaking, the older the person, the greater the aversion to further education. Age-homogeneous groups in training programmes help to overcome the general reluctance of older employees to engage in further training. For this reason, age-homogeneous teams are particularly recommended for reintegration training. However, such grouping must not lead to a 'two-tiered thinking', which would only reinforce the psychological barriers mentioned above.

In order to prevent *ghettoisation*, attention should, therefore, be paid to regular interaction with other learning groups to share experiences. In this context, the cooperation between staff developers and the line managers from the various departments is especially important.

(b) Building on Experience
Experience and previous knowledge play a significant role in learning. It is, therefore, very important to build on older employees' experience and to bring new things into a context that is meaningful to them. The learning materials should be clearly structured and contain many practical examples from everyday working life.

(c) Imparting Learning Strategies Instead of Prejudice
It is generally known that older people tend to learn differently from younger people, but that they do not learn any less well. The reasons for learning barriers are usually of a motivational nature and are based on a lack of self-confidence in one's own ability to learn. Older employees are often no longer used to learning and have to learn how to learn first. For this reason, before teaching content, consideration should be given to the appropriate learning strategies. In general, activating methods of self-directed learning will work much better than externally controlled teaching of learning materials; and this is particularly the case with older participants.

(d) Interactive Course Design
Instead of simply offering education-based teaching by means of lectures and PowerPoint presentations, the participants should become co-designers of the educational activities from the outset. This begins with the development of content and

the course materials, where the older employees' experiences from professional practice can be helpful. From a didactic point of view, exercises with a high degree of realism and a strong reference to the participants' life and working environment are recommended.

It should be noted that the current (pandemic-related) almost exclusive use of virtual training in the form of webinars can represent a certain obstacle, especially for older generations.

9.3.1.2 Ageing-Appropriate Staff Development

In contrast to the 'repair strategy' described above, staff development should always follow a forward-looking approach in which the qualifications and skills of the individual and the requirements of the organisation are subject to continuous review and adjustment (cf. Troger 2019). For the individual, staff development means lifelong learning and thus the maintenance of a learning arc that spans their entire working life.

This aspect gains particular significance when we consider the demographically driven ageing of most workforces and the general extension of working life. If the associated performance change is to be used productively for the respective company and individual's employability in general, what is needed is not only the employee's motivation and commitment to do well, but also an integrated and sustainable (in this sense age-appropriate) approach to staff development.

Integrated Staff Development Approach

Although the focus here is on education and further training, it should be emphasised once again that an integrated staff development approach goes much further. It begins with the selection of the employee whose skills profile best matches the requirements of the job, and continues with an equally effective approach to staff deployment and staff management—both for the employees and for the company. On the basis of a learning culture anchored in the basic values of the organisation, the employee is supported on his or her personal development path by individually tailored training measures.

A New Learning Culture

Learning in the sense of maintaining employability requires a company-wide learning culture, which is not limited to periodically planned education and training activities, but manifests itself both off- and on-the-job. This requires a more radical approach to learning: learning must no longer happen before, alongside or after the actual work, but must become an **integral part of work** to an even greater extent. This requires a work design that promotes learning, e.g., in the form of greater scope for employees and rotation programmes. Such learning-friendly work arrangements should be part of an overall health-promoting and age-appropriate work organisation, as described in Sect. 8.1.

Mixed-Age Teams

Many companies are already practising a demographically oriented approach in their daily business by specifically using mixed-age groups in projects. The aim is to combine the skills and qualities of the younger team members with those of the older ones. There is a continuous exchange of knowledge in the workplace and the exchange of experience further enhances the competence of all team members. This also helps to make it easier to deal with the departure of an employee. A prerequisite for the effectiveness of this form of self-organised learning is not only the right company culture and mutual recognition, but also a balanced number of younger and older employees.

Lifelong Learning

Although the banner of 'lifelong' learning has been on everyone's lips for decades, it only truly becomes topical in connection with (almost) lifelong employment and the resulting need to maintain employability. It is precisely this aspect that calls for the individual commitment of every single employee. Assuming personal responsibility for one's own professional development outside work is just as much a part of this commitment, as is exercising caution against over-specialisation and a subsequent resting on one's laurels. In this area, self-interest does not always align with the immediate interests of the company. For the HR manager, this means that they have to weigh up the laudable learning motivation of the employee against the benefit for the company.

Expert Pools and 'Tandem Learning'

Many companies today create pools of experts consisting of experienced, usually older, employees, whose tasks generally also include the education and further training of their less experienced colleagues. 'Tandem learning' works in a similar way, albeit only in teams of two, as the name suggests. An expert in one field works closely together with a colleague who is less experienced in this particular field. A variant of this is a tandem between two experts from different fields, who mutually benefit from each other's expertise.

9.3.2   Personal Development Plans

Age alone will, therefore, no longer be a suitable category for target-group oriented staff development. So where—apart from the technical specialisation to be imparted—can a common denominator be found for further training approaches? The skills and competences of employees can only be used optimally if the relationship between the requirements of the organisation and the performance and commitment of the employees is as balanced as possible in every phase of employment. Various factors and trends on both sides of this balance shape the relationship: On the organisational side, it is above all the general drive for progress that causes a continuous change in requirements. The half-life of knowledge is becoming shorter and shorter, especially in technology-driven companies, and this requires enormous efforts by the workforce to adapt.

The latter, in turn, must not fall into the so-called 'specialisation trap' and hope for an armchair career, or rely on the qualifications they once acquired while they were at university. On the contrary: due to longer working lives and easy access to knowledge, as well as its ever-diminishing half-life, it is now quite possible to have several careers within one working life.

9.3.2.1 Motivation and Commitment

For the most part, people only talk about performance; what about motivation and commitment? Changing framework conditions and career orientations—cf. Chap. 3—have led to career models and development programmes that are mainly geared to the employee's individual life cycle. Two things in particular stand out from my personal experiences of recent years: firstly, the greater consideration given to **non-work-related motives among employees above a certain age** (approx. 45–50 years) and secondly, the generally increased **importance of *work-life balance* among young employees** of the Y and Z generation (cf. Chaps. 1 and 3).

All this makes it necessary to adapt staff development to individual life phases in order to maintain the employability of the employees in the company, on the one hand, and to ensure their motivation and commitment on the other.

9.3.2.2 Individual Life-Phase Oriented Career Planning

This requires long-term development planning, which should start with the recruitment of young professionals and be an integral part of the organisation's Human Resources strategy. So much for the theory. In practice, things often look quite different: The interests of many young employees are very diverse, volatile and difficult to plan for. Very few can imagine a lifelong professional career in the company they currently work for. But that is exactly what staff developers should plan for, even if this long-term perspective is in clear contradiction to the fast-paced and dynamic nature of the economy and society described in Chap. 1.

9.3.2.3 Career Conversations

The only way out of this dilemma is to plan individual career paths between staff developer, supervisor and employee. The basis for this is an honest conversation about the future, in which the possibilities and necessities of the organisation are compared with the goals, abilities and potential of the employee.

The planning period for these career paths can cover 2 years or even 20 years, depending on the parameters mentioned above. In any case, a trajectory until retirement is never the goal of these career conversations (except perhaps for a 60-year-old shift worker). These 'work-oriented biographical perspectives' should also be addressed by the supervisor during the annual appraisal interview.

It will not always be possible to align the organisation's ideas with those of the employee, but an important goal has been achieved in any case: *transparency* about mutual expectations. An individualised plan of the employee's professional development based on these conversations will attempt to structure the requirements, pressures and incentives in such a way that a mutually beneficial working relationship up to retirement age becomes a possibility for both sides.

9.3.3   The Perfect Career Wave: Not Ladder!

For most people born before 1980, a career begins at the bottom left and ends at the top right of our mental chart (Troger 2019). The line is sometimes steep and sometimes flat, sometimes long and sometimes short. But it is always a straight line. Sometimes there is a dent in the trajectory, but generally this hurts and needs to be explained to a new employer. A wave, however, seems unimaginable. Why is this so? It is still socially frowned upon to interrupt one's professional career or to take a step back in order to learn something new, go on an educational trip or start a family. In some countries in northern Europe, however, this situation has changed in recent years: It has now become common practice for men to take time off, even for family reasons. More and more young people—including *high potentials*—are imagining their future in exactly this way: as a succession of career waves rather than a ladder.

Whether we like it or not, we will have to get used to non-linear career paths. How should we as supervisors and (strategic!) staff developers plan for the long-term under these circumstances?

9.3.3.1 Short-Term Planning Horizons
With regard to the approaches and methods used in staff development, planning will have to focus much more strongly on short-term horizons and work towards concrete tasks and tangible goals. It will make little sense to offer promising junior managers the prospect of a five-stage career development programme and in return make them promise to still be working for the company in 10 years' time.

9.3.3.2 Project Oriented Thinking
As recruiters we will have to learn to focus on the individual projects and achievements in the course of a career progression and not to pay too much attention to the time in between. It is not enough to 'generously' overlook a period of extended parental leave or to 'tolerate' the software developer's degree in psychology, instead, career choices of this kind must be met with respect and recognition. Perhaps together it will even be possible to develop a new perspective.

9.3.3.3 Plateaus and Waves
Given the longer working life, the vast majority of employees will sooner or later experience a so-called career plateau: daily routine, saturation, satisfaction with what they have achieved or the realisation that promotion is no longer possible. The reactions to this situation can differ greatly: Some want to take a *sabbatical*, others need a new challenge and start looking for alternatives on the labour market, and yet others decide to focus on their private life by reducing working hours. After a few years, the situation can look completely different for everyone. Only those companies that offer their employees prospects for the future in these times and

can react flexibly to their needs will achieve success in staff development. Companies that support and promote individual development paths and allow for career waves, will be attractive on the labour market and thus successful in recruiting.

9.4   Staff Development from an Organisational Perspective

Although staff development is *always* about effectively aligning the needs of the employees with the requirements of the company, we should examine the process again, but this time from the perspective of the organisation. Detached from the theoretical discussion as to whether organisational development should be seen as part of staff development or—as most contributors argue—vice versa, three areas are of particular importance in this context: employee retention, knowledge transfer and succession planning.

9.4.1   Knowledge Transfer

Continuous knowledge building and organisational learning are essential for a company to survive in a knowledge society. In view of the short half-life of knowledge and the dynamics on the labour markets, a secure and systematic transfer of know-how and skills is becoming increasingly important. This applies, above all, to the empirical knowledge of older employees, which is rarely written down or stored in a database.

One possibility to secure this knowledge for the future is to work in mixed-age teams. In addition to the already mentioned advantages of cross-fertilisation and a proactive approach to demographic developments on the labour market, these teams also represent an effective tool for a continuous transfer of knowledge between experienced and young employees.

Mentoring is another method of institutionalising the transfer of knowledge, given that the relationship between a mentor and a mentee is usually characterised not only by a difference in experience, but also by a difference in age. The special involvement of older and more experienced employees as mentors should, if possible, be detached from the usual hierarchical relationship between superiors and subordinates.

9.4.2   Succession Planning

Until a few years ago, succession planning in most organisations followed a standard pattern: shortly before retirement, dismissal or promotion, an older employee is assigned a young colleague, teaches him or her the rudiments of the job, and then leaves. Apart from an increase in frequency, this will not change much in the future, except that age will no longer have such a central role. *Old* can follow *young*, and *old* can follow *old*, depending on qualifications and skills. Due to the growing shortage of young talent, it is advisable to make a number of early plans for possible appointments to key positions that consider existing employees, including older ones.

Rotation models and horizontal careers should be established. The basis for systematic succession planning should be an **age structure analysis** which should be carried out at regular intervals and compared with the skills profiles of the individual organisational areas.

9.4.3   Employee Retention

This aspect has already been described at the beginning of this chapter: Staff development is not only an effective marketing tool for potential employees on-the-job market, but also helps the existing employees to decide whether they want to stay with the company or move on.

9.4.4   Career Planning Options

Individual-oriented career management focuses on the individual employee, while organisation-oriented career management focuses on the entire workforce and, even more so, has the development of the organisation as a whole as its primary goal. In simple terms, the aim is to ensure that the staff structure is aligned with the company strategy. Due to the shortage of skilled workers, the opposite—a **resource-oriented**—approach is increasingly common, i.e., aligning company strategy with the structure of the workforce. Using the standard portfolio procedure, the individual performance and ability profiles of employees are aggregated into personnel portfolios of individual departments or the entire organisation. In this way, bottlenecks can be identified at an early stage and counteracted with appropriate development measures.

There are three basic options for shaping a professional career in terms of content:

(a) Specialist Careers
This is associated with an increase in the complexity of the tasks and technical responsibilities as well as an expansion of the scope of action. Remuneration will also be adjusted to reflect these new duties. The aim of a specialist career is mainly to offer highly qualified specialists a prospect that is not tied to the management of other employees.

(b) Management Careers
A career path in management corresponds to the common perception of what a professional career looks like, as it provides for a vertical—and thus clearly visible—ascent within the company hierarchy. Taking on additional, more demanding,

tasks is associated with higher salaries and increasing responsibility in staff management.

(c) Project Management Careers

Project management careers are characterised by advancement in a horizontal (expansion of tasks and responsibilities within a project), vertical (senior project manager) or diagonal (new projects) direction. This is generally independent of company hierarchy and takes into account several developments of recent years: Firstly, the short-term nature of the work in many economic sectors, which is difficult to plan for, secondly, the lack of management positions in many companies due to the dismantling of hierarchies and the longer working lives of employees, and thirdly, the preference of generations Y and Z for clearly defined, scheduled work— i.e., work on a project basis (cf. Chap. 1).

9.4.4.1 International Careers

Irrespective of the need for cooperation across different groups, a transnational company structure offers interesting options for international staff development. Particularly in view of the above-mentioned lack of internal promotion opportunities and the increased need for internationally oriented managers, cross-national work assignments—horizontal, vertical or diagonal—will become increasingly relevant.

9.4.5   The Question of Return on Investment

Staff development must be worthwhile. Even the greatest humanist among HR professionals will agree with this statement—albeit perhaps from the perspective of the employees' benefit rather than that of the company. There is also agreement that the professional delivery of staff development has its price. Apart from the fees of the speakers, trainers and consultants, the valuable working time of the employees is also invested. What about the return on this investment? From the technical perspective of a management control system, it can be measured by two factors: the improved performance of the employee after the education initiative or their increased productivity and the time taken to deliver it. And precisely this last aspect is where the concerns of many entrepreneurs lie—concerns which are expressed primarily in two questions:

Does the time and cost involved still pay off for older employees? How can I ensure that the newly acquired skills will benefit *my* company and that the employee will not use the training initiative to increase their market value so they can look for a new job elsewhere?

The short answers to these questions are 'yes' and 'not at all'. The partial reimbursement of training costs by the employee in the event of his or her premature departure may be a small hurdle for a career-hungry high potential, but nothing more. This means that the aspect of **retention time** will become less and less important when calculating the return on investment of further training and that the short-term benefit in terms of **productivity** and **motivation** should be the decisive factor.[2]

In answering the first question, it is true that older employees generally entail higher staff costs (higher career levels, anniversary bonuses), however, they undoubtedly rank well ahead of their younger colleagues when it comes to the return on education and further training. One look at the low turnover statistics for employees over 50 is enough to conclude that this is indeed the case. The greater company loyalty of older employees, therefore, leads to a higher return on investment and to a higher chance that essential operational know-how is retained within the company. Particularly in highly specialised technology companies with time and cost-intensive induction and qualification periods, long-term employee retention is desirable from a business perspective because it maximises the return on education and further training.

Finally, in this context it is also worth mentioning the benefits of online training, which is the most used channel for staff development already due to the pandemic: The elimination of travel costs, travel time and savings on speakers has a positive effect on the return on these development measures.

9.4.6 The Actors

To round off the discussion on the wide-ranging field of staff development, it is worth taking a look at the actors involved, although I will restrict myself to the three most important ones—at least in terms of their personal involvement: the employee as the person directly affected, the immediate supervisor, and the HR department. Where relevant, staff representatives can have a role to play as well. Last but not least, the company management is, of course, also of central importance. In addition to approving the budget, the latter should also support the general principles of staff development.

9.4.6.1 Employees as Staff Developers

Christian Scholz (2014) saw the employee as an 'entrepreneur in his or her own right', whereas the supervisor or HR department assume more of an advisory role. In this context, the German HR visionary referred to the 'new economy', where this shift of responsibility onto the employee arose for the first time as a result of frequent job changes. I would add that this situation has indeed become much more acute today, given the volatility and individualisation of the workplace and the market power of workers. Twenty years ago, employers may have voluntarily allowed their employees to make decisions; today they have no choice but to give employees more autonomy while, at the same time, they try to assert the cost-benefit aspects for their company.

---

[2]This corresponds to the same logic as described above, with simple procurement and decreasing half-life of knowledge.

9.4.6.2 HR Departments as Staff Developers

In contrast to the classic role of the HR department—responsible for *all* matters relating to education and further training—I see its involvement today primarily in five instances of the staff development process:

First, the *strategic guidelines* of the organisation are established together with the company management and, if necessary, an overarching competence portfolio is defined. In cooperation with the heads of the departments, the skills profiles for the individual positions are then broken down. The next step, also in cooperation with the aforementioned heads, is to draw up the *staff development budget*, which is subsequently managed by the HR department.

When selecting the individual development measures, the HR development experts primarily act as *advisors* in an intermediary position between the employee and his or her line manager. They are also ultimately responsible for the overall *implementation of the development measures*. As the experts on methodology, they select the right tools and the respective internal or external speakers or coaches. During the pandemic, the most proactive staff developers stood out for their ability to organise the best online speakers and the necessary infrastructure to run the webinars in the shortest of times.

The final responsibility of the HR department in the development process, in my eyes, is to implement an **integrated management control system for education and training**. As described above, the focus is on the effectiveness of the measures and cost transparency with regard to the participant, his or her department, and the entire organisation. Together with the strategic guidelines and the budget plan, this should provide a numerical and content-related framework for the process.

9.4.6.3 Line Managers as Staff Developers

As the expert on the situation in the company or the internal development opportunities, and at the same time the most important point of contact for his or her employees, I see the direct supervisor as the central figure in the context of staff development. The supervisor experiences the employee in day-to-day business, sees his or her strengths and weaknesses, recognises whether they are underchallenged or frustrated that they cannot reach the next step on the career ladder, or whether they have reached an unexpected performance limit. As part of regular staff appraisals, the line manager plans the next career steps and any further training measures that may be needed with his or her direct reports. He informs them of management expectations and tries to reconcile these with the interests and needs of each individual employee.

Similarly, when it comes to putting what has been learnt into practice, no one can better judge the transfer success and thus the 'return on training', than the direct supervisor.

Although most HR professionals have long since left their supposed 'ivory tower' and are well informed about the day-to-day business in the various departments—the diversity and fast-paced nature of business processes make it impossible to react in time or even to anticipate such things as, for example, the desire of an under-stretched young talent to change jobs. Most importantly, in the course of the increasing individualisation of the working relationship, only the immediate supervisor is able to respond appropriately to the diverse and sometimes unforeseen expectations and needs of the individual. This is especially true since not only work-related aspects should be considered, but the individual's work-life balance should also be taken into account at all times.

9.5   Conclusions and Practical Tips

The staff development process is about bringing together the interests of the company or department with those of the employees. For the staff developer and the line manager, career planning means reconciling the future needs of the company or department (well-qualified management and specialist staff) with the individual career aspirations of the employees. The aim is to secure the company's long-term staffing strategy, on the one hand, and to support employees in achieving their professional and private goals, on the other.

The staff development process begins with the selection of the employee based on the best possible match between the company's person specification and the candidate's skills profile. In accordance with strategic business objectives and HR policy principles, employees are accompanied by their supervisor on their journey within the company and supported in their development. Somewhat in the background, the HR professionals coordinate and monitor the overall process and are available to employees and their line managers in an advisory capacity.

Is effective staff development a question of age?

Yes, when it comes to the way learning is done and the need for many companies and older employees to catch up. No, when it comes to the fundamental question of motivation and the commitment to learn in order to maintain one's employability in the long term. And also 'no', when we look at the effectiveness and the return on investment of education and training.

Finally, the main activities of the experts from the HR department and line managers in the staff development process are outlined (see Fig. 9.2) and some practical tips are given.

Practical Tips
1. Be proactive in your staff development! There are at least five central reasons for this:
   − The half-life of knowledge is getting shorter and shorter.
   − Performance has to be maintained as long as possible.
   − Staff development is seen as an employer value proposition.
   − People want diversity.
   − Entrepreneurs face the lack of qualified workers and the individualised workplace with perplexity.
2. Explore new paths in teaching skills and competences with *blended learning* approaches and do not let the virus stop you!
3. Ensure that the training initiatives are age-appropriate (without ghettoisation), but even more so that they are ageing-appropriate in terms of sustainable and lifelong learning.

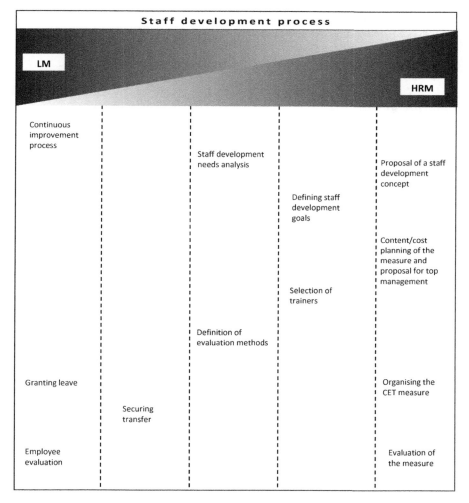

Fig. 9.2 Distribution of responsibilities and cooperation between line managers and HR department in staff development

4. You can expect performance capability, but not motivation and commitment. *Work-life balance* is complex and perceived individually.
5. Say goodbye to ready-made and standardised career plans. In an individualised working world, employees want to surf their own career waves. This requires individual and life-phase oriented career planning.
6. Return on training and further education generally increase with the age of the participating employees.
7. As a line manager, you are the first point of contact for the development and career planning of your direct reports.

8. Staff development largely means organisational development. Employee retention, knowledge transfer and succession planning are the three essential tools for this.
9. Make multiple succession plans for key positions, without regard to age.

References

Goleman, D. (1996). *Emotional Intelligence: Why it can matter more than IQ*. London: Bloomsbury.

Ilmarinen, J., & Tempel, J. (2002). *Arbeitsfähigkeit 2010: Was können wir tun, damit Sie gesund bleiben?* Hamburg: VSA.

Ilmarinen, J., & Tuomi, K. (2004). Past, present and future of work ability. In J. Ilmarinen & S. Lehtinen (Eds.), *Past, present and future of work ability. People and work*. Helsinki: Finnish Institute of Occupational Health. Retrieved October 15, 2020, from http://www.ttl.fi/en/health/WAI/multidimensional_work_ability_model/PublishingImages/work_ability_house_large.png.

Richenhagen, G. (2012). Demografischer Wandel in der Arbeitswelt: Ein internationaler Vergleich im Hinblick auf Arbeits- und Beschäftigungsfähigkeit. In T. Schott & C. Hornberg (Eds.), *Die Gesellschaft und ihre Gesundheit: 20 Jahre Public Health in Deutschland: Bilanz und Ausblick einer Wissenschaft* (pp. 367–383). Wiesbaden: VS Verlag für Sozialwissenschaften.

Rump, J., & Eilers, S. (2014). Demografieorientiertes Personalmanagement. Hintergründe und Handlungsansätze. In J. Rump & S. Eilers (Eds.), *Demografieorientiertes Personalmanagement: Hintergründe und Handlungsansätze* (pp. 11–12). Köln: Luchterhand.

Scholz, C. (2014). *Grundzüge des Personalmanagements* (2nd ed.). München: Vahlen.

Stock-Homburg, R. (2013). *Personalmanagement. Theorien, Konzepte, Instrumente* (3rd ed.). Wiesbaden: Springer Gabler.

Stöckl, M., Spevacek, G., & Strake, A. (2002). Alternsgerechte Didaktik. In D. Schemme (Ed.), *Qualifizierung, Personal- und Organisationsentwicklung mit älteren Mitarbeiterinnen und Mitarbeitern* (pp. 89–113). Bielefeld: WBV.

Troger, H. (2018). *Die Führungskraft als Personalmanager*. Wiesbaden: Springer Gabler.

Troger, H. (2019). Alters- und alternsgerechte Personalentwicklung. In H. Troger (Ed.), *7 Erfolgsfaktoren für wirksames Personalmanagement* (2nd ed., pp. 65–81). Wiesbaden: Springer Gabler.

Printed by Printforce, the Netherlands